Trude

from Lisl
Christmas 1959

D1325689

Crossing the Line

CLAUD COCKBURN

Other books by Claud Cockburn

Reportage
HIGH LOW WASHINGTON
REPORTER IN SPAIN

Autobiography
IN TIME OF TROUBLE

Fiction—*under the name of James Helvick*
BEAT THE DEVIL
OVERDRAFT ON GLORY

Satire
NINE BALD MEN
ASPECTS OF ENGLISH HISTORY

Crossing the Line

being the second volume
of autobiography by

CLAUD COCKBURN

LONDON

MACGIBBON & KEE

1958

Set in 10-pt Pilgrim
*Printed at the St Ann's Press,
Park Road, Altrincham*

Contents

Foreword

FICTION'S beginning, middle and end are easily decided. But where should autobiography 'really' begin? And the end presents an evident difficulty. There will be no one left to write it.

I wrote one piece of autobiography—Pekin, Herts, *Mitteleuropa*, Wall Street, London, Madrid, Munich. This is another piece. It could have been written first. There is no valid reason for not beginning in the middle, if one can speak of the 'middle' of an unknown distance.

The characters in this section, with exception of the author, are new. Nineteen thirty-nine was a new chapter heading in many people's lives.

Some say that because there are rather more characters, scenes and incidents than cogitations and internal monologues, one can have the impression of reading fiction, or the rough script of a play.

I hope that may be so.

For me, that is a way of approaching a true impression. So long as the people talk and act, the reader can form his own estimate of them and their environment, and of the author.

For example, I find it impossible to think of any deliberate action of my own as mistaken. How can I know what would have happened had I done something else? But the reader, unless smothered by excessive explanation, deafened by the beating of the breast, may judge quite otherwise.

André Gide wrote somewhere—I think in the notebooks of *The Counterfeiters*—that the writer should let the reader take advantage of him, feel in some sense more knowing and thus superior. True. And an autobiography should give the reader opportunity to point out the author's follies and misconceptions.

Characters appear in a shifting context of time and place, acting upon it and reacting to it. In this sense they are part of a series of 'period' pieces. Otherwise I think little of the handy trick of assigning people or ideas to periods such as The Thirties, The Fifties. But these are harmless over-simplifications.

Not harmless at all are the over-simplifications which dangerously confuse the issue of Communism.

That issue, naturally, looms large in this book, and would
do so even if people were not so eager to ask Why did you
become a Communist? Why did you cease to be one? How is it,
they ask, that while the U.S. Senate was listing you among the
world's most dangerous Reds, the Reds in Prague had you listed
as an organizer of the Western Intelligence Services?

The danger of over-simplifying the Communist issue is seen,
certainly, at its most numbing and corrosive in the United States.
But Britain, and the peoples of the whole Western alliance are
gravely infected too.

In 1914, people who felt uncertain or chilly about the rights
and wrongs of World War I used to be asked by enthusiasts,
'Would you stand aside while a German raped your sister?'

We have come a long way, and pessimism about sister's fate
has deepened. For years the question people have been told they
must answer is, 'Would you rather have your sister raped by a
man from the Kremlin or a man from the Pentagon?'

The person who replies, 'Neither, thanks, I have other plans
for her' is dubbed a treacherous neutralist; the sort of ditherer
who cannot make up his mind which part of Soho he would
prefer to be coshed in.

Mr Alan Valentine, high-ranking American University President and Governmental adviser, came back from an important
mission to India annoyed by Indian 'illogic'; by the denial that
genuine anti-Communism must involve membership of the
American alliance. An Indian leader said to him, 'The trouble
with Western logic is that it so often leads to a choice between
two unacceptable alternatives.'

The sustained and strenuous act of refusing unacceptable
alternatives—in politics or anything else—is called neutralism.
It is supposed to be 'passive' but is not. The earliest Christians
rejected the alternatives of Pharisaical Judaism and Romanized
paganism. They were, on that issue, 'neutralists'. But they were
far from passive and not ineffective.

In politics and in every other sphere some progress is achieved
by following Bernard Shaw's advice to 'get what you like, or
you'll grow to like what you get.'

I

Russian lessons

Y wife being then sixteen years of age, her mother, as climax of a general briefing on life-facts said, 'And when you marry and have a place of your own, remember above all things it's disastrous to let your head gardener *show*. If you do, he'll devote the whole place to getting winners at the county agricultural show or whatever it is. You'll never get so much as a strawberry or hyacinth or stick of asparagus for yourself when you want it.'

Sound advice, I dare say, and the only thing wrong about it that it was proferred at too late a date—late 1931.

Fortunately Patricia, taking a coolish Irish look at the way things were going in the world, never did think that the chances of head gardeners continuing to play a decisive role in many people's lives were much better than even. Two years later, head gardeners had gone still further out in the betting, and she said to her first husband that as there must fairly soon be a war, rather than settle down it would be better to see as much of the earth and its peoples as possible while the going was good. So they rode over the Canadian Rockies, lived for months in Tahiti, toured Siam and Malaya—Patricia by now fascinated by the unsolved problem whether the Negroes came from thereabouts to Africa or went from Africa thither—lived in New Zealand and the Congo, motored across the Sahara, and then were sometimes in a Riviera villa and sometimes in the black north of Finland, where Lapps in red caps used to drive miles across the snow in sleighs to learn the latest news of what ultimately had happened to the love affair of the ex-king of England. I met her for the first time immediately after she had returned from a lone trip to Ruthenia—then the ultimate eastern point of Czechoslovakia.

I had loved that neck of the east European woods too. Mr Sefton Delmer (who worked for the *Daily Express*) and his wife once—about Munich time—drove me down there from Prague, and we saw a man like Moses tending calves. One of the calves leaped a ditch and got itself struck by the car. It looked poorly, but we ran to and fro with our hats, getting water in them from the roadside ditch and throwing it over the calf's head. The patriarch looked on in sorrow and scepticism.

'Poor calf,' we said, fondling its ears.

'Not the calf is poor,' said the patriarch, '*I* am poor.'

We hardly knew it then, but it was the last smell of the old-time eastern European brew any of us were going to get for a long time. At Uzhorod we even talked to a 'Wonder Rabbi'—a Rabbi who worked miracles. Before him, there had been a more famous Wonder-Rabbi at Uzhorod, who, as a result of a vision, had defeated the Russians when they were sweeping in on the place in 1915.

The wonder-Rabbi we met was his son-in-law, had come from somewhere in Poland and married into the business. As son-in-law of the Destroyer of the Cossacks he had prestige too. Also he deserved it, because though Mr Delmer and I visited him at fairly short notice, when we got there he had a copy of the *Daily Express* on his desk. It had been rushed in during the twenty-four hours between our request for audience and our arrival. It was the first copy of the *Daily Express* ever seen in Uzhorod. But the Rabbi was at pains to tell us that he read the *Express* carefully every day. His favourite newspaper.

The courteous trouble taken made us, in our turn, feel very polite, very gentle. Nevertheless I had to say to him 'Do you, in fact, work miracles?'

He fluttered a white hand and very gently wagged a splendid black beard.

'I mean'—I said, or Mr Delmer said—'the people here most certainly suppose that you work miracles.'

'The common people,' said the Rabbi, 'have a tendency to superstition. Also they tend to confound the material with the spiritual. They see a man; a Rabbi; learned; a profound student of the Talmud; a holy man, in fact! So they think "the spirituality of such a man must be expressed in some unusual material powers." So they believe I can work material miracles.'

'And your own attitude to this mistaken tendency? You take steps to counter and expose such false conceptions?'

'You would do well to remember,' said the Rabbi, stroking his beard, and looking with an air of interest at the *Daily Express,* 'that every false conception contains, nevertheless, a kernel of truth.'

In that small nick of time that was still left to that kind of Europe, we also visited a Jewish seminary—though that perhaps is not the right word. It was perhaps the equivalent of the highest class of monastery. I asked a blazing-eyed young man with a red beard, who reminded me disconcertingly of a former sub-editor of *The Times,* what he felt about the Hitler menace. What, if any, preparations were being made for resistance or escape? Or did he think nothing would happen?

He tilted his head back, and looked at me over the curling tip of his beard with that searing look of mixed compassion and disdain with which men of God cannot help regarding the earth-bound. He was familiar, said he, with the existence and activities of the man Hitler, but as for himself he was interested in certain Talmudic studies and had little time to spare for the kind of question I was asking.

Most of the Jews in that section of the continent were mur dered not long after. Yet who shall say that this man, getting on with his thinking and studies, and sarcastically damning the eyes of the approaching murderers had got things wrongly summed up? It is a 'Grand Perhaps'.

He was, it seemed, one of those who exist, if the situation may be so expressed, vertically, or intently, rather than horizontally. What is important, they think, is the achievement of today, and the petty pace of the tomorrows—even though it creeps day by day towards the gas chambers—should not be allowed to interfere or distract.

By the time, a couple of months later, that Patricia toured those parts, things had got so tense that anyone who asked questions—and to ask questions was part of her purpose in travelling about—was suspect of being up to no good. The anti-Nazis and the pro-Nazis, Russians red and white, and apparently the Wonder Rabbi, too, thought she must be the original beautiful young woman spy everyone had read about and should be on guard against. They put her in jail, and the Chief of Police dropped in every morning to explain his philosophy of life, his heroic *Weltschmerz*, his clear-eyed understanding that civilization was going to the dogs.

For the cynics, the depressed, and the bloody-minded, the period was indeed a field-day. It offered an easy-to-use X-ray of the supposed innards of human nature. Original sin was likewise clearly discernible. For idealists the time was stimulating, too, because they had always said that if things went on this way something horrible was going to happen, and now it was happening. For instance, you spent two years saying at the top of your voice that unless the governments of the Western Democracies assisted the Spanish Republic against the forces of Fascism, the Western Democracies would soon, themselves, get it, as it were, in the neck. Probably there were saintly people about who, though their pleas had gone unheeded, sincerely hoped that their prophecies would be unfulfilled. Not so, I think, the majority. There was to be found a melancholy, perhaps really vicious, satisfaction in the ever-more apparent fact that the Pharisees were not going to get away with it.

Some noble American politician, famed in annals, said when accused of making an unpopular statement of truth which might lose him votes: 'I would rather be right than President.' Just so, there are those who would rather see a horror they have predicted come to pass than have to face some unpredicted improvement of the situation.

Those were indeed, in Clarendon's bitter phrase 'reproached and condemned times'. In other places and periods, people might have felt that the only thing that could suitably occur next would be the end of the world. One did not, in the winter of '38—'39 have to be so fanciful. The war would do the trick. The gas-mask was the expression of people's faith in the accepted apocalypse. Chlorine would give the final quietus. The expectation of those stinking and lethal clouds rolling round the Ringstrasse, the Boulevard des Italiens, and Piccadilly Circus, was serviceable, too, as affording a satisfactory explanation of why it was so much harder for us than for the members of any previous generation in all history to do those things which ought to be done. It accounted, also, for cultural inertia, alcoholism, sexual muddle, and cold feet.

At some meeting about that time of statesmen—in Paris or

Geneva—a French black-and-white artist said to me, 'I am by profession a caricaturist, but here photography suffices.' It struck me as poignantly true then, and has often so struck me since. Reality goes bounding past the satirist like a cheetah laughing as it lopes ahead of the greyhound.

Sourer, even, than my friend the artist was another esteemed friend and benefactor, Robert Dell, an old man with the voice of an embittered crow, who looked like a mix-up between a cavalry officer of the Edwardian Age and the late Sir Max Beerbohm, and was in fact the diplomatic correspondent of the *Manchester Guardian*. At the age of seventy-something, he still danced all night and worked all day—chiefly at sticking poisoned arrows into the Foreign Office. He would recount with malign gusto the story of some outrageous piece of baiting and provocation he had been engaged upon, and then, his snow-white brows knitted in bewilderment, would say, 'And do you know, Claud, they *didn't like it a bit.*'

Towards dawn, in Montparnasse night-clubs, as young, vigorous girls wilted in his arms, gasping with the exhaustion of the unending dance, the stale air would be cut by his raucous, amazed cry : 'But we can't go home *yet*, it's only a quarter to six.'

On one such morning, as we at length relaxed at breakfast by a brazier on the terrace of the Café du Dôme, he said to me, 'Do you want to get—I know the idea of the "scoop" is horribly out of date, everyone is so awfully nice and co-operative these days, don't you find?—but still, do you want to get what used to be called a "scoop" for your horrid little paper every day?' (The 'horrid little paper' was, of course, the *Daily Worker*, whose diplomatic correspondent I then was.)

'That would be nice.'

'Well then, all you have to do is to read all the continental papers available every morning, take lunch with one or more of Europe's leading politicians or diplomats, make up your mind what is the vilest action that, in the circumstances, the French, British, Italian or German Government could undertake, and then, in the leisure of the afternoon, sit down at your typewriter and write a dispatch announcing that that is just what they are going to do. You can't miss. Your news will be denied two hours after it is published and confirmed after twenty-four.'

It was a particularly encouraging piece of guidance because at that time the *Daily Worker* was excluded from the newspaper trains which sped other London dailies across the country, so that I had to telegraph or telephone my messages hours before rival correspondents.

It was a time when one experienced a sharp need for some kindly lights amid the encircling gloom—a gloom which somehow seemed worse in London (where a lot of people still thought you were a tedious maniac if you said there was certainly going to be war), than in Paris where most people thought you a bore, and raving at that, if you pretended to suppose anything else. For a while I had been more tethered to London than I cared to be because my friend Michael Koltzov, foreign editor of *Pravda*, had recently appointed me London correspondent of that newspaper.

In this situation there was, from the outset, an element of embarrassment, because people supposed that in such a position I must have special facilities for getting to understand Russian attitudes, 'inside' sources at the Russian Embassy and so on. People sought to pump me about Russian policies, and were suspicious and offended when I said I knew no more about it than anyone else with a reasonable amount of common sense and appreciation of the fantastic. No one in London (where you must always put your needle in a haystack if you want anyone to find it) would have believed the truthful statement I could have made about my stint with *Pravda*.

Soon after I had started writing daily dispatches for the paper, the administrative people at the Moscow office rang me up and instructed me to open an office in London. I said it was entirely unnecessary—the correspondence could be done from my own flat, or on a typewriter here and a typewriter there. The simple fact was that I do not like to have an office and secretary and all that implies. In an office of your own you either get through your work early, and then you feel guilty because you are not fully utilizing office and secretary, and so you start dictating letters which otherwise need never have been written; or else, particularly in London, you want to work through the night and then charwomen and caretakers come and peer at you with hatred and suspicion.

But the *Pravda* people were annoyed because, not understand-

ing these phobias, they thought I was being a little insulting in a
western kind of way; suggesting, in effect, that they, with the
largest circulation of any newspaper on the turning globe, could
not afford to hire a smart piece of Fleet Street. What they
wanted was something with prestige to it, a classy type of job,
as for instance a half-floor in the Reuter building. If I had suggested negotiating for a penthouse above the *Daily Telegraph*
they would have thought the better of me. Money, they made
clear, was no object.

I still dragged my feet a little and was soon not sorry to have
done so, because the next thing that happened was that various
wives of Koltzov—he had wives in several western capitals—
started to telephone me to say that they had heard on the grape-
vine that Koltzov had been arrested and was due to be shot any
day now. Many of Koltzov's wives were known to me—three of
them had been in Spain. All of them were lovely, intelligent
women, all in love with Koltzov. They hoped, because they were
in love with him, that I would do something to save him. Because
they were intelligent they understood at once that there was
nothing whatever that I could effectively do.

It was true that I talked daily with *Pravda* when I telephoned
my article or articles to Moscow, but I did not feel that a sudden
plea from me : 'Do not shoot my boss and friend of my bosom,
he is innocent' would carry a lot of pro-Koltzov weight in the
Kremlin. It was well known that for several years he had been
the personal mouthpiece and trouble-shooter for Stalin in Spain
and other *partibus infidelium*, and in Moscow Stalin's intimate.
One had but to remember the truth of the American saying to
the effect that the bigger they come the harder they fall. He was
shot.

(Mr T. Driberg, in his little book about Mr Guy Burgess,
mentions—in reference to my account of Koltzov in the first
volume of this autobiography—that Koltzov has recently been
'rehabilitated,' which is one of those things which may be said
to be very nice so far as they go. The notion of what might be
termed posthumous pardon—execution first, revision of sentence afterwards—is one which would certainly have amused
Koltzov himself.)

A little later *Pravda* took my by-line off my articles and news
stories, which now appeared anonymously. I was dispropor-

tionately upset by that, because I recalled the loving care Koltzov had taken to try to find the absolutely correct Russian transliteration of the name I then wrote under—Frank Pitcairn. It was a question of differentiating, in Russian, the sound of the 'a' in Frank from that of the 'ai' in Pitcairn. He was a lover of language, and he liked to think about such things and get them right.

The articles continued to appear daily for a while, and then stopped. For a while the salary cheques arrived as though nothing untoward had happened, and then they stopped, too.

I did not, of course, know at the time whether Koltzov had even been arrested, let alone shot. A lot of sapient people said the whole thing was a blind and he had been sent to China on a secret mission of the highest importance. Since he had told me in Prague at Munich time that he expected to go to China, I half-believed these tales. On the other hand, *Pravda*'s behaviour to his appointee in London seemed, to say the least, suspicious.

I had no means of knowing whether I was supposed to continue telephoning daily to Moscow, firing words into the void, and whether the stoppage of pay was supposed to mean something, or was merely the result of some technical hitch or muddle of a kind which would surprise nobody at all accustomed to the bumbling workings of the Comintern.

Besides, what about the office, for which I had just begun to negotiate?

I asked questions on the telephone. The man at the other end said he had no information about anything. I wrote to Moscow. There was no answer. I visited M. Maisky, then Soviet Ambassador in London, and asked his advice. He was sympathetic and at the same time sardonically amused at the spectacle of my encounter with Russian bureaucracy. He said if I would write once more to *Pravda* he would give me a covering letter, explaining my sense of bafflement. I wrote and he wrote, but no reply was ever received. (It occurs to me now that quite a lot of people were probably arrested and jailed or shot just for getting a lot of letters from me. It would have been Stalin's idea of being on the safe side.)

I remarked to Maisky that I was glad that at least I had not gone out on a limb with that glamorous office. He said he admired my instinctive sense of balance.

All this caused me to wonder sometimes how right or wrong people were when they asserted that I had special knowledge of Russian attitudes.

Oddly—or perhaps not so oddly, because I have always liked Americans, and the sort of man that likes Americans is liable to like Russians—a prominent light in my part of the gloom was my old friend Mr Vladimir Poliakoff, formerly diplomatic correspondent of *The Times*. (It was he who had first, perhaps inadvertently, provided the information which ultimately led to the discovery—or invention, as some said—by *The Week*, of the famous—or notorious, as some said—'Cliveden set'.)

With the head of a Slav generalissimo, and a get-up vaguely suggestive of Homburg about 1906, this Vladimir Poliakoff strode and occasionally tiptoed around and about the diplomatic world of the twenties and thirties like a panther, which duller creatures deem merely picturesque or bizarre until they note what a turn of speed he has. Among his other notable qualities was an infinite capacity for taking pains to do everyone, from ambassadors to train conductors, small but unforgettable favours. A colleague, who regarded the very existence of Poliakoff with jealous disapproval, declared that there was not a Foreign Secretary in Europe whose mistress's dog had not been smuggled across one or other frontier by Poliakoff.

I met him for the first time in 1929 when I was tenuously attached to *The Times* office in Paris. The atmosphere in the office on that day was sulphurous. The chief correspondent, on calling to see the Minister of Foreign Affairs, had been informed by the *chef de Cabinet* that 'Your chief has just been with the Minister for an hour.' The correspondent was at first merely amazed that the editor should have come over from London without informing the office. Later, to his disgust, he learned that the supposed 'chief' was the peripatetic Mr Poliakoff on a quick trip to Paris. By virtue of a certain manner he had, he was quite often taken by foreign statesmen to be the 'man behind' everything from Printing House Square to Whitehall, and his sincere denials merely confirmed their belief.

Furthermore, the assistant correspondent had been apprised by friends in London that Poliakoff was accustomed to refer to him slightingly as 'the office boy with the silk moustache'. As a result of all this, the chief correspondent shut himself up in his room,

C.T.L.—B

his assistant put on his hat and walked out, growling, and I, to my alarm, was left alone with the internationally distinguished Poliakoff. I saw him examining me with attention, and feared he would ask me high diplomatic questions which I should be unable to answer, and thus become discredited.

He said, 'What you have is the grippe. Your temperature—I am not accustomed to be wrong about such things—is a little over a hundred.' Astonished, I admitted that this was precisely the case. The tails of his grey morning coat flapping suddenly behind him, he bounded from the sofa.

'A-ha!' he shouted. 'I am the one to cure that. A special remedy. Ordinary ones are futile. I proceed at once to the chemist on the corner to give my instructions. Relax. I shall return.'

In ten minutes he was back and, seating himself beside me, took from his tail pocket a small clear-glass bottle from which he poured a few drops of liquid on to a huge silk handkerchief.

'Breathe deeply. Inhale the remedy of Poliakoff.'

He had his arm round my shoulder and held the handkerchief to my nose with the air of a field-marshal succouring a stricken private. The result was immediately beneficial. But I noticed, too, that the smell and general effect were exactly those produced by a well-known, widely advertised popular remedy, the name of which I have forgotten. I was sufficiently curious to enquire later from the corner chemist whether a certain gentleman—Poliakoff was easy to describe and unforgettable—had, a little earlier, bought a bottle of this well-known product and arranged for it to be specially decanted into a plain bottle. Such had, the chemist said, been the case.

I found this little manœuvre, this taking of so much trouble to please, both impressive and endearing, and years later, when I had left *The Times*, was delighted to renew acquaintance with Mr Poliakoff at some diplomatic reception in London or Paris. He had a house in a square in South Kensington and there I used to drink Russian tea or vodka with him, or walk round and round the gardens while he exercised his two small Afghan hounds and talked to me derisively, in his harsh Slavonic accents, of the international situation. Even when he later brought a libel action against me our walks and talks continued amicably.

Being a supporter of what was called 'the Vansittart line'—
the notion that by a friendly policy towards Mussolini it might
be possible to split the Axis and isolate Hitler—he was fervent
in denunciation of those powerful personalities in England who,
on the contrary, saw in Hitler a bulwark and potential crusader
against Bolshevism and thought friendship with the Nazis both
possible and desirable. The vigour of his campaigns and intrigues
against such elements was naturally heightened by his knowledge that some of them lost no opportunity to convince everyone that he himself was a hired agent of Mussolini.

His sources of information from anti-Nazi factions in the
British and French Foreign Offices were thus first-rate, and the
stories that came from them had that particular zip and zing
which you get from official sources only when a savage intra-
mural departmental fight is going on.

I rushed about between London, Paris and Brussels, supple-
menting and checking such stories from other sources. Vigorous
anti-Nazis in the City, too, and on the so-called Churchillian
wing of the Conservative Party were also very ready with
'inside information.'

At length I thought I had enough and more than enough to
write in *The Week* (the little mimeographed news-sheet I ran at
the time) a longish 'think piece' about the nature and aims of
those in high places who were working, sincerely perhaps, but
as it seemed to me disastrously, for the 'appeasement' of Adolf
Hitler. There were, of course, several references to gatherings
at the Astors' Thames-side house at Cliveden. When I published
the story, absolutely nothing happened. It made about as loud a
bang as a crumpet falling on a carpet. A few weeks later, I ran
the whole thing again, in slightly different words, and with
similar result.

And then about a month later I did it a third time. There were
only trivial additions to the facts already published but the tone
was a little sharper. But it happened that this time it occurred to
me to head the whole story 'The Cliveden Set' and to use this
phrase several times in the text. The thing went off like a rocket.

I think it was *Reynolds News*, three days later, which first
picked up the phrase from *The Week*, but within a couple of
weeks it had been printed in dozens of newspapers, and within
six had been used in almost every leading newspaper of the

Western world. Up and down the British Isles, across and across the United States, anti-Nazi orators shouted it from hundreds of platforms. No anti-Fascist rally in Madison Square Garden or Trafalgar Square was complete without a denunciation of the Cliveden Set.

In those days, if you saw cameramen patrolling St James's Square at lunchtime or dusk, you could be nearly sure they were there to get a picture of the Cliveden Set going in or out of the Astors' London house. Geoffrey Dawson, then editor of *The Times*, and a prominent member of the 'Set,' comments petulantly on this nuisance in his diary. If you talked to American special correspondents, what they wanted to know all about was the Cliveden Set. Senators made speeches about it, and in those London cabarets where libel didn't matter, songsters made songs about it. People who wanted to explain everything by something, and were ashamed to say 'sunspots,' said 'Cliveden Set'.

And throughout it all the members of the Cliveden Set, furiously, wearily or derisively, maintained that they were not members because there simply was not any Cliveden Set to be a member of. It was a myth.

And the fact was that, however it started, it presently became a myth. Within a year or so, the Cliveden Set had ceased to represent, in anybody's mind, a particular group of individuals. It had become the symbol of a tendency, of a set of ideas, of a certain condition in, as it were, the State of Denmark. It had acquired a powerful and alarming significance for people who could hardly have named three of those who frequented Cliveden. The phrase went marching on because it first had dramatized, and now summarized, a whole vague body of suspicions and fears.

Occasionally, moderate-minded intermediaries who felt the story was stirring up dangerous thoughts urged me to tone it down in some way—curb the monster I had set loose. I had to reply that in the first place I thought the picture essentially a true one, doing more good than harm. In the second place, even supposing that, contrary to my own convictions, I were to get the B B C to permit me to announce personally to the listening millions that the story had no foundation, that I had invented it, no one would pay the slightest attention. People would come to the conclusion that I had been nobbled by the Cliveden Set.

I was certainly taken aback by the wild improbabilities which some correspondents were writing about the Cliveden Set. It looked as though quite a lot of people were getting involved, were being branded as subtly scheming political intriguers, who would not have known a plot if you handed it to them on a skewer, and quite possibly had gone to Cliveden simply for a good dinner. But then, I reflected, if one is as ignorant of political goings-on as some of them claim to be, is it very wise, even for a very good dinner, to go at all? I am prepared to believe that a lot of the people I had cast as principal figures were really mere cat's-paws. But then a cat's-paw is a cat's-paw and must expect to be treated as part of the cat. Or, as the Chinese proverb puts it: 'Do not tie up your shoes in a melon field, or adjust your hat under a plum tree if you wish to avoid suspicion.'

What ultimately interested, and still interests, me about the entire affair were not the facts about the Cliveden Set but the journalistic detail—the way in which a phrase can 'trigger' to explosion a lot of facts which, for the most part, were already known to hundreds of people, but remained, as it were, inert.

'Newspaper writing,' said the great Thomas Barnes, mid-nineteenth-century editor of *The Times*, and its true creator, 'is a thing *sui generis*; it is in literature what brandy is in beverages. John Bull, whose understanding is rather sluggish—I speak of the majority of readers—requires a strong stimulus. He consumes his beef, and cannot digest it without a dram; he dozes composedly over his prejudices which his conceit calls opinions; and you must fire ten-pounders at his densely compact intellect before you can make it comprehend your meaning or care one farthing for your efforts.' A newspaper story, he concluded, 'wanted a little devil in it.'

Poliakoff was a good man to help one put 'a little devil' into one's stories. Staid people naturally loathed him, as being an adventurer, a rapacious semi-oriental pirate upon the English seas. They had loathed in the same way the incomparable de Blowitz—and, indeed, one of the aspects of Poliakoff which gave me great pleasure was that his mind and personality, even his clothes, seemed in some way to connect the world of Henri de Blowitz, of the Second Empire, of Bismarck, and the Dreyfus case, with our own.

Probably this, too, was in part, at least, a courteous trick, a stage-show put on for my benefit, since he was always alert to note what people wanted, and then, if possible, give it to them.

'You,' he warned me several times, 'are a romantic. It is dangerous. On the other hand, it cannot be helped. Every man should be allowed to choose the brand of razor he cuts his throat with. A minimal human demand.'

As a result of this intense attention to other people, he learned, almost before I knew it myself, of an occurrence of great importance in my life. On a gusty morning in February, 1939, we were in his study, drinking a little vodka, and talking partly about the Government and partly about the unaccountable *malaise* of one of the Afghan hounds, when he said suddenly and angrily, 'Pointless to talk to you this morning. Of what use the wisdom and experience of Poliakoff? You are addled. You have fallen in love.'

And it was, oddly enough, the morning after the party at which I had for the first time met Patricia. I agreed that his diagnosis was correct.

'English?' Poliakoff asked. 'You would never understand an English woman.'

'Not at all. A glorious Irish girl who has just come out of jail in Uzhorod, Ruthenia.'

'Excellent,' said Poliakoff. 'I advise you to press forward. The omens seem favourable for your happiness.'

2

Spirits of the Age

ILENTLY released—if that is the word—by *Pravda*, I had
resumed my habit of travelling at least once a fortnight to
Paris, partly for the reason I have already indicated, partly
because news of the kind I wanted to get was more 'available'
in Paris than in London (where one would so often spend hours
seeking to penetrate what one supposed was the discretion and
'English reticence' of some leading figure, only to discover that
he knew nothing anyway) and more particularly to consult and
exchange information with such old friends and fellow-workers
as Otto Katz (then operating under the name of André Simone),
and that revered genius, Egon Erwin Kisch.

Though he died abruptly at the end of a rope, pronouncing
me responsible for his misfortune, historians ought not to forget
Otto Katz. No portrait gallery—rogues' gallery, some would say
—of the period would be quite complete without the putty-
coloured visage of that most talented propagandist and
intriguer.

Pretty soon every schoolboy will think he knows all about
that time, certified as having been full of starry-eyed do-gooders
with pink illusions which, when darkness came at noon, blew up
in their faces and turned them a neutral grey or else deep blue.
Not so much, probably, will be heard of the late Katz—a man,
nevertheless, reeking of 85 per cent. proof *Zeitgeist*, and producing some pervasive practical effects upon events. Manuals of
journalism for schools should have a bit about him, too.

He had sidled into my life in the summer of 1932, when he
was acting as a kind of assistant director of the great anti-war
congress of that year.

After the closing session, I found myself at midnight sweating
horribly in an hotel bedroom where Mr John Strachey, Mr

Gerald Hamilton, a vigorous Hungarian woman, and myself
were translating the official German text of the congress mani-
festo into English which must be, all agreed, as jolly popular in
style as the *Daily Mirror* and as rigidly exact as the Athanasian
Creed. Just how I got into the act I cannot remember, and it
certainly was exhausting.

The Hungarian woman knew German so much better than
the rest of us that she concluded she must know English better,
too, and made this clear. Mr Hamilton, whose natural prose
style was Edwardian, became so discouraged that he took off his
wig and sat silently nursing it on his knee, his head gleaming
like a new-laid egg. Mr Strachey seemed near to tears of vexa-
tion at the stubborn ineptitude of everyone else.

Every so often, a grave smile and a light sigh floated in from
the corridor, both brought to us by a smallish, light-footed man
with a big head and abnormally broad shoulders hunched in a
way to suggest that his burdens were indeed heavy, but he could
bear them, and yours, too, if you cared to confide them to him.
His smile said that whatever might be the faults of others working for peace that night, our little group was the salt of the
earth—so brilliant and devoted that we should certainly
produce splendid results, dead on time, if it killed us. He had the
air of a stage manager going round the dressing-rooms of
a troupe on the verge of hysteria.

When I asked who he was, they said, 'You don't know who
Otto Katz is? Oh!'

After the sleepless night, he invited me at breakfast-time to
drink brandy with him on the terrace, and we talked about the
congress. I spoke with enthusiasm. He ascertained that I had
been, until recently, a correspondent of *The Times* in the
United States. Presently he went about his business, which, as it
turned out, was to prepare and issue to the continental news
agencies an interview with 'the distinguished former foreign
director of *The Times*,' who heartily endorsed all objectives of
the congress, and had some sharply disobliging things to say
about the British Government.

I protested to Mr Katz, demanding corrections and denials of
the story. People, I said, would think Wickham Steed had turned
Red in the night. He said: 'But as a sincere supporter of our
cause and experienced journalist, you appreciate that any

retraction could be damaging to the excellent effect already obtained. *The Times* will doubtless issue any denials necessary. It will all help to stimulate discussion.'

'But it's preposterous to describe me like that.'

'I felt the phrase made a clearer impact. In journalism,' he said, fluttering his hand in a stagy gesture, 'one should try for clarity of impact.'

His staginess had a basis in experience. He had worked in various capacities for provincial theatres in northern Bohemia. Almost the only way to anger him was to doubt his story that at some time during that period he had been married to Marlene Dietrich. You could abuse him with impunity, but, if you doubted those nuptials, he became passionate, challenging you to go to Teplice, or wherever it was, and examine the records.

Along some political or journalistic channel—it was certainly a career open to talent—he had moved into the tumultuous Berlin entourage of the late Willi Muenzenberg, whom many people took to be the main dynamo of the German Communist Party. Whatever may be the truth about all that, Muenzenberg—who claimed to be an illegitimate nephew of Kaiser Wilhelm II—had made a vital impact upon the political life of Europe. He had snatched the journalism of the extreme Left from the hands of the pedants, insisted that a modern revolutionary newspaper could be as 'popular' in today's terms as an old-time revolutionary broadsheet, and that the technical tricks, skills, and 'appeal' of the stunting, pandering, sensation-mongering capitalist press were to be not despised, but learned. His success, particularly with the picture paper *AIZ*, which for a time was the largest-circulation weekly in central Europe, had important consequences in Italy, France and Latin America. Muenzenberg's offices in the Wilhelmstrasse, across the way from the Foreign Office, were also the centre of those numerous international organisations (the League Against Imperialism for example), which, while the Communists supplied the inspiration and driving force, did at moments of crisis rally many sorts and conditions of non-Communists and anti-Communists who wanted to get moving and found no other bus going their way.

In all this, Otto Katz was first the pupil, later the right-hand man and, ultimately, it was often asserted, the inspirer of Muenzenberg; he was certainly the chief engineer of the Muenzenberg machine. After Hitler moved in on both sides of the Wilhelm-strasse, Katz, who now called himself André Simone, operated from a series of headquarters in Paris. He padded about Paris, Geneva, London, New York and Chicago, exercising and developing an almost necromantic capacity for getting people who naturally loathed and suspected one another organised for joint action. The nature of the—so to speak—material he worked on seemed not to interest him greatly: he was as happy welding mutually hateful novelists and poets into a literary League for the defence of this or that, as he was when arranging for a couple of Tory Lords and someone from Transport House to turn up on a platform with the editor of *l'Humanité*. The more improbable the *combinaison*, the more it charmed him. Indeed, after a visit with him to the United States, the Roman Catholic Prince Loewenstein told me that, though prepared for anything, he had, after all, been startled when he saw Herr Simone-Katz 'genuflect three times and kiss the ring of a cardinal to whom he then presented a Marxist professor just out of jail in Rio de Janeiro.'

All this time Katz was busy, too, as a very sharp-shooting press agent and public relations counsellor for the organisations in which he was interested. Almost weekly he brought off the tricky shot of planting a damaging anti-Fascist story in a pro-Fascist newspaper, and under his original impulse his stories ran about the world like snooker-balls. They certainly had 'impact'. He regarded journalism simply as a means to an end, a weapon. In this I found him sympathetic. Long before, in New York and Washington, I had come to the conclusion that the real humbug of the press begins only when newspapers pretend to be neutral, impartial fact-purveyors, 'servants,' so help me, 'of the public.'

Arriving in Paris from Spain unexpectedly one day during the Spanish War, I telephoned Katz at the office of the *Agence Espagne*, the news agency of the Republican Government which he organised and directed. As was usual when one telephoned any office run by Katz, an excited voice said, 'Si, si, mais, s'il vous plaît, be so good speak deutsch, bitte schoen, momentito,' and then Katz came on the line shouting, 'Thank God you're here, come at once, urgent.' He plunged immediately into business. 'Have I ever told you that you are considered by many, myself included, the best journalist in the world?'

'Often, when you wanted to get something for nothing out of me.'

'Well, what I want now is a tip-top, smashing, eye-witness account of the great anti-Franco revolt which occurred yesterday at Tetuan, the news of it having been hitherto suppressed by censorship.'

I said I had never been in Tetuan and knew of no revolt there.

'Not the point at all,' he said impatiently. 'Nor have I heard of any such thing.' The point, he explained, was that a crucial moment had been reached in the supply of arms to the battling Spanish Republicans.

Occasionally, despite non-intervention, the government of Léon Blum, under pressure from the Left, agreed that all concerned should shut both eyes tight while military supplies were rushed across the Catalan frontier. At this moment a major battle was being mounted in Spain. On the frontier a big consignment of field guns was ready. The outcome of the battle might depend on its getting through. Next morning a strong deputation of Communist deputies and others was to call on Blum, asking for a little shut-eye. Blum, naturally, was always more malleable when anything happened to suggest that Franco might, after all, lose the war. It was thus essential, Katz pointed out, that a jolt of that kind should be administered now. Something with a clear psychological impact. What better for the purpose than news of a sudden revolt against Franco at the very origin and source of his first onslaught, Spanish Morocco? Why not, for instance, Tetuan? That, he said, would have impact.

There seemed to be just a chance, and we worked on that story at a high pitch of anxiety and excitement. Our chief anxiety was that, with nothing to go on but the plans in the guide-books, which were without contours, we might have Democrats and Fascists firing at one another from either end of an avenue which some travelled night-editor would know had a great hump in the middle. The fighting, accordingly, took place in very short streets and open squares. As we saw it, an important feature of the affair was that sections of the Moorish soldiery, sickened by losses in Spain, had joined with civilian victims of colonial oppression and Spanish anti-Fascists in united, if desperate, action. It meant that the same thing might happen in Spain itself. Katz was insistent we use a lot of names, of both heroes and villains, but express uncertainty over some of them—thus in the confusion of the struggle outside the barracks it had been impossible to ascertain whether the Captain Murillo who died so gallantly was the same Captain Murillo who, months ago in Madrid. . . .

In the end it emerged as one of the most factual, inspiring and yet sober pieces of war reporting I ever saw, and the night editors loved it. When the deputation saw Blum in the morning he had been reading it in newspaper after newspaper and appreciating its significance. He was receptive to the deputation's suggestions. The guns got through all right, and the Republicans won that battle.

(I should say here that when, a little while ago, I published part of this story in New York, a defender of Blum wrote a furious denial that such could have been his attitude. He purported to know—I have no idea how—that no such motives could have actuated Blum. He may, of course, be right. Perhaps, for instance, Blum was interested because a revolt in Tetuan would shake the faith of betwixt-and-between Franco supporters in France, who thus would be less liable to make a scandal about the dispatch of arms to the Republicans. The defender I refer to wrote with such assurance that one is forced to suppose it at least possible that he really did have some knowledge not available to other people. The supposition is at least strong enough to make it seem only fair to put his view—which I still think quite mistaken—on record here.)

Many people to whom I have at one time and another told this little story of the Tetuan revolt have been themselves revolted, profoundly shocked. Or at least they said they were. When I first published it as part of an article in a weekly paper, Mr R. H. Crossman, Labour Member of Parliament, referred to it with disgust in a piece he wrote for the News Chronicle. Aware that Mr Crossman had himself played a considerable role in British wartime propaganda, I was in turn taken aback. Was it, then, possible that throughout the life-and-death struggle with Hitler our propagandists had all along taken the view that their paramount duty was to be gentlemen, and not to tell lies, however damagingly misleading these might be to the enemy? What about, I thought as I noted Mr Crossman's disdain for the Tetuan trick, the 'Man Who Never Was' and suchlike episodes?

Reading on, I was fascinated to find that what fretted Mr Crossman was not that the thing had been done, but that I seemed to be quite happy, retrospectively, to have had a hand in it. According to him, it was true that he and colleagues had done that sort of thing during the war, but they had done it with gentlemanly distaste. ' "Black" propaganda,' wrote Mr Crossman, 'may be necessary in war, but most of us who practised it detested what we were doing.'

A comfortable ethical position, if you can stop laughing. To me, at least, there seems something risible in the spectacle of a man firing off his propaganda-lies as, one presumes, effectively as he knows how, but keeping his conscience clear by 'detesting' his own activities. After all, if he does not think the cause for which he is fighting is worth lying for, he does not have to lie at all, any more than the man who sincerely feels that killing is murder is forced to shoot at those enemy soldiers. He can become a conscientious objector, or run away. 'Paris vaut bien une messe,' and I do not recall that Henry of Navarre ever claimed that he had detested his own 'cynical' behaviour.

At any rate, Katz had none of these inhibitions and did his work con amore. He had, of course, his failures, most of them, so far as I could observe, resulting from a quality rather often found in people of his background, namely a tendency to get in a muddle about the English. I do not have that background, but I am conscious of being in a muddle about them too. He could simultaneously attribute to them almost super-human cunning and intelligence, and sub-human stupidity and credulity. He would thus sometimes spend time shooting, so to speak, at gun-emplacements which did not exist, and at others imagine that he had duped people by some manœuvre which the simplest could see through.

He was very proud of having secured for whatever office it was he was finally running in Paris—I have forgotten what name it went under—the services of a young Czech who, Otto claimed, could pass anywhere as an absolutely typical young Englishman. I forget, too, just what benefits were supposed to accrue from this—perhaps the idea was that in this role he could better effect contact with voyaging V.I.P.s, make friends and influence people. A little difficulty was, that for reasons no doubt sufficient, the young man would have had trouble in get-

ting a visa to go to England to get the 'tip-top' English clothes
which Otto, by now quite intoxicated with his particular Pyg-
malion act, thought desirable. However, a Paris tailor was found
who claimed to understand, more or less, what was considered
correct for business or *le sport* by English chic (in both senses of
the world) types. And they rigged that poor young Comintern-
commando up in an outfit of which it could be said that anyone
who did not immediately discern on seeing him coming that this
must be some Czech dressed up in a Frenchman's idea of an
Englishman would have needed his eyesight tested.

I said as much to Otto, who was offended and became moody.
Then a fine idea cheered him.

'Are you so sure,' he said gently, 'that you yourself understand quite what is the correct thing in England? After all, my
friend, you have lived so much of your life in central Europe, in
the United States. And even in London, do you see a great deal
of the right people, socialites and such? It is easy to lose touch
with English Society. It is not,' he added kindly, 'your fault. All
the same, in my view Tommy looks absolutely . . . what is the
word? . . . pukkah.'

He laughed, repeating 'pukkah' with pleasure.

'Tommy?' I asked, incredulously.

'I want,' said Otto, 'us all to get used to calling him "Tommy".
A good, non-committal name.'

Irked, I could only remark that the address of his new office
was, in every sense, a good one—it was in the Rue de l'Ancienne
Comédie.

I never knew just how Otto Katz got out of France a little
while before the twist of events which produced in turn the
Nazi-Soviet Pact and the suppression of the French Communist
Party. He escaped the fate of those refugees who were first
arrested by the French and then killed by the Germans. He spent
the greater part of the war, I think, in Mexico, returning later,
after the German defeat, to Prague where he became a kind of
foreign or diplomatic adviser to the official Communist newspaper *Rude Pravo*.

Some years later he was hanged by the Communists, and just
before he went to the gallows made a confession saying that he
would have done well enough had he not, at an early date, been
misled and recruited by me as an agent of the British intelli-

gence service. The statement made quite an impact in Prague, and several dozen people were arrested, and some of them tortured, for just having known me at one time or another.

Our friend, Egon Erwin Kisch, of whom I saw a good deal in that period before the war, had, so I believe, died before these events took place. At the time of his death or until just before it, he had been Mayor of Prague.

Polgar says somewhere of somebody that 'his dearest wish would have been to have been born in Czernowitz, and, since he is a darling of the Gods, even this has been granted him.' In the same way I dare say that Kisch, who loved Prague with a passion unsurpassed even by the passion of those who love Edinburgh or Dublin, would have considered that to be born in Prague and finally become Mayor of that city was about as final a consummation of dreams as any man could expect—except that he had, for most of his life, less than no reason to expect it, considering that as he grew up there he was spat on by all high authority as a loathsome little radical newspaperman, Jewish into the bargain, and later had to fly for his life, an exile who, were he to return after the Germans had taken over, would be not merely spat on but tortured and hanged.

Perhaps, if he had lived long enough, he might have ultimately joined Katz on the gallows, for in that panic 'purge' nobody was safe. However, Kisch was less vulnerable than Katz, being a sort of municipal, if not national, hero, his writings loved and admired by people who totally disagreed with him politically. Because his books were world-famous, the Prague people saw in him a world-wide advertisement for themselves.

Though little known in England, Kisch was an important phenomenon in the history of European journalism. For it was he who first introduced to central European journalism the western, Anglo-American conception of reportage. Until his bustling, thickset figure, vehicle for gypsy-sharp eyes and an enquiring nose—he looked rather as an Aberdeen terrier would look if it were Jewish—first hustled into the back streets of Prague (streets which in the end were so long that they took him to Pekin, Madrid, and Sydney), the term 'reporter' was not noble in Europe. Noble was rather to sit in an editorial office writing 'think pieces', or else—à la Française—conduct huge-scale enquêtes into situations of various kinds, in which

observed phenomena served as sparse pegs on which were hung
a whole wardrobe of political speculation or general philosophy.

Within weeks of its first appearance Kisch's first book of
articles—'The Rushing Reporter'—changed all that. It sold more
than a million copies. To be a reporter became the fashion, and
quite old men who hitherto had signed their articles as 'Doctor'
this or 'Professor' that, proudly proclaimed themselves 'repor-
ters' and claimed to be out for the facts.

As in the careers of all men who succeed in doing what they
want to do and somewhat more, luck played in Kisch's career a
notable role. He was, of course, lucky not to be assassinated in
China or Mexico—lucky, indeed, as he said to me once 'being a
central European Jew of the twentieth century to have lived a
long time without being tortured even once.' Personally I have
always been very interested in luck, and, to me, more impressive
than these later instances was the luck he had in connection
with his first great journalistic coup in the strange and lurid
affair of Colonel Redl.

Colonel Redl may well have been the greatest *agent double* of
the twentieth century, so far as it has gone. Or else, perhaps he
merely seems so because he was one of those who ultimately got
caught. In such cases, as with murderers, it is only possible to
assess the relative qualities of those who, in the long run, did
not quite make the grade.

At any rate, he was good enough in that role to have achieved,
a few years before the outbreak of World War I, the distinction
of being simultaneously the chief of the counter-espionage
system of the Austro-Hungarian Empire, and the chief of the
Russian espionage system against the Austro-Hungarian Empire.

His start on the ladder to this eminence was commonplace
enough—young officer of middle-class background trying to
keep up with the aristocratic von Joneses, needs money, spotted
by international spy-ring, gently lured, then trapped, then black-
mailed. Homosexual too. The story so far is pure corn. However, what happened next was more unusual, and a tribute to
Redl's personal qualities. He seems to have been one of those
men who could make a virtue—if this is not a contradiction in
terms—out of the most dire of necessities. He freed himself
from the squalid international spy-bureau in Brussels by getting
the people in St Petersburg to buy him out, promising them that,

given enough money, he could get them their money's-worth many times over. From this point on, the ladder became a double ladder, like something in a circus act, and with astonishing aplomb Redl made each ladder co-operate with the other, all to the swifter advancement of Redl. Thus he pointed out to the Russians that it would be a great advantage from their viewpoint if he were to get on to the inside of the Austrian military counter-espionage organization. But to do so, and to get to any worthwhile position in it, he would need to render some services. Why not, for instance . . . ? The Russians saw the point immediately and gave Redl the names of a couple of their own spies in Austria-Hungary whom he then 'unmasked'—earning in Vienna the reputation of a smart man. The process continued until he was right at the top of both ladders. He would give little 'briefings' to Austrian spies going into Russia, telling them how patriotic and heroic they were. They were not to know that their jobs were even more risky than they supposed, since Redl had, when it suited him, tipped off St Petersburg to their identities, and they were shot almost before the Carpathians were out of sight behind them. Information and lives were swapped to the satisfaction of both intelligence services, both of which were able to prove—in St Petersburg as in Vienna—that they were getting results.

The result for Redl was that he became a member of the 'inner council' of the General Staff of the Austro-Hungarian Empire, and—*pari passu*—the most important Russian agent in the world. And in 1913 he sold to the Russians the whole of the Austro-Hungarian 'order of battle', laboriously worked out over many years, for the event of war on the eastern front.

One part of the climax came because of something which one may evaluate as one will—either as the spatulate bumbling of Russian bureaucracy, the casually criminal inefficiency of all intelligence services, or simply the fact that it is almost always almost fatal to pin any faith to the belief that the professionals in any line, from newspaper-proprietorship to the Field-Marshals, have much idea of what they are up to.

However that may be, the Russians sent off the preliminary payment for the big sell-out in an envelope addressed to 'Opera Ball Thirteen,' Poste Restante, Central Post Office, Vienna. And Redl's own men, who naturally had no notion of their chief's double role, happened to intercept the document. The sum inside was so large that Redl was asked at a meeting of the 'inner council' whether he did not think that this must be the clue which would lead to the apprehension of whatever individual or group was responsible for numerous leakages which had recently occurred. He was forced, as a loyal member of the General Staff, to arrange for two detectives to be permanently on duty at the General Post Office, with a bell rigged up to inform them so soon as anyone came to claim that letter.

Naturally, Redl could not resist the suggestion. The detectives were placed in the back office with a bell. And Redl could have sat down to wait for ever, or until the heat went off, to collect his money, had it not been for his friend—a stable boy whom he had financed into an expensive cavalry regiment—who at this moment reminded him that he (the young lad) was madly in love with an actress, and that he proposed to see nothing further of Redl, unless Redl could see his way clear to buy one of the new-model Daimler cars and take him—the stable boy—on a glamorous motor trip through fashionable resorts in Switzerland and on the Riviera. Otherwise, true love would triumph, and it would be the actress. And the friendship-trip in the Daimler, if it was to come off at all, must come off now—at the most in a week.

Without the Russian payment Redl could not buy the Daimler. He took a chance. Just before the General Post Office in the Stefanstrasse closed, at five o'clock in the afternoon, he took a taxi thither, went in, asked for a letter addressed to 'Opera Ball Thirteen'. The clerk, as instructed, handed him the letter and at the same time rang the bell notifying the detectives that the big moment had come. But, as so often happens when the big moment comes, the detectives—already bored by their seemingly senseless vigil—were now reflecting that it was Saturday night, that the post office would be closed in a few minutes, that in an hour or so they would be escorting their girl-friends to the Prater. They had their trousers off and were ironing them to give the chic crease. It took them just that little while after the bell rang to leap into those trousers.

Nevertheless they did get into their trousers and out of the building just in time to espy the number of Redl's taxi; they had the good luck, a quarter of an hour later to encounter that same taxi homeward-bound across the Stephan's Platz; they traced, point by point whither the fare had gone; and they found, as they cruised, down behind the back cushions of the taxi, a leather sheath—the sort of small leather sheath that would, in those days, be used for a paper-knife. He had needed it to cut open the Russian letter.

That was how they traced him to the Hotel Herrenhof, where they told the man at the reception desk they were looking for a spy, and he laughed, and they asked 'Why does that make you laugh?' and he said, 'Because this is the Vienna residence of our biggest spy-catcher—did you not know?—Colonel Redl.'

Nevertheless they asked the receptionist to show the little sheath to every guest who went in or out, and enquire whether he had lost it, and when Colonel Redl—in civilian clothes, and all ready for the trip to Switzerland and the Riviera—came down, they perfunctorily showed it him, and he said, 'My God, yes, that's mine, now where did I . . . ?'

Then he saw the detectives, watching him. He walked about Vienna all evening, and by the time he returned to his hotel there was a military commission there to hand him a revolver. He waited until six in the morning and then shot himself. The military commission took off for Prague where Redl had his headquarters, and a communiqué was issued to the newspapers announcing that Colonel Redl had died suddenly of a heart attack. The Imperial Government was particularly anxious to keep secret facts which, if known, would provide propaganda ammunition to the Czechs, the Yugoslavs, the Socialists and all those others who proclaimed the régime rotten at the core.

This was where Kisch's luck came in. The day at whose dawn Redl shot himself at the Herrenhof in Vienna, was a Sunday. And for that day had been scheduled an Association Football match in Prague between a team from Dresden City and a team representing the Prague newspaper *Bohemia*. The advance betting was all on the *Bohemia* team, but they lost, because at the last moment their goalkeeper did not turn up and could not be found anywhere.

The Editor of *Bohemia* at the time—and if this did not make him a darling of the Gods nothing could—was Egon Erwin Kisch. Late that Sunday night, after the bitterness of the lost match, Kisch at length interviewed the missing goalkeeper—

who excused himself by saying that he had had an urgent job to do. He was, by occupation, a locksmith.

'A job?' snarled Kisch. 'On a Sunday? Why not come right out with it and admit you were too drunk to get out of bed in time for the match?'

The locksmith told him things had not been like that at all. A military commission had been there—searching the personal headquarters of Colonel Redl, and they had needed the services of a skilled locksmith to force dozens of locks on Redl's private desks and drawers. Wide-eyed, the young locksmith told Kisch of the things discovered in those drawers—the autographed photographs of young men, the bundles of letters, the conversation about these matters that went on between the members of the commission.

By this time, Kisch had forgotten his displeasure at the defeat on the soccer field. He questioned and cross-questioned, and the next issue of *Bohemia* carried a démenti which ran to several columns length. Because of the censorship it had to be couched in a certain form. 'It is entirely untrue that Colonel Redl, who died a perfectly natural death of a heart attack on Sunday morning, was in fact . . .' The facts, all denied, then followed. And even at that more than half the issue of the paper was seized and burned by the police.

It was thus that Kisch, in his way, like—though in other ways so unlike—Poliakoff, for me linked past Europe with the present Europe and helped to make the present Europe more bearable, more intelligible. Whatever astounding and even dismaying things seemed to be happening, they were no more astounding or dismaying than a lot of things that had happened before.

We used, in that strange spring before der Pakt and the war which we all, erroneously thought, was going to be the end of everyone, to take, sometimes, the pleasant air of Touraine, in the company of a man whose real name I have never known nor asked—he was called simply Monsieur Bob. His parents were wine-growing peasants in Touraine, and he himself—I have been told, and I think it is true—was an officer of some French cavalry regiment which was attached (either as guard or demonstration) to the French Embassy in Russia at the time of the revolution.

Whether it was cavalry or not, the fact was that when the showdown came—when the French were supposed to rush at the revolting proletariat—this young officer refused to order them so to do. Indeed he ordered them, and they seem to have acted with vehemence, to assault the other lot—the Reds. At any rate, whatever it was he did was heinous, and he was sentenced to death in France, should he ever return to the jurisdiction. In the end there was an armistice on that sort of thing—I suppose as a result of the Franco-Soviet Pact (these things always seem of life-and-death importance at the time and afterwards you forget what on earth the sequence really was). So there he was in France, a gentle, dapper little man cocking a Touraine peasant's eye at the Comintern of which he was a principal agent.

I had met him a couple of years before in Spain where he had arrived suddenly on a tour of inspection. I had expected someone grim who, probably, would weigh me in the balance and find me much wanting. I took a terrible chance by recommending to him—a Tourangeois—a certain Catalan wine I had discovered, telling him that it was as good as a medium-grade French claret. Fortunately, for he was a fastidious little man, he thought so too, and we became friends over the first bottle.

Occasionally, when there was time, he would drive me and one or two other wine-lovers such as Kisch, down to his parents' vineyard. They were a gnarled old couple, looking as though they had been toiling in that vineyard since about the time of Voltaire. And although neither of them had ever been farther from home than Tours, they thought their son's sensational and even bizarre career quite a natural thing to happen in the world. On account of their almost rigorous hospitality, after a couple of hours at their farm-house one lived in a golden haze. They would open a bottle of their wine, give you a glass and ask what you thought of it.

You drank and commented admiringly—and it really was very good.

The old man would look at you as though he had found himself entertaining an escaped lunatic.

'Good? You think that good? But my dear sir, forgive me for asking, but where have you been all your life? Now permit me to draw your attention to *this* bottle. You will see the difference.'

You drank a glass or two of the next bottle, and you did see the difference and said so.

'Wonderful!'

'Wonderful? You can find that wonderful? Good, yes, I agree. But not wonderful. Now nearer to being wonderful is this.'

Bottle after bottle was opened on a deliciously ascending scale, until the peak of the sublime was reached. Once, ignorantly, I remarked of the last, the most sublime bottle of all, that it must fetch an enormous price in Paris. My host jumped as though at an indecent suggestion.

'Sell *that* to Paris? My dear sir. That is our best wine. We can't sell that. We drink it ourselves.'

It was during one of these golden interludes that Monsieur Bob first sought to convey to me, with infinite discretion, the possibility, theoretical as yet, of something in the nature of a German-Soviet Pact. To most of us at that time the notion was both outrageous and incredible. And if rumours were heard, we supposed them to have been put about by reactionary agents.

'But if,' said Monsieur Bob, sighing deeply and stroking the stem of his wine-glass, 'the British simply do not want to come to a serious agreement with Moscow?' (This must, I suppose, have been in late May or early June.) 'Suppose,' he said, 'that *le patron*' (it was the way Stalin was always referred to at that time) 'suppose *le patron*—on the basis, you understand, of information received—believes that secretly the British still hope to come to an agreement with Hitler themselves? An agreement which will send him eastwards instead of westwards? What do you think *le patron* would do? What could he do, except perhaps turn the tables on them and buy a little time for Russia by sending him westwards first, *en attendant* the real battle in the east?'

'But good God—an agreement with Hitler? With that aggressor and murderer, the leader and organiser, after all, my dear Bob, of anti-communism everywhere?'

'Are all Scotsmen,' asked M. Bob, oddly echoing Poliakoff, 'somewhat romantic? I would draw your attention to the fact that we are talking about serious international politics. But of course nothing of the kind may ever happen. Perhaps London will all at once come to its senses. I have great faith—perhaps it is I who am now being romantic—in English common sense.

Perhaps'—and it was a phrase you heard over and over again in Paris at the time—'perhaps they will send for Churchill and put an end to all this fooling about.'

Perhaps it was the wine, perhaps it was the fact that Patricia was due to come over to Paris in a day or two—for whatever reason, I paid at the time too little attention to this conversation in which, as I saw later, my friend Bob was seeking to offer me, from his own inside position, a cautious pre-view of the possible shape of things to come. So that when, a good many weeks later, the first unmistakable indications that 'der Pakt' was going to be a reality came, soon after midnight, over the tickertape at the Savoy Hotel in London, I was almost as startled as anyone else.

Nevertheless, when the earthquake occurred, I found that Bob's warning had subconsciously prepared me for it. Also his manner and personality were strong antidotes to panic. He was one of those who, at moments of exhaustion and darkness of mind, revive one's confidence in the human race. He had the virtues, such as courage, clarity of mind, and firm philosophy, which were to be found among the best Comintern agents, without the occupational vices of many of them, such as rigidity, pomposity, affectation, parrot-talk and the arrogance born of basic insecurity.

He was one of those men who really do love their fellow-men like brothers and are, literally, prepared to be martyred for their sakes. He accepted the most rigid discipline because he considered it necessary to victory. Some march in step because they find it easier than walking alone. Monsieur Bob was not one of those. He was one of those, however, who in shedding their illusions do not also shed their hopes.

3

Pop goes the weasel

A MAN who claims to have been present at the time told
me recently a poignant story of a discussion held in
the Kildare Street Club, Dublin, in the last week of
August 1939. I suppose if you amalgamated the London Carlton
Club and the Athenaeum and then stuffed the end product with
moth-balls, you would get something resembling the Kildare
Street Club. (It is, for instance, the place where two men quar-
relled for life because, due to acoustics and confused mentality,
while Mr A was making bitter comments on the coldness of the
bath water, Mr B understood him to be aspersing, as frigid, Mr
B's daughter.)

However, by the late August of that year the news that some
kind of international conflict might well be brewing was already
known at the Club. The late Earl of Wicklow, mulling over the
situation with friends, said they could take it from him that
the whole idea of war was nonsense.

'Austria-Hungary,' said he, 'has learned her lesson from the
last war. If Hitler were to attack, Austria-Hungary would take
him in the rear, and he knows it.'

With regret, his friends reminded him that Austria-Hungary,
as such, no longer existed, and that its disparate portions were,
directly or indirectly, under the control of Hitler himself.

The Earl reflected briefly and then said, 'Well, be that as it
may, Hitler will still not dare to act. He has to reckon with the
Serbs. The Serbs, and mark my words, the Serb is a good fighting
man,' said he, 'hate the Boche. Serbia will take Hitler in the rear,
and he knows it.'

Sadly they told him the situation regarding Serbia—how it
had ceased to exist as a separate nation, been merged into Yugoslavia, and how, for various reasons, Yugoslavia was in no

sort of shape to be conducting decisive attacks upon Hitler's rear.

'In that case,' said the Earl of Wicklow, 'the whole thing is reduced to an absolute farce.'

The idea that the whole thing had been reduced to an absolute farce was, with more or less justification, according to your viewpoint, the first reaction of millions of honest Britons to the news that 'hammer' Molotov and champagne merchant Ribbentrop were together in Moscow, arranging to be friends for evermore. Witty, encouraging and inaccurate to the last, the British Foreign Office spokesman said, 'All the Isms are Wasms.'

No one old enough to have been politically conscious at that time is likely to forget the bubble of passions, the frantic accusations and counter-accusations, the 'agonizing re-appraisals', the re-affirmations of faith, the hubbub of emotions, which thereupon broke out. And, of course, people too young to have been there must by now find a lot of the excitement irrelevant and incomprehensible. It was real enough that night.

The *Daily Worker*, where it was axiomatic that reports of any agreement between Hitler and Stalin were vile Fascist inventions, had long since gone to press, and I was having supper at the Savoy with my tempestuous friend Mr Wilfred Macartney —another man who, criticise him as you may (and there have been times when he seems to have positively gone out of his way to get criticised), was certainly an incarnation of the *Zeitgeist*.

I have been told that he was the youngest Captain in the British Army in World War I, and he was, at the time, fairly rich, too—something to do with the ownership of tramways in Malta. He worked, later, in the Aegean under Compton Mackenzie, then a principal British 'secret agent' in Athens, doing espionage or counter-espionage and smuggling and sabotage—all fine piratical stuff, very uplifting at the time but probably bad for you afterwards, like marijuana.

In London later, bored and—as the saying was in those days —'disillusioned', he became arrested as a Soviet spy, trying to give (not, one should emphasize, sell) British naval secrets to the Kremlin. He got seven years, and served five or a bit more of them at Parkhurst. He was a man who had always lived rather lavishly in the physical sense, and the deprivations of jail told upon him severely. When he came out, he wrote a book which became a best-seller—it was an account of his prison experiences called *Walls have Mouths*. It made him almost rich again, and no one would have blamed him had he decided to take a little time out and catch up on the caviar and champagne.

To his eternal credit, this boisterous, unaccountable, lovable and exasperating man did nothing of the kind. He immediately volunteered to join the International Brigade to fight in Spain, and was the first commander of the British Battalion of that strange force. It was at its headquarters, in Albacete, that I met him—a gay-looking man, though with a touch of oddness, because although his face remained youthful and rubicund, his hair, during his stretch in prison, had turned chalk-white.

There was a lot of trouble in Albacete at the time—the trouble you cannot get away from with a revolutionary army which some people have joined on revolutionary principles, and others for what they think is going to be a free ride. (On the other side there was an Irish Brigade, raised to fight for Franco, which had a record unique, I should say, in military annals. It was the only force which returned from a campaign with more members than it had when it set out. The losses they suffered were remarkably light in comparison with those of the International Brigade. But when they came to leave, a number of Irishmen— seamen and others—who found themselves in straitened circumstances in Seville and Cádiz, availed themselves of the opportunity of a trip home.) Quite recently, in Youghal, Ireland, I was talking to a postman, a Mr Fitzgerald, who was one of those in the Irish Brigade who did get into the front line. After a lot of note-comparing we found that at one moment we must actually have been firing at one another from behind opposing rocks. 'My God, Mr Cockburn,' said Mr Fitzgerald, 'if we'd both been better shots there'd have been a terrible loss to civilisation.'

The trouble at Albacete was partly political (too much Communist control was alleged), partly non-political (if anything in this day and age can be so described). The 'non-political' part of the row was about the shortage of tea at the time when civilised Englishmen drink tea, and the fact that, try as you might, you —a man born and bred in Glasgow—could not get the same kick out of a bottle of Spanish brandy as you could get out of a bottle of Scotch.

André Marty who, though he had been the able leader of the French naval mutiny in the Black Sea in 1917, was, in my opinion, at this time mad as a hatter—he once chased me right around the lounge of the Florida Hotel in Madrid seeking to shoot me on the ground that I had recognized him (he was incognito) and started to converse with him—was at this period chief Political Commissar at Albacete, and to have Marty in charge of anything was worse than having half the hard cases in Glasgow roaring at the Adjutant's door.

I never sorted out what precisely happened in Albacete, but whatever had happened Macartney was, so to speak, elected to carry the can back. Whether, as some said, he was officially instructed to inflict a crippling wound upon himself, so that he could be returned to Britain without scandal or annoyance, or whether, as others have firmly declared to me, a minor political commissar saved him the trouble by unexpectedly firing a pistol bullet through his elbow joint as they rode together in a car, the fact is that the next time I saw him, in Valencia, there he was with his arm in a sling and on the way home.

When I too returned some considerable time later, he told me with intelligible satisfaction that his doctor had absolutely forbidden him to drink anything but champagne at any time—breakfast, lunch, dinner and midnight. One very early morning he exuberantly cashed his usual cheque at the Savoy but—it was one of those things which seemed more amusing at the time than they afterwards turn out to be—wrote on the borrowed cheque form the address of Barclay's Bank as '16 King Street', headquarters of the Communist party. As a result of some confusion (there was probably a new, unknowing man in the accounts department), the Savoy people took him to court about it. He had no difficulty in explaining the innocence of the prank, and the magistrate pointed out that apparently the head-waiter knew Mr Macartney very well and was regularly in the habit of cashing his cheques for him.

'Why,' said the magistrate, 'did you do that?'

'Well, sir,' said the waiter, 'I had been given to understand that he was Editor of the *Daily Worker*.'

After seeing the news on the ticker I went home and brooded much of the night, and in the morning took the telephone off the hook—it was sufficiently evident what the various people who would ring one up would, respectively, and in contradiction of one another, say. And indeed they have been saying it ever since.

In those days I had, perhaps, a rather more childlike confidence in the judgment of Stalin than—by pure hindsight—I have now. That is to say, I did not grasp to what extent he was the victim of excesses of occupational insanity. Even now, I cannot see that there was anything else he could have done in the matter of the Pact—and nobody on the British side has, so far as I know, ever produced a single official document to show that the British statesmen concerned were seriously interested in an Anglo-Soviet alliance, and were not more interested in an Anglo-German alliance. It is, of course, no crime on their part to have preferred the chance of one to the chance of the other. From their viewpoint and from that of many of their associates, they were justified. They would have gained a few years by launching Hitler eastwards, and, had he won, there would still have been a few years more before, with European and probably part of Asiatic Russia under his control, he would have swallowed up Britain and France.

Yet, despite these considerations, people became, at the time, quite frenzied with indignation. I recall a distinguished and sincere fellow-traveller of long standing, who, during those days, could not bear to leave the offices of the *Daily Worker*, where he daily beat his breast, except to visit the precincts of the Communist party at King Street, where he beat it more. Choking with emotion, tears often on his cheeks, he totally neglected his own very lucrative business as he tottered bewilderedly up and down the stairs at both places with, it seemed, the general idea of telling everyone concerned—editors and functionaries of one kind and another—that something must be done. What he thought should be done never emerged, unless it was that the British Communists were suddenly to proclaim that they were going to quit the Comintern as speedily as the European Socialists had retired to their national fastnesses when the earlier trouble broke out in 1914.

The memories of 1914 were, indeed, among the troubling factors. It would be interesting, if anyone had the time to do it, to make a study of events and dates which have reached out a long, paralysing hand to grip and twist future history. The

French very notably, for a century and a half, surrendered themselves with apparent enthusiasm to this vicious mauling by the
hand of history. It sufficed to suggest that somebody was acting
like a 'man of the 18th Brumaire' or of the '11th of July' or
whatever date it may be upon which some horrible thing was
done, to set people against that somebody, or at least to lay
on him the burden of proof that he was not up to something vile.

The English are victims (or beneficiaries, according as to
whether you think this procedure by historical analogy a good
thing or a bad thing), of the same tendency. For years and years
the Labour party was—perhaps to some extent still is—
governed by the memory of how in the early 1930's Ramsay
MacDonald split them and betrayed them to form the National
Government. And, in 1939, the thinking of everyone on the Left
was subtly or crudely influenced by the recollection of how, in
1914, the Second International, after its Congress at Brussels in
which its member parties from every nation had solemnly gone
on record with the declaration that under no circumstances
would they support their Governments should those Governments lead their countries into war, almost immediately went
home and supported their respective Governments by voting, at
the outbreak of World War I, for the war credits necessary to
the financing of the conflict.

Perhaps, so far as its long-term effects are concerned, it was
above all the dramatic nature of the reversal, of the betrayal
of declared principle, which gave that proceeding its importance, its historical 'authority'. For just as a phrase can
ultimately be more important than a fact, so the degree to which
an act is conducted dramatically can be decisive in affecting the
total, historical, impact of the act itself. Ramsay MacDonald,
for example, by being, at the moment of his 'betrayal', the
visible darling of Lady Londonderry—so that the late James
Maxton asked in the House of Commons whether the anthem
of the Labour party was now the 'Red Flag' or the 'Londonderry
Air'—dramatised the whole business as effectively as if he had
written a folk-ballad about it. The Defender of the Poor, the lad
from Lossiemouth, sells his birthright for a mess of pottage—
lets the poor go hang for the sake of a reception at famed Londonderry House, with ambassadors and peers jostling one
another on the marble stairway.

It is strange to find people still occasionally playing the 'if' game. On television, not long ago, somebody asked a lot of experts what would have happened if the Romans had not conquered Britain. And, believe it or not, the experts replied to the question as though there were some way of making a sensible answer. A very expert thing to do. And people still ask me what I think would have happened had Franco's attack on the Spanish Republic been defeated. When I tell them that I do not have the least idea what would, in that event, have come to pass, they look at me askance, as though I were concealing something.

Nobody can judge whether an historical event, an order to an army, a diplomatic manœuvre, was a catastrophe or otherwise unless he is prepared to say at the same time what *would* have happened if that thing had *not* happened. And since nobody is in a position honestly to make such a statement about what the alternative would have been, the question is in the nature of things unanswerable and otiose.

Anyone can argue—and every articulate person over the age of thirty has so argued—pro or con the Nazi-Soviet Pact. Suppose Stalin had thumbed his nose at Hitler, been attacked, collapsed, forced to surrender the rich spaces of Russia to the Germans, after which, with those resources behind him, Hitler had gone for the west? Suppose it—but you cannot know that it would have happened just like that. Or suppose Stalin had been just a little more trustful of Chamberlain and Daladier and Colonel Beck? And suppose that in that case they in turn had agreed that the Red Army could advance through the eastern border States—the point upon which, ostensibly at least, and, in view of what since has happened, intelligibly, the negotiations broke down. Hitler might, in that case, have been finally encircled and suffocated, and there would have been no World War II. One is certainly at liberty to suppose that.

But, to return to that harassing day in London in August, 1939, when history is moving along at a fast clip there is really no time to indulge in these speculations. Like Napoleon, when some ponderer asked him for a thoughtful statement about the *finesses* of military strategy, one can only say, disappointingly, 'Well, you join battle, and afterwards you see.'

Personally, if the matter is still of any interest, I thought that either the pact would scare the British and French Governments into revising their attitude to Moscow, or else they would have to face such consequences as are liable to ensue when you bet you can take on a continent and a half and lick it. (It would be incredible, were it not on record, that there were publications —the *Nineteenth Century* under the editorship of that defender of the English homeland, Mr Frederick Voigt, was one of them— which, while deploring the Russian attack upon Finland, found some comfort in it, on the ground that now we could go to war with Russia as well as Germany, thus tidying up the entire situation.)

It is the work of an instant now, of course, to attribute everything that went wrong to the wickedness, criminal lunacy and general mental debility of Joseph Stalin. I am bound to say that I did not think anything of this idea at the time, and admit I do not think much of it now. It is easy, then as now, to understand just why the British and French Governments were prepared to risk defeat by Hitler rather than do anything which could in any way favour the interests of Communism. But if you said, in those days, that the leaders in London and Paris believed that the struggle against international communism was more important than the struggle for individual national survival—if you suggested, in fact, that we were moving out of the period of the 'nation state' which had dominated life and politics since the end of the Middle Ages—you were regarded as a foolish doctrinaire, and slanderer of the London Government.

Robert Byron, who, in his high stiff collar and severely tailored clothes looked—and intended to look—like everyone's idea of an Old High Tory, which he most sincerely was, once in my presence delivered one of the finest left and right verbal blows I have ever heard to an expatriate American, son of some squalid manufacturer in Ohio, who had made a packet of money out of buttons or underpants or whatever it was, and become an English politico of sorts, and a figure in English Society. He was, it need scarcely be remarked, an admirer of Hitler and a fervid supporter of the policies of that British Government which interminably sought an accommodation with Hitler.

'I suppose,' said Robert Byron, his big, pale, fierce eyes popping at this creature across the dinner table, 'I ought not to be surprised to see you betraying the interests of your adopted country in the supposed interests of your adopted class.'

It was the impending and inevitable loss of the friendship of men like Robert Byron—and in point of fact there were very few men like him—which somewhat depressed me at the moment of the news of the Nazi-Soviet Pact. For a long time there had been a loose, entirely informal, but exhilarating alliance between the extreme Left and people such as Byron who, I suppose, could be described as 'Churchillian Tories'. Now all that was going to end in bitterness and recrimination. (Even that, as things turned out, did not last very long, because soon Robert Byron was sent on an intelligence mission to the Aegean, torpedoed, and drowned.)

On that morning of der Pakt I went down to the *Daily Worker* deliberately rather late—I had my own mind made up and I thought it would be tedious to have to watch a lot of other people making up theirs.

At that time, the *Daily Worker*, after being evicted from the Dickensian barn it originally inhabited in Tabernacle Street, where the electric light was constantly failing and much of the work had to be done by candle light, was housed in the City Road, and the public house we used, just across the road, was the original Eagle where the weasel went pop.

Naturally, being so situated, we had done a lot of research into the origins of the rhyme and what exactly the weasel was. Our consensus, for what it is worth, was that the 'weasel' was one of those big tailor's irons. A hundred and fifty years ago, the City Road was a road leading through fields and open country-side to pleasure gardens somewhere in the neighbourhood of what is now Camden Town—or perhaps still farther out. In any case, to go 'up and down the City Road' was a practice indicating dissipation and extravagance, and the expense was increased by the habit, fashionable it seems among the City apprentices and their masters, of breaking the journey by a halt for drink at the Eagle. And the outcome was that the out-of-pocket tailor had to pawn or 'pop' the principal tool of his trade, the weasel.

The public house was lavishly decorated with drawings by the *Daily Worker* cartoonist Rowney—formerly of the army in India and later killed in Spain. He had a strong, rough line, very suitable for harsh political cartooning and seen to great advantage on the walls of a profoundly Cockney public house. There was a large one of a tailor actually popping his weasel which was particularly admired by the proprietor, who had rubbed Rowney's slate clean of heaven knows how many unpaid drinks when the drawing was delivered.

The place did good business in those days—partly because the *Daily Worker* staff and people from King Street who had come along to advise and supervise, and people from all over who had come to wheedle from the paper free publicity for their bazaar or protest march, all used it, and partly because, in consequence, there were rarely less than three plain-clothes men from the C I D, putting their whisky down to expenses inevitably incurred in the pursuit of important political secrets such as might be expected to drop from the lips of the subversive types regularly there assembled.

I remember remarking, as we sat that August morning in the gritty sunshine that came in from City Road, that it certainly looked like being a hard winter. For it was already evident that, however necessary the Pact may have been to the Russians, by signing it they had effectively dynamited everywhere all the Popular Fronts, the vague but comforting alliances between Reds and anti-Nazi Conservatives. We were out, from now on, in a very cold cold. The demonstrations in Trafalgar Square and Hyde Park, faultlessly organised by the Communists, with Trade Union leaders and Liberals and even Tories on the hustings, the letters to newspapers which I had so often 'ghosted' and then had signed by impeccable figures in our public life, the private solicitations in clubs and other places where they plot, had somehow failed to make the grade—failed, that is to persuade the British Government to do enough to persuade Stalin's Government that an Anglo-Russian alliance with teeth in it was a practical political possibility. (No one would deny that what Stalin considered 'enough' was an awful lot.)

I was, it goes without saying, powerfully and instinctively moved to take that opportunity to break with the Communists there and then and brigade myself with the 'Churchillian Tories'. Personal considerations swayed me in that direction, not least among them the fact that Patricia had just run away with me and I felt that now, as a result of the latest turn of events, I was getting her to jump into a much deeper hole than she could have foreseen a few months before. On the other hand, quite apart from the high political rights and wrongs of the matter—

and I was uncomfortably undecided as to who was right and who wrong—I was dominated by the feeling that I had, of my own free will, joined, so to speak, a regiment and that I had better soldier along with it, particularly at a moment when it was obviously going to come under pretty heavy fire.

It seemed to me that in those dead days of the Popular Front I had had a rather easy time being a Communist, and it would be, to say the least of it, shabby to quit now.

And, of course, there were other powerful reasons in favour of fighting things out on whatever line the Communists might finally determine to adopt. You cannot work closely with people for years without enmeshing yourself in a network of personal—sentimental, if you like—loyalties and affections. All this, obviously enough, is a clear instance of what is now called, in the jargon of the American sociologists, 'other-directedness'. They suggest thereby that, whereas at one time people were overwhelmingly influenced by tradition (in particular religious tradition and belief), and at a later period by their own inner convictions on ethical and political questions, nowadays they are above all swayed by their 'group'—the organization or community with which they are most closely associated.

It has never seemed to me that the theory explains anything much, or tells anyone much that everyone did not know already, but it is perhaps a useful stimulant and guide to one's thinking.

Nevertheless, the fact that a person is swayed by his 'group' does not answer the question how and why—assuming that he had a choice in the matter—he got into the group in the first place. And in this matter I think that a good many people in England whose business it should be to understand why people become Communists are the prisoners of their own propaganda —always a dangerous situation and, in this case, useful only to the Communists themselves.

For years people have been going around and about saying that in Britain Communism is an alien thing, that it is repugnant to all but the physically starved or the mentally distorted or those who may imagine that they are going to float on a high tide of troubles.

Such an account of the situation is patently untrue, or at least miserably inadequate, and therefore, as I say, dangerous. The reality—and it is a serious matter—is that Communism can and does have deep affinities with British radicalism. Manchester and London did as much to shape Karl Marx and Marxism as did the Rhineland or the Paris Commune—perhaps more. And, paradoxical as it may seem, Communism has—or at least very often has—a particular appeal to people brought up in the British public schools and universities, especially people with a classical and Christian education. The Greek dramatists and both the Testaments smoulder with passages which, at any rate to a young man, are incitements to revolt against orthodox society, to throw in his lot with the 'have nots' against the 'haves'. And if you ask me what first—long before I experienced central Europe in the inflation time, or attended the American crash of 1929—'conditioned' me to be susceptible to the appeal of Communism, I should have to say that it was, for example, the Magnificat I listened to every Sunday at evensong in the village church, and Antigone's defiance of Creon in Sophocles' play.

To draw attention to the putting down of the mighty from their seats is by no means an innocuous proceeding—unless, of course, the congregation is asleep at the time and does not notice what is being said.

All the same, it was somewhat melancholy to sit there in the Eagle and reflect that at least half one's friends were soon going to stop speaking to one, perhaps for ever. I recalled a sentence written by my great-grandfather, then Lord Cockburn, who was a young Whig in the Edinburgh of the early nineteenth century, a time when, as he says in his memoirs, 'even in private society a Whig was viewed somewhat as a Papist was in the days of Titus Oates. Very dear friendships were in many instances broken, and although the parties may have survived till age and changed times made longer severance absurd, the reconcilement was always awkward and never true. This incompatibility of public difference with private cordiality is the most painful recollection that I have of those days, and the most striking evidence of their hardness.'

It occurred to me that world events were conspiring to make a lot more difficult even than it had looked at the outset any reconciliation between Patricia and her parents, of whom she was profoundly fond.

On the news that she was running away with me, her mother

had said, 'Do you realise that, if your brothers were in the diplomatic service, a scandal of this kind would force them to resign?'

Patricia said, 'But in fact they are not in the diplomatic service.'

'That,' said Mrs Arbuthnot characteristically, hammering the floor with her stick, 'is not the point.'

Major Arbuthnot voiced a different objection. He had been proud, he said, of holding a certain record at the Carlton Club—he was the only member who had three sons and a son-in-law, all of whom were members too. Now, though Patricia's first husband would no doubt remain a member, he would cease to be the Major's son-in-law, and the record score would have to be wiped out.

Though endearing and nostalgic, these reactions seemed, at first, those of people imprisoned on the stage of a period piece. I soon found that the contrary was the case. Regretting the ruins of their Edwardian period—including the loss, first gradual, then sudden, of the greater part of their fortune—they yet managed a singularly lively and alert existence in the present. Like all honest and lively elders, their attitudes were annoyingly unpredictable to contemporaries suffering from arrested development. Major Arbuthnot, indeed, who could take pleasure in quite contradictory ideas at the same time, considered it his congenial duty to *épater* people of pompous or rigid mind wherever he found them. Mrs Arbuthnot, who superficially seemed the archetype of the Edwardian *grande dame*, was in profound sympathy with Irish nationalism, detested 'colonialism' and 'racialism', and first warmed to me when she learned that I had actually fought against Franco whom she despised as a disloyal officer and a puppet of the disgraceful Hitler. Both of them had that warmth and openness of heart which is the product of a deep inner self-assurance.

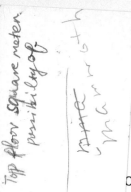

Top floor square meter. possibility of

4

ong, cold winter

I HAD been right in surmising that, politically speaking, it was going to be a hard winter, though, of course, in every other sense it was a much harder winter for those who were sweating out the 'phoney war' in the Army. There are people who will sincerely contend that the mental and spiritual tribulations of people wrestling with grave political and personal problems, but doing their wrestling on a desk chair or a sofa before the fire, can be worse than those of the people who are out in a field with the Army, being cold, wet, poorly-fed, dog-tired, nagged, bullied, ordered around and well aware that the next thing that may be going to happen is that you get savagely opened up by a shell, bullet or bayonet, or you get a letter from home saying your loved one has been bombed or gassed or become weary of it all and gone to America with a more promising type of man than you seem to be at the moment. I have often reflected upon each of these general situations, and personally I will face the trouble at the desk.

Still, there was trouble enough.

Naturally—and I mean naturally, in the sense that no one else could have been expected to take any other attitude than they did, so that there was cause for unhappiness, rather than resentment—the situation which had become uncomfortable at the time of the Pact's signature became as painful as prickly heat when, after at first supporting the war, the *Daily Worker* received through the Comintern instructions to denounce it as an imperialist one.

Again, gripped by memories of 1914, I could not feel that the Comintern was necessarily wrong, although not to be encouraging one and all to go for Hitler seemed hopelessly wrong too. But then, I would reflect, sincere Socialists like Blatchford had felt, in 1914, that that war, too, was an exception to the rules he had been brought up on. It must, he thought, be wrong not to go for Hunnish Kaiser Bill.

Also there was at work in the minds of many people on the extreme Left at that time a general feeling that if, for example, Neville Chamberlain was on one side of a question and Georgi Dimitrov, hero of the Leipzig trial, was on the other, then the probability was that Dimitrov was right and Mr Chamberlain was leading one up the garden. Neville Chamberlain was saying that the war was necessary and just—that we were fighting 'the evil things'. Dimitrov was on record with a Comintern statement—he was secretary of the organisation at the time—which concluded with the declaration that 'the working people of the world must put an end to this war after their own fashion, in their own interests, in the interests of all labouring mankind.'

As things turned out, and given the attitude of the working people of Germany and other lands, the statement—in so far as any practical international relevance was concerned—was meaningless. At the time, partly because I had a profound admiration for Dimitrov—he was one of those true heroes who really had been out in the wind and the rain, facing day after day the probability of torture and murder by Goering's young men—I considered it inspiring. But nobody under the age of forty or so today can possibly have any notion of what Dimitrov was to us in the way of a symbol, a flame in darkness, a proof that, however bad things seem to be, the courageous, even the apparently foolhardy backers of a 66 to 1 chance may still win.

Reasonably enough, people used to ask me how I could bear to be pushed around and about by an international body like the Comintern. Today, when it is known that Stalin was not quite all that some people thought him to be—though I would not like to pretend, as some do, that all the virtues of Communists were their own, and all their faults Stalin's—and in the light of truly illuminating events in, for instance, Hungary, it is easier than it was then to regard 'subservience' to the Comintern as more crassly wrong-headed than it seemed at the time.

The way I looked at it was that if an international organisation was needed at all—and it seemed to be—then the organisation had to have a place to meet (and Moscow was the most

logical), and it had to have some power of discipline, of imposing its decisions on its members. What, otherwise, was the point
of it? And the fact, which genuinely did bother a lot of English
proletarian Communists, that the majority on the central committee of this organisation was composed of a pack of bloody
foreigners, did not bother me at all. Put like that, of course, the
statement that it did not worry me suggests that it was ridicu-
lous and parochial for anyone to be worried by it. Such is not
quite the case. We should have worried more, because of the
certainty that the Russians, having shown how to win the game
would always dictate rules of play. In the same way, it is reasonable for a sincere Roman Catholic to worry about the prepond-
erance of Italian influence at the Vatican.

My own complaint about the Comintern was not that it
operated with the 'ruthless and sinister efficiency' attributed to
it by some propagandists, but that for so much of the time it
wobbled along in a muddle which was frequently comical but,
at the same time, depressing.

Nobody, for instance, could ever persuade them to grasp—
not, at least, for more than a week or so—that when people at
the *Daily Worker* tried to write in a 'popular' manner; when
they said that English people did not much like to read column
after unbroken column of solid news and speculation about the
international position, or the state of industry and agriculture;
when the suggestion was made that, even if the thing came out
a little bit 'off-line', a good popular story was going to do more
good to the cause in England than the literal translation of a five-
thousand-word statement by *le patron*, the propounders of these
suggestions were sincere.

I recall an occasion, soon after I became associated with the
Communists, when the English-language edition of the international weekly that was the organ of the Comintern appeared
with a 'directive' by some Muscovite genius which some other
Muscovite genius had translated into the words 'the lower
organs of the party in Britain must make still greater efforts to
penetrate the backward parts of the proletariat.'

In the effort to explain why the British Communist party had
refused to circulate that issue of the publication, a lot of people
learned the hard way how very difficult it can be to explain to a
half-dozen Russian and German Professors of Marxism why

something they have said amounts, in English, to a rather dirty joke, particularly as while you are explaining it they are think-ing 'Nonsense, it is not a dirty joke at all. How could it be? A simple political directive. This objection is an attempt at Men-shevism, not to say direct sabotage.'

Strictly by hindsight, though hindsight might, in this case, not be purblind, it would be possible to attribute a good deal of the Comintern's fumbling zig-zag—its confusions and its rigidities, its general atmosphere of a morality play in which the Good and the Bad are fighting it out—to personal intrigues and ambi-tions of Joseph Stalin.

As I recall, the first time I sniffed a really gamey whiff of what Khrushchev, so belatedly, decided was a wicked 'personality cult' was when a well-meaning man, a devoted man, wrote a piece in our paper which was intended to explain to the English reader why Stalin was not a dictator in the same sense that Hitler and Mussolini were dictators, and why Socialist construc-tion in Russia differed from Fascist or Nazi construction in Italy or Germany.

He was misguided enough to suggest that among the differ-ences between a personal dictatorship and the dictatorship of the proletariat was the fact that if, for instance, our beloved leader and comrade Joseph Stalin were to pass away tomorrow, that sad event would not ruinously affect the structure and progress of the Soviet State.

There was the father and mother of a row. Stalin, it appeared, had interpreted the statement as a direct instigation to the assassination of himself—an emphatic assertion that he was entirely expendable. For a considerable time the *Daily Worker* was banned in the Soviet Union. English enthusiasts landing at Leningrad and waving it joyously in the face of the Customs men, to show that they were absolutely on the right side, not mere capitalist sight-seers, found themselves under lock and key in very short order. And for a long time everyone connected with the editorial department of the paper, responsible for this heinous deviation, was regarded by all good and true members of the Comintern with the gravest suspicion. It looked to them very much as though *perfide Albion* were up to her old tricks.

I had, certainly, been warned. When many sorts and condi-tions of friends first saw me moving, under pressure of many experiences, many hopes and aspirations, towards the Communist party, they gave me from their sharply varying viewpoints their notions of why such behaviour was a mistake. They disagreed about almost everything except two points.

They were at one in declaring that the Communist party was both ruthless and muddle-headed. Since I had spent years in newspaper offices, had closely observed many Foreign Offices and Embassies, and had been, for a while, an unofficial adviser and loose associate of an investment trust in New York, I found it difficult to see how these qualities could at all sharply differentiate the Communist organisation from any other with which I had been connected.

The second point, of which at least the simpler-minded of my friends were sure, was that 'Moscow Gold' was pouring through the British Communist party like water. Indeed, sitting almost penniless one day in the old Café Royal, I was accosted by an agreeable acquaintance—a Russian banker, refugee from the revolution—who said to me, 'I hear on incontrovertible authority that you are paid £2,350 per year by the Soviet Government for your services as Editor of *The Week* and diplomatic correspondent of the *Daily Worker*.'

In those days £2,350 a year was a more comfortable sum to try to live on than it would be now, and the mere idea of such a pay packet went to my head.

'Waiter,' I shouted with enthusiasm, 'bring this gentleman a large brandy and soda.'

When I came to pay for it with my last shillings it occurred to me with a sharp sense of deprivation that the exhilarating tale of this subsidy was a myth.

It would, evidently, be naïve to suppose that the Russians do not pay out large sums to agents in Britain. It would be strange if they, unlike every other Government in the world, were to abstain from buying whatever and whomsoever they can afford. My doubt, based on first-hand evidence, is whether they pay anything—beyond the aeroplane fares for international junkets and rest cures at Crimean Sanatoria—to the Communist party or the *Daily Worker*. If they did, you would think that in the interest of efficiency they would pay more. The point, it appears to me, has some small importance because, here again, the comfortable notion that English Communism would collapse or fade away, cease to be a problem or menace, if it were not financed by Moscow, is, in my opinion, another of the risky illusions I have referred to. If the problem of Communism is important at all, it is important to have this sort of facts about it right.

When I was at the *Daily Worker* the paper was more or less continuously on the verge of financial ruin—except during a short period at the very end of the war and in the first months of the peace, when, chiefly as a result of the battle of Stalingrad, Communists everywhere could enjoy some reflected sunshine.

Pay-day in the City Road was something like a game of hoop-la, with a lot of players and not enough prizes. Rarely indeed was there enough in the cash-box on Fridays to enable everyone to get paid their full weekly wage—which was grimly meagre anyway. The total was shared out by the manager, a humorously tough type from the Elephant and Castle district who later was killed in Spain, on the basis of a kind of inverted means test. Staff members whose wives were about to give birth, or the ceilings of whose kitchens had caved in and had to be repaired at heavy expense, got a bit more than others.

Once, after that manager had been killed, I found a new, temporary manager sitting in his office on a Thursday morning apparently half dead of apprehension. He had looked at the available funds, and their low ebb had scared him. He felt it would be terrible to have to face the staff on the morrow with such more than usually bad news. And just as he was feeling like that, a man—sent he thought at the time by Providence, but by this morning he feared it might have been the Devil—had come in and given him a sure-fire tip on a 20-1 outsider running on Thursday at Haydock Park or wherever it was. And the temporary manager had taken half of all the money available for the wages and backed that horse with it.

'Should that animal fail,' he said, trembling—the tension was such that he felt he had to confess his rash act to someone—'the lads 'll about kill me.' However, the tipster had not been the Devil but Providence, and that week everyone got full pay and even some arrears.

I do not have, I think, the qualities which go to the making of a 'good Communist'. Or, indeed, a good party man of any denomination.' A good one, I mean, in the sense of the person who really operates happily with the machine. There are enthu-

siastic Conservatives, Labour men, Democrats and Republicans
—but a lot of them are not what the party, whichever one it
may happen to be, considers 'good'. That is something special,
and needs a special sort of mind. And it is arguable—in fact it is
more than just arguable because I personally have seen a lot of
evidence to support the view—that there is basically more in
common between two 'good' party men of diametrically
opposed parties than between two men of the same party one
of whom is 'good' and the other just doing his best for what he
presumes to be a good cause. In this connection, Walter
Duranty, long years ago a famous Moscow correspondent of the
New York Times, wrote that 'there is more in common between
the Communist party' (he was speaking of the Russian one) 'and
Tammany Hall, than either Tammany Hall or the Communist
party would care to admit.'

There he certainly had a point.

As for me, discipline, unless operated by very remote control,
gives me claustrophobia. Nor do I care at all for any form of
discussion 'in committee'. I have never known a 'committee
discussion' decide anything serious—either you and another
man know what you are going to do whatever happens, in
which case you are wasting the time of these other men who are
sitting there voicing opinions to which, in practical terms, the
real operators are not going to pay the least attention, or else
the purpose of the gathering is to find out which way the wind
is blowing and then sail as close to it as you dare.

I am not saying that 'collective decisions' are impossible or a
waste of time; I am only saying that I do not know how to take
part in them. I feel similarly about cricket—I have no urge to
suppress cricket, or even to shun cricketers, but I do not understand, or wish to participate in, the game. I wished always to
participate in the game of journalism and propaganda, but I did
not want the business of writing a piece postponed until a lot
of people who probably could hardly write a sentence that anyone would bother to read, let alone remember, had discussed
the whole matter. Or rather, I wanted them to discuss the
matter, which I can see they had to do, without bothering me
about it, and then tell me what the problem was, and I would,
as the phrase goes, 'get in there pitching'.

In other words, I am deeply interested in what people have to say—I am even interested in the expression of their faces as they say it—I like to hearken and observe the workings of high politics and business, I like to talk a lot because talk is the animation, the lighting which dramatizes the actors on the stage for you, but do not enjoy becoming involved in such discussion otherwise than as hearkener, observer, and, ultimately, projector.

At that time—the time I mean of the outbreak of war—people said to me, more or less accurately, 'Look, you are a principal journalistic propagandist of the Communist party. You are, we believe, a high-powered agent of the Comintern. You have many unique contacts, levers, ways to know a man who knows a man. Why not, when you meet with the big chiefs say this and say that? Argue, sway policy. Take, for example, advantage of the fact that Mr Pollitt is on one side, and the toughest Comintern boys, headed by Mr William Rust, are on the other. Your influence could be decisive.'

This was just wilful thinking. My 'influence' at that time could not have come within a hundred miles of being decisive. If a lot of things that had happened had not happened—for instance suppose that Koltzov by some miracle had still been foreign editor of *Pravda* and perhaps, like Shepilov later, being groomed for the Foreign Secretaryship at the Kremlin, that kind of advice might have made a little sense. As things really were, and as I knew them to be, it made none at all.

What I liked was to make up my mind what cause I could advocate, and then listen to the 'good' party men telling me how they wanted their thoughts put into powerful English that would achieve a telling impact upon the masses with its colour, popular touch, and mass appeal.

Certainly one reason why people on the outside of the organization presumed me to have a key position and an influence which not only did I not have but which, in fact, nobody could have had, was that subconsciously they thought that an upper-class individual who had thrown in his lot with the Communists must, automatically, have such a position—the Old School Tie would put him there, while the proletarians filled the lower echelons where their proper place was.

Disconcertingly enough, it was just about this time that a friend and fellow-traveller, whom I had introduced to King

Street with the suggestion that he might prove the very man for some mission they had in mind, told me that while there he had been given a word of warning about me—the functionary who interviewed him indicated, not too subtly, that there was good reason to suppose that I was, in reality, a particularly dangerous agent of M I 6. I made some enquiries and found that the man who, for the time being at least, was most convinced of that, was that same very tough comrade who was alleged, rightly or wrongly, to have put that bullet through Wilfred Macartney's elbow. It became increasingly apparent that I had been right when I said that it was going to be a hard winter.

In the whirl of events, editors succeeded one another in a hurried silence like that of a film in the days before sound. Right at the outbreak of war, Mr Pollitt moved down from King Street. Although in general I do not care for orators—perhaps I subconsciously see them as unfair competition to the writer—and Mr Pollitt is, or was, above all else an orator in the oldest English radical tradition, I liked him much; he was a slave-driver with a flattering tongue instead of a lash. His technique, well worth study by any executive, was to tell you he was about to make an outrageous demand of you, go right ahead and make it, and then remark that he would not have ventured to make such a demand of anyone else because no one else had the ability, courage, unselfish loyalty and heroic powers of endurance that you had.

He once persuaded me that I could get to Oviedo, Spain, live a fortnight there in the middle of a near-revolution masquerading as a mere tourist, and return to London all for the sum of £12. 'A pity if you couldn't,' he said, 'because that is all we have in the kitty.'

Much later, I did, at some party, say to him that I sometimes wondered whether anyone could really be as ultra-English and as forthright a down-to-earth human-hearted Englishman as he —even by the normally hostile newspapers—was so constantly reported to be. Was it not, I queried, all due to the happy circumstance of his having a strong Lancashire accent? His expression at that moment reminded one of George Robey blandly getting away with murder.

Mr Pollitt's editorship was enjoyable but short-lived, because soon the Comintern chiefs had their notable meeting, and the

British delegate or representative—a cheerful ex-sailor with a head like a cannon-ball who once told me that in the course of a very tempestuous and danger-fraught life nothing had ever really upset him except piles—came back from Moscow with the news that the war had been assessed as an imperialist one. The reason was evident enough—it was supposed that the 'phoney' war was going to be permanently 'phoney'; that therefore, somewhere along the line, an agreement would be reached by which the Germans, with open or tacit British support, would attack Russia; and that therefore the main effort of the Communists must be to harass and, in the final event, totally hamstring or overthrow the Governments concerned. In other words, it was the evident view of the Comintern that the declaration of war did not change the essentials of the situation existing during the period of 'peace'.

It was certainly quite a gamble—because, as everyone was quick to point out, supposing the French and British Communists succeeded in the preliminary objectives, and then Hitler after all attacked the west and took over, what sort of shape would Communism and Soviet Russia be in? My own impression at the time was that the tangle of suspicions and counter-suspicions had become inextricable. You could not persuade a British Conservative—still less a Labour man, who had more immediate motives for hating and suspecting Communists than the Conservatives did—that in reality the Russian Communists and the German Nazis were not permanently and diabolically in league to achieve and share the domination of the world—and it is true that Stalin and his friends at that time did much to encourage or deepen that conviction. Equally, you could not persuade a Russian—and nothing the British or French Governments had done in the past year or so made the persuasion any easier—to believe that each and every action of those Governments was not a cynical trick designed to speed the day when the grand alliance of the west, with Hitler as its spearhead, would move in on the Soviet State. And the situation was unquestionably complicated by the fact I mentioned earlier in relation to Otto Katz—the fact, that is, that something in the English character makes it nearly impossible for central and eastern Europeans to figure out whether the English are besottedly foolish or plain crooked.

By hindsight, all these factors and calculations are clearly visible. But at the time the situation was inevitably rancorous. It was easy, decades after the event, for someone like, for instance, Lord Rosebery, to take a balanced and even sympathetic view of Napoleon Bonaparte and to show what follies were committed by the British Government in their ultimate attitude towards him. And Rosebery himself, from his superior vantage point, does explain that after all Napoleon's France had cost the British in question a terrible lot of effort and money. In the same way, the fury occasioned by the change in the Comintern line in 1939 is entirely intelligible.

A few days later I met Mr Pollitt on the stairway landing and made some casual remark. He waved in a gesture half-clowning, half-serious. 'Farewell, my old companion in arms,' he said; and when I got into the office there was Mr Campbell, sourly, dourly humorous—one of those Scots who make you feel that real Scotsmen are more different from the English than Chinese—peering at me from the editorial chair with a sardonic smile illuminating his gravity; an expression which, as was so often the case with Mr Campbell, said nothing and told everything.

One could not look at Mr Campbell without one's mind travelling back over a considerable, and considerably bumpy, stretch of recent history. He stood and walked, for instance, in a stiff, stumpy manner, and that was because his toes had been blown away in gallant action during the awful battle of the Somme. which—because of the gigantic manslaughter occurring on both sides, manslaughter on a scale the world, since the days of Genghis Khan, had not conceived as a present possibility—has been rated by many commentators as the true dividing line of our age: for, they say, it was the Somme which finally took the gilt off war's gingerbread, which awoke Britain, France and Germany to the realities of twentieth-century conflict, to the notion that it was not only a minority of fighting men that could be wiped out, but a whole generation, and that the bell tolled for them all. It was, they affirm, at the Somme that a big section of the European masses, as distinct from zealots and theorists, consciously or subconciously took the turn into that angry despair of the present, that compensating, messianic hope of a violently realisable future, which for so many subsequent years dominated the mind of Europe.

At any rate what Mr Campbell had following the Somme were a medal for courage, broken feet, and a new view of life.

Some of that may even be true.

Mr Campbell, this thoughtful, profoundly sceptical man—a man, that is to say, capable of devotion without loss of scepticism—had also been responsible, partly by direct action, partly by indirect consequence, for the downfall, in 1924, of the first Labour Government. At that time he had been editor of the *Workers' Weekly*, forerunner of the *Daily Worker*. He had written, or at least published, an appeal to soldiers not to shoot strikers. He was prosecuted for sedition. From Socialists throughout the country came a gale of protest, the fiercer because, although the Campbell case was important in itself, it was felt to be still more important as a symbol of the way the Labour leaders were going (an attitude to life and politics summed up a few weeks later by Mr Ramsay MacDonald in the assurance that Labour 'would serve the nation in Opposition as they had served it as a Government . . . It will still be a fight of gentlemen.')

Prime Minister MacDonald dropped the charges against Campbell, was accused of so doing under political pressure, a blow at the very foundations of British justice, lost the support of the Liberals in the House of Commons, was defeated, resigned, went to the country, and was defeated again—partly and perhaps mainly because of the timely forgery by the Intelligence Service of the 'Zinoviev letter' which, like all successful political forgeries, was effective because it expressed and dramatized an already existing idea and half-truth—the notion of the Comintern reaching out to control or manipulate levers of British public life.

Mr Campbell's editorship of the *Daily Worker* just after the outbreak of the second world war was a strictly caretaking affair. Everyone was to mark time, or vamp till ready, until the battle between the supporters of the war and the supporters of the Comintern had been fought to a decisive conclusion. When that came to pass, with Mr Pollitt and Mr Campbell both in the wilderness, a new face, the skin of it seeming to be stretched as tight as a balloon by the bursting energy inside, hung like a rising red sun above the editorial desk. Mr William Rust had arrived. He was the most apparently supple, and yet capable of being the most rigid, of Communists I have ever known. Just so, he was the most cockney of cockneys, and yet —at least for a long period of his life—his thoughts, and still more his writing, were moulded almost completely by Moscow.

Later, particularly after a long stint with the International Brigade in Spain, his remarkable and at first contradictory qualities appeared quite suddenly to integrate.

I knew people who saw him as the typical party functionary —informed, energetic, and as cold as he was dry. Since that was the picture of him given to me before he moved into the *Daily Worker* office, I looked forward to his editorship with dull dismay. The apprehension was unjustified, and not for the first or last time I had a vivid appreciation of luck—a feeling, that is, that no one soldiering along through the Vale of Tears could possibly deserve to encounter so many good friends in so many places as I did. George Jean Nathan, the New York dramatic critic wrote—or else he told me, I forget which—a series of bitter animadversions on his many, many friends and acquaintances, explaining how this or that little trick or tic which they had made it impossible to stand them any longer, and he was forced to sever relations with them. In the end he had only four friends left. 'And I often wonder,' he mused, 'how in God's name those four stand me.'

I do not know how easily or otherwise Rust stood me—but he did it, and often defended my attitude and actions at a good deal of discomfort and (at least once) of danger, to himself. Whatever you might think of his opinions at a given moment, he was a man to go, as the saying is, tiger-shooting with. He never, for instance, abandoned you to fate and then explained that he had been forced to do so on principle and was very, very sorry. When he thought he was going, for his own reasons, to let you go out on a limb and leave you there, he told you so in advance. He had, besides a good head on his shoulders, a streak of the urchin and a bigger streak of the pirate. In other words, when, as sometimes happened, he was monstrously hypocritical, or lying horribly, he did these things with full consciousness, using these tricks as weapons. He had no 'lie in the soul', and, to my mind, one of the major differences in life is between those people who lie on purpose and those who do not even know whether they are lying or not.

Qualities such as those of the late William Rust were, of

course, particularly exhilarating in an organization of an evangelical character, like the British Communist party, where, inevitably but depressingly, there is always a lot of space occupied by characters similar—and similar for sound historical reasons —to the Evangelical clergyman, Mr Slope, in Trollope's *Barchester Towers*.

'He is possessed of more than average abilities and is of good courage. Though he can stoop to fawn, and stoop low indeed, if need be, he has still within him the power to assume the tyrant; and with the power he has certainly the wish. His acquirements are not of the highest order, but such as they are they are completely under control, and he knows the use of them. He is gifted with a kind of pulpit eloquence . . . he deals greatly in denunciations, excites the minds of his weaker hearers with a not unpleasant terror, and leaves an impression on their minds that all mankind are in a perilous state, and all womankind too, except those who attend regularly to the evening lectures in Baker Street. His looks and tones are extremely severe, so much so that one cannot but fancy that he regards the greater part of the world as being infinitely too bad for his care. As he walks through the streets, his very face denotes his horror of the world's wickedness; and there is always an anathema lurking in the corner of his eye.'

For a while after Mr Pollitt and Mr Campbell broke ranks, we had a situation best summed up, or so it seemed to me as we all argued and argued, in the words of the once world famous Mr Dooley—the Irish-American philosopher dreamed into existence by the Chicago journalist Finley Peter Dunne.

'Whin ye see,' said Mr Dooley—whose observations on political life were first drawn to my attention by my father when I was eleven or twelve years old, and made a big impression upon me—'whin ye see two men set in opposite corners while one mutters "thraiter" an' th' other hisses "miscreent", ye can bet they're two dimmycratic leaders tryin' to reunite th' party.'

Fairly soon, however, the Government put an end to our more overt troubles by suppressing the *Daily Worker*. There came an afternoon in 1940 when one of those C I D men who had so often and so attentively watched us playing the pin-tables at the Eagle came across the road and presented us with the notice of suppression. Noticing me among those present, he displayed a certain embarrassment, and presently revealed its cause.

He was a busy man. On that same afternoon he had another paper to suppress—namely my weekly newsletter, *The Week*. But it appeared that, under some British regulation attached to the Act which enabled them to suppress at all, there was also an obligation to serve the notice upon the owner or responsible publisher in person, and in that responsible person's own place of business. That, at least, was the policeman's interpretation of his duty, and so what were we to do? Here was I—also a busy man, and due to be busier still when we had to deal with the situation that would arise from the suppression—and we were in the City, and the offices of *The Week* were literally miles away in Victoria Street.

Asked, courteously enough, by the policeman whether I would engage myself to meet him a little later in Victoria Street for the sake of being put out of business a second time, I pointed out that I was likely to be working pretty hard in the next little while. It was an allusion which he perfectly understood, for it was obvious that the moment the *Daily Worker* was suppressed we should all be getting busy issuing illegal versions of it, which was going to be a dangerous and time-absorbing business.

Finally, the Inspector asked me whether I would care to have him drive me down in the police car, so that *The Week* could be suppressed with a minimal loss of valuable time. I thought for a moment that it could be considered unseemly for me to go cruising on such an errand at the expense of Scotland Yard. But, after a moment's reflection, I accepted the offer and we shot across the town in the police car, making excellent time between the suppressed *Daily Worker* and about-to-be-suppressed *Week*.

Within the hour, they had shut up *The Week*, and as they did so I had that peculiar sense of relief one sometimes has when they finally tell you you have to take to your bed, or go to hospital. You may be in pain, but the administrative side of things, the awkward decisions, are their pigeon now.

For a little while we did run an illegal *Daily Worker*—a tiresome business because one was aware that in fact the thing was a mere gesture, the publication reaching hardly anyone. And yet you could get five years hard labour if you were caught at it, just as though you had been pouring criminal incitements into the ears of millions.

I daresay the affair was almost as annoying for the Special Branch of the C I D as it was for us—for in this strange charade they too had to pretend that whatever we were doing was of vital importance, and during that nasty butt-end of winter they had to follow us about in all weathers. One day I was trying to make my way to the place where the product was put together, and the two C I D men following me seemed to be unusually keen. None of the usual routines for throwing off the 'tail' seemed to work. When I got a taxi, they always seemed to find another one instantly available; when I jumped into a tube-train just before the gates closed, they seemed always to be able to squeeze in through the doors of the next carriage just in time.

At length, somewhere under St John's Wood, in one of the trains wherein I had been shuttling back and forth for what seemed like hours, I overheard a fellow-passenger say that the fog outside was so thick you could not see your hand before your face. At the station I was out of the train and bounding up the escalator with a reasonably good start on the Law. And sure enough the fog outside was just as the man in the train had described it. I took off my shoes and ran in stockinged feet through the pea-soup, and, after running some while realised that, although I had certainly lost my 'tail' I had also lost myself.

I was creeping along, tapping my fingers on the wall beside me, when I saw, a little above my head, a figure which seemed familiar. It was a statue, in bronze, of a young woman—a nude representation of Atalanta crouching slightly behind her hounds. At once I remembered that at one time Clare Sheridan, the sculptress, had asked Patricia, in Paris, to sit as a model for such a statue. And the more I examined the statue before me—it was, so far as I recall, on a kind of arch over the gateway— the more it seemed to me that this was certainly Patricia and that therefore this must be Clare Sheridan's house, the address of which I knew. (I have been told since that although Patricia's figure had been there for a time, Mrs Sheridan had—by the date of which I am writing—made another statue of another girl. If that is so, the physical resemblance was certainly extra-ordinary.)

At any rate, the sight of this mysterious bronze girl, her limbs in the posture of a runner at the start of the race, and her gaze intent upon the fog ahead, helped to orientate me.

I realised that I was much too far from the scene of my intended enterprise to make worth while any attempts to get there that morning. On the other hand, I was quite close to my home. By this time somewhat exhausted, and still carrying my shoes in my hand, I thankfully made my way to my own house. I entered as cautiously as possible, thinking that the C I D men might still be lurking somewhere. The caution proved use-less. I was sharply bitten on the foot, and then, through the fog, there was audible for miles around an astounding noise as of a lost soul yodelling. It was produced by a dog called Zig which Patricia had brought back from Central Africa—one of the first Bezengis ever to come to this country in good health.

The yodelling was one of the qualities which were thought likely to recommend this breed to flat dwellers—the dogs could not bark: just yodel. They are, in their native place, used as lion dogs. Though no bigger than a small, lightly-boned terrier, they nose out lions for the hunters and give this yodelling cry. They are clever and also enjoy embarrassing people. Zig, for example, used often to sit quietly in the room beside me until she heard Patricia at the door and then suddenly set up the most dreadful, heart-breaking screaming, implying that the wicked new master, the brutal second husband, was torturing the innocent African, beating her half to death for no good reason.

She sensed, evidently, that she had an excellent opportunity to tease me now. The noise was dreadful, and to quiet and calm her I had to raise my voice. Sure enough, one of the C I D followers had been lurking—supposing, no doubt, that the secret publishing office of the illegal *Daily Worker* was actually located in my house. He came in and searched the house from cellar to attic, fawned on by Zig, whose manner suggested that she was indeed glad a representative of respectable society had called at last, and that if he would follow her carefully she would lead him to the hidden sources of fearful crimes. I hate anthropomor-phism. I just note what her manner suggested.

5

Diversions in the dark

I LIKE dogs, provided that they have a certain wit, and do not sulk too much when things go awry, and this Zig, always on the look-out for the opportunity to drop, as it were, a metaphorical banana-skin under one's foot and laugh, in her high-pitched African fashion, as one crashed spiritually or socially humiliated, was a high class of dog. In fact I never encountered an animal I esteemed more until, in Ireland about ten years later, I became the owner of the oldest donkey in that island. He had been named, by his previous owner—a Mr Heffernan, who could remember just when he bought him, so that I can state his age with accuracy—'Jacky', and, when I first got in touch with him, was forty-four years of age.

I use the phrase 'got in touch', because that is the way it was. The thing came about because my mother-in-law was trying to save the Protestant school in our town of Youghal. Only about five per cent—it may be less—of the population of this ancient and beautiful town are Protestants, but a school is maintained for their children, and, with the tolerance which marks the Irish Government as unique (since it is a tolerance combined with a passionate conviction that the Protestants are utterly mistaken and, in the long run, dangerous enemies) it is the law that, provided the school can show, over a given period, an attendance of a minimum of twelve pupils, it qualifies for all the Government grants available to the Roman Catholic institutions.

At the period of which I speak—in the late 1940's or early 1950's—the fate of the school hung in the balance. Four crucial children lived a matter of five miles out of town at a place which used to be called Dean's farm until the plight of Irish farming forced the Deans to emigrate to Lincolnshire; whereupon it was

70

bought by a refugee from Communist Czechoslovakia, who raised eggs there with an efficiency which was the admiration of all, although there was never an adequate market for all the eggs he raised, so that he went off and took a big job with one of our rising Irish industries and the farm changed hands again several times. The children did not have any means of transport to town, failed to attend school regularly, and endangered the grant.

Mrs Arbuthnot, one of the few rich Anglo-Irish who supported Mr de Valera, considered, so far as I could ascertain, that the main, if not the only, thing that was wrong with Irish nationalism was that the Roman Catholic Church had inevitably gained an undue influence on this otherwise sound political movement —a situation resulting, as she justly pointed out to me, from the failure of Protestant Parnell.

Being of practical mind, she gave thought to the school situation and concluded that the way to solve the problem was to provide the Dean family with a donkey and a tub cart. The cart was already available, and contact with the donkey was at length established by myself and the Rector, who was, in that capacity, ultimately responsible for the success or failure of the Parochial School.

The price demanded for this aged and sagacious beast was three pounds, and my mother-in-law and I shared fifty shillings of the burden, with the Rector contributing ten—on the ground, as my mother-in-law very wisely said, that it would enhance his interest and attention to business if he had a financial stake in the enterprise.

For a whole school term the donkey took the children to and from school, but at the end of the period Mrs Arbuthnot— who felt a love for and responsibility towards our fellow-animals —noted that the donkey had been ill, or at least carelessly, used. He had sores and lice, and was emaciated. He was in consequence removed from the care of the Deans and accommodated on lavish pasture at Mrs Arbuthnot's house, where he browsed very cheerfully under that Oriel window in Youghal from which Spenser records that he looked out as he wrote the first stanzas of *The Faerie Queen*. (The house, at that time, belonged to Sir Walter Raleigh who, among other functions, held the position of Mayor of Youghal.)

The day came, a very hot day in mid-summer, when the re-habilitated donkey, clean, sleek, beautifully coated, was to be returned to the Deans in readiness for the approaching autumn term. I was to go along with him and make a little speech, ex-plaining to the careless children just how a donkey should be taken care of, drawing their untutored attention to the state the donkey had been in before and the state he was in now.

My sister-in-law came along to drive the trap, but Jacky, who —if this is not too anthropomorphic a way of looking at the animal—seemed to resent the circumstance of being used as an example of what care and thought can do for our dumb friends, refused to work. We had to get out and pull him and push the trap up hill and down for the whole of those miles. Within sight, at last, of the Dean farm, we saw that the Deans had observed us from afar, (or else, more likely, they had been notified in advance by the Rector that they were going to get their transport back but would have to take a speech with it) and they were assembled at the road-gate of the farm.

I mentally rehearsed my little exhortation, which was simul-taneously to do much for the animal cause and save a section of Irish Protestantism. The donkey's expression became more and more resentful, and as we drew nearer to the gate he staggered slightly and then reeled in a positively spectacular manner. I was at once aware of an ominous resemblance between him and Mr John Betjeman who, in earlier days, used to em-barrass pompous friends by pretending to have an epileptic fit in Bond Street or Whitehall or the foyer of the Ritz Hotel. He once played a trick of that kind on an ambitious cousin of mine who expected to become the private secretary of Sir John Simon, then Foreign Secretary. My cousin was talking to Sir John in a sapient, well-bred, discreet kind of way, which made me and Mr Betjeman feel a little sick, when Mr Betjeman started to do his act, first trembling a little, then foaming at the mouth, then trembling a lot more, and finally falling down, writhing on the pavement of Parliament Square.

'Stop it, Johnny,' snarled our political aspirant, who knew perfectly well that the thing was a malign trick, a wicked act of deflation. It was the beauty of that trick that the victim always knew that it was a trick and could do nothing about it or, if he attempted to do so, got himself into worse trouble.

It was what happened on this occasion. A small crowd had, of course, collected, and the honest human hearts of these by-standers were intelligibly outraged by the sight of one man in epileptic agony on the pavement, another actually laughing, and a third, with chill indifference, trying to go on talking to the Foreign Secretary about Manchukuo.

'Look at your poor friend,' they shouted at my cousin who was trying to make such a good impression on Sir John. 'Can't you see he's ill? Having a fit he is. Can't you do something?'

Seeing his hopes of a fine political career deteriorating fast—for Sir John Simon was a particularly respectable class of man who would certainly not care to have as his private secretary one who consorted with people apt to have epileptic fits almost in the doorway of the House of Commons—my cousin, exasperated, interrupted his conversation with the Minister long enough to kick Mr Betjeman savagely in the behind.

The onlookers were at first incredulous, then indignant nearly to lynching-point. 'See that? See what he did? Kicked his poor friend. *Kicked* him while he's in a fit.' Furious humanitarians rushed forward to get Mr Betjeman to his feet, others argued noisily about how best to call an ambulance, two men dashed into the outer lobby of the House of Commons howling for assistance, and the Foreign Secretary, to whom a scene in the street was a lot more shocking a thing to be involved in than a war in the Far East, disappeared. My relative's climb up the political ladder had ended almost before it had begun.

My reminiscent suspicion of Jacky's behaviour on the lane leading to the Dean farm was justified. Within a dozen yards of the gateway, where all the Dean children and their parents were drawn up in an attitude of respectful expectation such as is due to a man who is partly responsible for salvaging a donkey and the Protestant school, this donkey not only reeled, but, reeling, fell. With the air of a stricken hero, determined to struggle forward to the goal despite all, he somehow slid himself a couple of yards through the dust. Then, with a look at me which seemed the equivalent of a malicious wink, he allowed himself to collapse entirely and, for good measure, ejected a small dribble of blood from the side of his mouth.

My speech died on my lips. Twenty minutes after I had left the farm, so I was told later, the donkey recovered completely.

Later, I bought out the Vicar's and Mrs Arbuthnot's interests, and he lived and worked with us another seven or eight years and appeared, with dignity, on a British Television programme, being interviewed by Mr Malcolm Muggeridge. Throughout all those years he took any opportunity he could find to tease me if he thought I was getting at all above myself, or taking anything for granted. A year or so ago he went to Blarney Castle, as companion to a young horse who had become so attached to the donkey that nobody could get him into the horse-box unless the donkey went too, and would have pined away without his aged companion. The donkey finally keeled over and quietly died after standing a long time gazing, so the groom at Blarney told me, up at the Blarney Stone.

The central African lion-dog, Zig, had a similarly astringent effect. At a time early in the war, when hardly any human in London could find a taxi, this dog used to find them and ride about in them at my expense—she would trek miles across London, get weary and lost, catch, with her exotic and endearing appearance, the eye of one of the rare taxi-drivers, and (her address being on her collar) be chauffeured back home, laughing, it seemed, unrestrainedly as I paid the fare.

(In the very early days of television she, like Jacky, appeared on the screen. My wife had been asked to talk about Central Africa and to bring the strange dog. But, unlike the donkey, Zig did not behave with dignity. Far from it. She first turned her back on the audience and then, it was her idea, I suppose, of a joke, relieved herself in the sight of all. She also pretended to hunt for fleas, although she was kept perfectly clean and had none. She wanted, I suppose, to suggest to the audience that with Patricia she lived in squalor.)

She was, unfortunately, a kind of drug addict—she would do anything to get hold of wool and suck it. She could smell wool through a thick cardboard box, and bite into the box until she could get her teeth and nose into the wool.

This addiction, which was soon imitated by her puppies, rendered her unfit for the society of children—she was capable of jumping into a pram and dragging the clothes off a baby to get at the wool, and, though a few minutes later she would scream with remorse for the possible injury done to the child, she could never resist doing it again when the craving came upon her. For this reason, among others, when my eldest son was born we had to give her away.

There had been reasons for doing so even before that. Her sardonic impishness led her to find ways to make us even more unpopular and suspect in the neighbourhood than, as a result of the Communist Party's change of line, we were already. The house whose back garden abutted on our back garden was occupied by a woman who was suspicious of her neighbours at the best of times, and, on finding that she had Communists at the bottom of her garden, became nearly hysterical and used to call up the police in the middle of the night to say that she had seen us signalling with electric torches to invisible enemy aircraft. Zig used to get into the garden at night and yodel, and, by an odd association of ideas, our neighbour somehow formed the impression that even the dog was communistic and that its cries had some sinister significance—perhaps it had been trained to signal to other subversives in adjacent streets. She would call up the police about the dog, too, and once, considering that they were lacking in zeal, she herself crept into the garden and attempted to kidnap the little creature.

Though this person could not but remind one of that sort of people who, in the first world war, used to throw stones at dachshunds, the general atmosphere of suspicion and hostility in which we lived was, of course, natural enough, and at least we were not in jail. I had, however, been afraid lest Patricia might find it intolerable; an inconvenience, too, of her new way of life which she could not have been expected to foresee. She had, however, been brought up in Ireland, a circumstance which had conditioned her to take a more realistic view of the twists and viccisitudes of political existence than she otherwise might have done; and, in addition, she had developed an acid scepticism about anything that any British Government might do, support, or proclaim.

Her home itself, properly named 'Myrtle Grove' but still locally called 'Raleigh's House', told a sufficiently realistic political story. It was from here that Sir Walter had first plundered Munster, and here that he had himself been plundered by the first Earl of Cork, who bought his estates for a song with apparently the understanding, at least on Raleigh's part, that the Earl would in turn lend his support to save Raleigh from execution for treason. If he did have such an understanding, he was fatally mistaken.

Generations later what had very probably attracted her grandfather, Sir Henry Blake's, favourable attention to the place was that it was, above all, defensible. He was a former officer of the Royal Irish Constabulary, penniless at the start, but handsome, able and adventurous—a character, indeed, more native to the eighteenth than the nineteenth century. He married an heiress, whose parents immediately disinherited her. But she was a woman of energy—a legacy, perhaps, from her mother who, at the age of seventy or thereabouts, suddenly decided to learn ancient Hebrew, and did so—and she managed to manipulate the influence of her powerful clan (her sister was Duchess of St Albans) so successfully that Henry Blake became successively Governor of Newfoundland, Jamaica, Hongkong, and Ceylon, and rich into the bargain. The subject races of the Maldive Islands paid annual tribute in the form of millions of tiny yellow cowrie shells; the British Government obligingly lent Sir Henry one of Her Imperial Majesty's cruisers to ship them home in; and Sir Henry used them to gravel the walks of the flower garden at Myrtle Grove.

As an ex-policeman and colonial Governor, Sir Henry did not take much stock in English theories as to the love and loyalty with which the Irish people at large—as distinct from agitators and small bands of extremists—were supposed to regard the ruling class (particularly such of its members as happened to be of native Irish stock, but operating on the side of the Ascendancy). He did not greatly care for the look of those lovely Georgian houses with huge windows—well enough in their way, but very uncomfortable if the populace should prove unloving and turn up with firearms. He chose instead Myrtle Grove, largely on the ground that this early Tudor dwelling was girt, for the most part, by the mighty old town wall of Youghal and was, in any case, right inside the town, conveniently near to the garrison, not isolated somewhere where the natives might have time to express themselves violently before succour could arrive.

A good deal of Patricia's childhood was lived during the war of independence and the subsequent civil war, when there were standing orders at Myrtle Grove to the effect that any man appearing in the grounds after dark without due authorization was to be shot at sight, with no time-wasting questions asked. Her parents, in point of fact, sympathized with the Irish cause, at least to a much greater extent than was usual among the Anglo-Irish, but it was never certain whether that much sympathy would be an adequate protection; people often enough got shot as a result of a misunderstanding.

An addition to the defences was the belief that Lady Blake had the power of the evil eye. This weapon was in her case thought to be so potent that when the old lady sat, as she often did, at the window of the library on the ground floor, the gardeners, when they had occasion to pass in front of the window, did so in a crouching posture, or actually on all fours, for fear of encountering that terrible beam.

This background perhaps made it rather easier than would have at first seemed likely for Patricia to accept, or at any rate not to be startled or repelled by, unorthodox, violent or extreme political views which, by habit and tradition, so many English people found it almost impossible not only to accept, but even to examine seriously. She had the further advantage of having spent only a few weeks at an orthodox upper-class school—she was sent to one in London when her parents lived there, but she was allergic to it. It made her scream in the night and run a temperature and she had to be sent over to Ireland and her notably unorthodox grandmother, who nourished her physically with large doses of claret and port wine, and mentally with encouragement to make good use of the large Myrtle Grove library, and in general to look upon the acquisition of factual knowledge on subjects ranging from primitive religions to the geography of China as a desirable and, in the fullest sense of the word, amusing activity, so that Patricia after her day's hunting, of which she was passionately fond, would spend what she considered a pleasantly relaxed evening drinking port and studying *The Golden Bough*, or a learned article in the *Encyclopaedia Britannica*.

Indeed, it was a civilized kind of house where it seemed natural to be gay and serious at the same time and where the library was deemed as important as the stables.

Still, despite general unorthodoxy of opinion, readiness to examine anything new, and inveterate suspicion of all acts of the British Government, she was sceptical and suspicious of the Communists too, and their sudden opposition to the war made her profoundly uneasy. However, she was prepared to give them and me the benefit of the doubt—and, at the time, there seemed to be enough doubt as to the realities of the international situation to make a quarrel on the issue less than worth while. You could see plenty of flaws in the Communist case, and plenty of hypocrisy in the statements that came from Moscow—but then you looked at London and Paris, and the general pattern of western war policy, and you saw the same things there. Also, Patricia shared with me what I suppose could be called a certain laziness of mind; a preference, at any rate, for getting ahead with some available form of action, rather than becoming involved in more or less talmudic arguments about whether to act and what direction to act in. I took pleasure in polemical political writing, satire, and militant reportage not, certainly, with quite the detachment of a barrister in relation to his client, but with an attitude something like that—it was the marshalling of the case, the strategy and tactics of the written word which basically interested and excited me. And Patricia felt something of the same.

Her introduction to the war itself at least was sufficiently English. She had long been in training with the ARP, and, now at the moment of the outbreak was working in the underground —allegedly but not actually bomb-proof—communications-room of the Area Control Centre in Praed Street. Chamberlain droned his Sunday morning announcement over the radio, the first air raid warning droned after him. People thought there would be a holocaust any minute now. Patricia's telephone rang, and a profoundly shaken voice cried, 'This is St Mary's Hospital. Whatever am I supposed to do now? I've lost the keys to the bloody mortuary.'

After the abandonment of the illegal *Worker* there followed a period of inexpressible political dreariness. With no papers to write for, I felt as though I had been suddenly castrated. I worked, irritably and ineffectively, as a sort of Public Relations and Press Officer for that congeries of loud-mouthed committees called the People's Convention. I detest committees, conferences and public speaking, and since the People's Convention involved a non-stop experience of all three I used sometimes to wonder at that period whether I had died without noticing it and was in hell for my sins.

Much of the activity of the organisation consisted in what, on a much later occasion, Mr Wilfred Roberts, M.P., described to me—he was speaking of a Liberal party conference—as 'an attempt to avert a split between the dupes and the fellow-travellers'. The only interest or amusement I ever extracted from the People's Convention was in the reading of a secret report upon it, prepared for the Labour party or the T U C (I forget which) by some 'expert', a copy of which had been stolen for us from Transport House. From this I gathered that our proceedings, which seemed to me almost totally futile, in reality constituted a serious menace and were a powerful source of political evil.

When Hitler with bomb and tank finally convinced Stalin that the Nazis were not as friendly as they looked, the Communists immediately dynamited the Convention, which blew to pieces with an almost inaudible pop.

During that time of relative isolation you needed not only lights in the darkness (there were really quite a lot of them) but barometers to tap and thermometers to read, so that you could feel you knew rather more about the state of the weather than you could learn from the newspapers or the meetings of the faithful.

In this respect I found much pleasure, comfort and utilitarian advantage in the society of a Mr Harry, who kept, in our neighbourhood, a big public house which combined a rich Edwardian cockney flavour with a faint element of up-to-date garishness, according well enough with the big motor cars of military men in his yard by day, and the aircraft overhead dropping incendiary bombs into the roadway by night.

Apart from keeping this public house Mr Harry was a member of a family vaguely connected with what might be called the down-to-earth side of cockney entertainment. Through a cousin he had an interest in a boxing establishment or prize-ring somewhere, and another cousin had a piece of a music-hall, and someone else of the clan was promoting some other little show in the provinces. In token of all this, Mr Harry himself wore spectacularly expensive suits, had a carnation regularly in his buttonhole and smoked—right through the worst of all the shortages so far as I can recall—big cigars.

He was a man who felt that the first business of an inn-keeper is to be tolerant to all who do not actualy disrupt by their conduct the harmony and comfort of the inn—and in time of war, and savagely aroused political feeling, to maintain that kind of balance is a considerable achievement. Mr Harry liked to achieve it, so that without much danger of being suddenly assailed by a fellow-drinker as a Moscow-minion, a fifth-columnist and probable Jew-baiter in disguise, I could spend a couple of hours there taking the temperature and tapping the barometer of what people were really saying, sometimes in the saloon bar, sometimes in the public. It was understood that I was an eccentric who refused to be 'typed' as an unfailing *habitué* of one or the other.

Mr Harry himself liked to make people at home. But he was also a busy man, and often did not take time to find out whether some vague rumour he had heard about one of his clients was true or not. Thus, when I first took to going there, he had picked up from somewhere or other a report that I was a former diplomat currently doing hush-hush work of a military nature. He at once told me that, at an unspecified period of his early youth —at the time I speak he must have been in his late forties or early fifties—he had been in the Indian cavalry.

'Had my white charger, old boy,' he said, drawing luxuriously on the cigar,' and rode all over India on it. Glorious. Never mind about the bombs—the old Empire will come through.'

Learning, a little later, that his earlier assumptions had been mistaken, and that I was something to do with 'the literary game', he told me, at a rather intense period of the blitz, that he himself had been, until very recently, a 'great reader'.

'Used,' he said, 'to like nothing better than settle down with something good.'

'What sort of thing did you read?'

'Well,' said Mr Harry, 'Thucydides, Dante—that type of thing. But d'you know,' he said mournfully, listening to the sirens, 'this thing's got on my nerves. I can't settle to that sort of thing nowadays. It's changed my reading habits altogether. Can you imagine what I read now?'

I tried to imagine what an enthusiast for Thucydides and Dante might be reduced to when his nerve broke.

'Dickens?' I guessed. 'Or some of the modern novelists?'

'Nao,' said Mr Harry, his cockney broadening in disgust at my naïvety, my under-estimation of the nerve-shocks he had received. 'Nothing but the back numbers of *Men Only*.'

'The *back* numbers?'

'Yus. Just the back numbers. The up-to-date ones get on my nerves. Too much of all this around us. Too much war.'

When Mr Harry admitted to himself, as he must have known with one half of his mind almost from the outset, that I was in some way mixed up with the Communists, I knew that the political climate of Britain had considerably changed. It must have been a month or two after Hitler's attack on Russia that he mentioned to me that he had always been a close student of politics, and that he had always felt 'some sort of Socialism or Communism' to have a particular appeal.

'After all,' said he, 'you have to consider elementary human justice. Don't forget that, Claud, old boy.'

Because it was sometimes used by groups of fire-watchers the public house could on occasion, without interference by the police, stay open half the night. In an unusual upflare of common-sense it was thought better that an incendiary bomb should be dealt with by a man who had been notably infringing the licensing laws than that it should be left to burn the neighbourhood. At one such moment Mr Harry and I were standing alone in the bar, very late, and he said to me, 'I can see it coming, Claud. The Communists are going to take over the country when this little lot's finished with. And I don't say they shouldn't. I don't say you haven't common human justice on your side, Claud. All I ask of you is just one thing.'

'What's that, Harry?'

'All I ask, Claud, when you and your pals take over and make that great revolution, that you'll just leave me my King, my constitution and my country.'

He had tears in his eyes, and it was hard not to be able to offer him a binding guarantee.

A year or more after the war was over, Mr Harry took a trip to the Channel Islands—the only bit of the British Isles actually occupied by the Germans during the conflict. He was enthusiastic. He described some huge beer cellar which the German military had remodelled and decorated in the Munich manner—a magnificent place, which, by its existence and the amenities it could offer to the English visitor, showed that out of evil some good could come.

I made some disobliging remark to the effect that I had read somewhere that a good many of the Channel islanders had made quite a good thing out of the war—had collaborated with the invaders 100 per cent, given them lists of local Jews so that these could be deported, and so on. Mr Harry said he had heard similar reports in the islands, and judged them to be well-based.

'But you don't understand, Claud old boy,' he said, 'at the time they did that, those people thought the Germans were going to win.'

Within a couple of weeks of the German invasion of Russia, Mr Rust had begun to organize what turned out to be one of the most remarkable 'mass campaigns' in the history of the British Left—the campaign to lift the ban on the *Daily Worker* and, incidentally, *The Week*. With extraordinary skill he fused the enthusiasm for the Russian fighters, the general belief of millions of British working people that now a lot of real tough friends had come to their senses and were fighting shoulder to shoulder with them, with the immediate objective of getting the ban raised. I was told at the time that, from quite an early date, Mr Churchill had expressed himself as in favour—or at least not opposed—to such action. But, as a result of what could seem a paradoxical structure of British politics ever since approximately 1924, it was the leadership of the Labour party which most strenuously resisted the move, and used all its influence and knowledge of Left politics to dissuade the rest of the Government from doing anything of the kind.

It was not until, to the visible and aghast astonishment of those on the platform, the Labour Party's own conference at Central Hall, Westminster, in the winter of 1942-43, voted against the ban by a small but respectable majority, that the final event became inevitable.

The Week was told it would be allowed out, too.

At this moment a curious episode occurred. Half casually, half intently, Mr Rust asked me whether I did, in fact, propose to re-start *The Week*. I was astonished. We had been campaigning for the freeing of both papers for months. He then said that there were some people at King Street who felt, or might be expected

to feel, that *The Week* constituted an anomalous phenomenon
—one which could even be embarrassing, I enquired in what
sense that could be so? He explained that what was anomalous
was that on the one hand, as a result of recent events, *The Week*,
which hitherto had, so far as a lot of its subscribers were concerned, been seen as merely radical, and even anarchistic, was
now rated as an organ of the Communist party. Yet, except in so
far as its Editor was associated with the *Daily Worker*, the Communist party had no real say-so about *The Week*, no editorial or
financial control. He made it clear that this was a situation which
gave many people at King Street nightmares. And I could see,
in a way, why. It was made clear to me that nobody would
take it amiss if I just failed to take advantage of the lifting
of the ban and devoted myself in future exclusively to the
Daily Worker.

In some ways the notion was attractive, for I could see that
the situation, which was so entirely different from that which
The Week had been founded to exploit, and of which it had so
successfully taken advantage in the 1930's, no longer existed—
and had not, in fact, existed since, at the latest, the end of the
'phoney war'.

On the other hand, the cool suggestion now made irked me
and caused me uneasiness. I had a feeling it might be better to
keep my tiny boat in seaworthy condition. I could hardly express
that thought very clearly to Mr Rust—who would have been
quick to appreciate it—because it would evidently have confirmed whatever suspicions about my possible goings-on were
harboured at Headquarters. It was desirable to emulate that
Chinese General who, in the days before the Communists took
over, was suspected by his Commander-in-Chief, Chiang Kai-
shek, of moving over to the other side.

'Be not afraid,' cabled the General or War Lord from some
fastness in West China. 'I have no thoughts of my own.'

I did, however, say to Mr. Rust that I really could not put
myself in the position of having stumped the country for
months, demanding, in the name of British justice and the
elementary freedoms of the press, that my paper be released from
the ban to carry out a task indispensable to the proper informing of public opinion and the health of the nation, and then, the
ban being raised, walk away with a shrug saying that on second

thoughts I deemed it a waste of time to take advantage of our arduously re-gained liberty.

William Rust, whose sense of humour you rarely appealed to in vain, accepted the argument as valid, and—or so I was told—put up a vigorous fight on my behalf against those who looked upon the existence of an 'independent' paper which also purported to be Communist as a gross, and even alarming, contradiction in terms.

6

L'homme qui rit

UNLESS you are in actual combat, or in some commanding position where you can play chess with it all, most of a war is apt to be horribly boring. It does not fill up your time interestingly, and yet it is too intrusive to let you get ahead with anything else. There are exceptional people who, under stress of war, seem almost literally to rise, as the phrase used to go, above it; people who can force themselves to turn the beastly necessities of war into virtues, and, in addition to combat, do whatever else they do—such as painting, or thinking, or designing engines—better in that atmosphere than in any other. They make, I believe, the finest fighting men and I suppose they are at the same time the people who in war time really do 'save civilisation'. Personally, I have encountered more of them among the British and French than anywhere else. There were several such—together, naturally with numerous scoundrels and poltroons—in the entourage of General de Gaulle, and, by a twist of the whirligig of time which now seems bizarre, there was at that time in London a working alliance between the Gaullists and the Communists.

Mutually they suspected that the British and American Governments were, even then, favouring collaborationists and appeasers in France, on the gound that they would, in the long, long run help London and Washington solve their grievous—genuinely grievous—problem of how to defeat Hitler without letting the Communists win.

As a consequence it could be surmised that they might be prepared to a certain degree to strangle or squeeze the windpipes of those sections of the resistance movement which could be proved to be, or strongly suspected to be, under Communist control. It would not have been an unreasonable behaviour on their part. Nobody can be amazed at people doing what they conceive to be in their own best interests. And if these people choose to place their bets that way—to gamble that they could afford to hobble some of the French resistance for the sake of other objectives on more distant horizons—it was their privilege to do so. As things turned out, they did bring about approximately the situation they were surmised to have in mind. The situation in France today cannot be fully understood without some reference to the policies prevailing and the struggles undertaken on one side and the other in the London and Washington of the early 1940's.

Nobody will ever know now how correct was that surmise, or what weight the people who held those views really pulled at the time. You could sift for months the official and unofficial records, the published and unpublished memoirs, and you still would find that your busy historical sieve had holes in it. Although the first Henry Ford was mistaken in thinking that history is simply 'the bunk', he was right in supposing that when people write history they have a temptation—conscious or subconscious, but seldom resisted—to put some bunk into it.

Any important and lively phenomenon of history is like the horse in Dickens's *Hard Times*.

' "Girl number twenty unable to define a horse!" said Mr Gradgrind, for the general behoof of all the little pitchers. "Girl number twenty possessed of no facts, in reference to one of the commonest of animals! Some boy's definition of a horse . . . Bitzer," said Thomas Gradgrind, "Your definition of a horse."

' "Quadruped, Graminivorous. Forty teeth, namely twenty-four grinders, four eye-teeth, and twelve incisive. Sheds coat in the spring; in marshy countries, sheds hoofs too. Hoofs hard, but requiring to be shod with iron. Age known by marks in mouth."

' "Now, girl number twenty," said Mr Gradgrind, "You know what a horse is." '

But those engaged—in both the English and French senses of the word—in any form of immediate activity are, as it were, riding the horse and can hardly hang about until it has been defined to the extent where it is known that in marshy countries it sheds its hoofs. At that time we were all riding horses, and nobody had time to bother much with defining the hoof-structure of Gaullism, or Communism either.

The '*mystique*' of Gaullism and de Gaulle was a word much in vogue at the time, and rightly so. It is strange that although the British have as much susceptibility to '*mystiques*' as do the French—though the British will commonly deny it, and slightly deride the French for that susceptibility—there is no word for it in our language. This lacuna—could it mean that a whole language can suffer from an inhibition?—is a problem for psychoanalytical semanticists, and they should get on with it.

The highlights of life and history are produced by the occasions and personalities which make two times two equal seven. That is a function of '*mystique*.'

It was in that sense that there was a '*mystique*' of the Spanish war, and with the emergence of General de Gaulle from the squalor and horror of the 'phoney' war and the subsequent French disaster, followed by a noise from Paris as of apes intriguing and disputing about coconuts while the extermination chambers trundled and a little farther westwards, there sounded a pure and lyrical note which (though neither the Communists nor the Gaullists would admit it now), suggested to some people that Europe had not gone entirely tone-deaf at the moment when the Spanish Republican cause came to its dead end at Figueras.

The people who never can see how to make more than four out of two times two, and settle for that as the best that can be done with the arithmetic of life, had a jolt. France, like Evadne in *The Maid's Tragedy*, had brought many people near to

> ' . . . that dull calamity,
> To that strange misbelief of all the world,
> And all things that are in it.'

General de Gaulle, and all that he implied, were an escape from dull calamity.

I have just said that there was a working alliance between the Gaullists and the Communists, and in the practical sense of the term—the sense that a co-operation of this kind existed and had effects—it is true. But both the Gaullists and the Communists may be right when, as they often do nowadays, they deny the existence of any such thing. Perhaps it was just an alliance between individuals who found one another sympathetic and thought that for the time being they were going the same way. So far as I was concerned my ally was that journalist and propagandist of genius André Laguerre (a very French Frenchman brought up in San Francisco, because his father was French consul there). After escaping from France and for a while tramping the pavement of Carlton Gardens with a rifle on his shoulder, on sentry-go for the Free French, he became—as a result of his energy and some unknown person's perspicacity—Public Relations Officer for the Gaullists.

At that time, the Gaullists were far from popular in London— partly because they were still less popular in Washington where President Roosevelt took the view that, in terms of Rooseveltian philosophy, the relatively small de Gaulle bottle must be marked 'dangerous, to be taken only under American doctor's directions', like the much bigger bottle in which Roosevelt thought he smelled the inveterate imperialism and colonialism of Winston Churchill. The much over-simplified impression one had at the time was that Mr Churchill, who had his own troubles with Mr Roosevelt—not to mention the general and real undesirability of doing anything which might be difficult to explain to Mr Bernard Baruch—saw no good reason to compromise British policies by getting their name too closely linked with that of General de Gaulle.

Liberals and Socialists in France and England were suspicious of the General, too. Indeed, I suppose that if you made up a composite figure of every available element that would annoy, discompose, and arouse the suspicions of an orthodox English Labour Party leader, the General would have about filled the bill. He may have made, from time to time, some enthusiastic speech about democracy or the century of the common man, but, if so, I do not recall it. And the omission was a serious political mistake. It was one which M. Laguerre and myself did our best to repair.

We were not much assisted by the attitude and actions of some members of the entourage. De Gaulle himself, though declared by his enemies to be as vain as a peacock, was no easy client for publicity men. And then there was a Colonel Passy (it was not, naturally, his real name, but in the course of the years I have forgotten what his real name was), a counter-espionage *policier*, who could never grasp the difference between that sort of killing which the public think is murder, and the sort they accept as a form of national defence.

He murdered, or arranged for the murder of, a man in Duke

Street. He believed, rightly I have always thought, that this man —representing himself as a devoted adherent of the Free French —was in reality a German spy. The victim, after death, was strung up in this room in Duke Street, and the police were supposed to believe he had hanged himself.

The police found it difficult to understand why a man would have beaten himself up in a savage manner before stringing himself up. Also, since it was the ordinary police who had been called in to find the body of the alleged suicide, the case had been automatically placed on the conveyor-belt of the 'due processes of law'. There had to be an inquest.

It was the sort of point which Colonel Passy was liable to overlook. Perhaps he would have been more careful about it if he had not misunderstood—and who shall blame him?—the nuances of the British political scene. He did not, evidently, understand that in British political life it is almost essential to be a Christian even when you are an atheist. 'Being a Christian' in this sense means that, though you may proclaim total disbelief in the doctrines of the Church, you must at the same time indicate that you are in favour of Christian 'ethical values'.

To sneer at this as hypocrisy is cheap. There is hypocrisy in it, certainly. But, when the people across the street are running up their extermination chambers and getting to take torture for granted, this sort of hypocrisy has a value. Wilde said hypocrisy is the tribute vice pays to virtue. Such tributes, and the recognition that they ought to be paid, have a civilizing influence.

Being, in this sense, Christian, British public opinion—and more particularly Left opinion—is implacably opposed to war. When, after announcing its opposition, the Left, as in the last two world conflicts, finds itself vigorously supporting a war, it understandably prefers that it shall not have its nose rubbed in the facts of war more than is absolutely necessary. It requires, for instance, that if, in the interests of the war effort, a man has to be done to death in Duke Street, the murderer shall wear kid gloves and leave no finger-prints. Enemy agents, like the ex-husband of the heroine of *Gentlemen Prefer Blondes*, are not murdered, they become shot.

A disclosure that the Gaullists considered it natural and reasonable to murder a man in a backroom in Duke Street on the ground that they thought him an enemy agent was going to be meat and drink to de Gaulle's enemies. Liberals and Labour people were going to react with horror on general principles. And a lot of other people who would have thought nothing of doing the same thing in similar circumstances were going to exploit what one of them once deliciously described to me as the 'layman's reaction' zestfully for their own purposes.

The case has always fascinated me as being one of those affairs which have effects similar to that which imminent drowning is supposed to have, except that in these cases it is not the past which is projected in a sudden illuminating flash, but the present. By just watching the reactions of people—of those, that is, who knew or guessed the truth of what had happened—you could acquire a detailed geographical survey of the mind and face of political Britain, a sketch of trends and tendencies you could not have got from innumerable 'public opinion polls'.

Characteristically completing the picture, General de Gaulle and Colonel Passy simply could not see why, once the body was literally on view, the British authorities could not dispense with an inquest, or else instruct the local police to say that the man had been picked up dead in the street, or tell any other story of the kind which would avoid any type of political unpleasantness. Indeed it was one of those episodes which helped to convince the Gaullists that the British Intelligence Service—for whose assistance in burying the matter quietly they immediately applied—was positively working against them. Otherwise why wasn't an agent sent round to the police station or the Coroner with instructions as to what the police witnesses and the Coroner were to say or do? *On est trahi.*

Although I did not think so at the time, I have been assured since that a maximum was done in that quarter to smother the affair. But although, by skilful use of the security regulations, the barest minimum of fact got published in the newspapers, the story circulated widely by word of mouth and André Laguerre, with such assistance as I could offer, had to work overtime trying to keep the General's picture among the political pin-up favourites of the public at large.

Things would have been easier for us if it had been true, as was so widely asserted, that the General had no sense of humour. He was represented as an austerely unbending, rigid type of man who 'joked with deefficulty'—who could not, it was said, joke at all. To suppose so was to misjudge him seriously. In my estimation, at least, he could not resist a joke even when to play it was obviously against his best interests. Most of his jokes were about as harmless as a hand-grenade after the pin has been taken out. His amusement at seeing other people abruptly debunked or deflated often reminded me of my dog Zig. They were both, in this sense, highly astringent.

Cardinal de Retz, in his incomparable memoirs, records how he, after weeks of more or less successful intrigue in Rome at the time, 1655 or thereabouts, of the election of Pope Alexander VII, did himself grave harm because he could not resist making malicious jokes at the expense of M. de Lionne, French Ambassador Extraordinary, whom he should have been trying to conciliate. 'I observed on this occasion,' he notes sadly, 'though too late, what I have since observed in others, namely how extremely careful one ought to be, in great affairs still more than in others, to curb the pleasure one is inclined to take in telling funny stories.'

It is not apparent that de Retz ever subsequently acted in accordance with this sage axiom, and I dare say that even if Laguerre had, at my suggestion, presented General de Gaulle with a marked copy of the de Retz memoirs, having this passage underlined, it would have made no difference. Mirth is a habit-forming vice.

At one time, the Free French employed in London—much in the way that people employ hard-up peeresses to lead their daughters round the Season—a highly-connected but quite broke socialite to run a sort of *salon* for them. She gave lunch parties and dinner parties where loyal Free Frenchmen met English men and women of influence. (M. d'Astier de la Vigerie, who used to parachute, near-suicidally, in and out of France like a ping-pong ball, told me once of attending a dinner of this kind when an English Cabinet Minister and his wife were present. They were not unaware of the heroic doings of M. de la Vigerie. 'Are you,' the Minister's wife enquired, 'planning to return to France soon?' M. de la Vigerie, hardly able to believe his ears on hearing this fantastic indiscretion, replied to the general effect that that was as might be. Undiscouraged, the Ministress pursued her investigation. Would he, as and when he dropped from the skies into occupied France, be going anywhere near Bourges?

Thinking, 'Good God, are these people having a war or not?'
Vigerie replied that all things were possible. 'If,' said the Minister's wife, 'you do happen to be in Bourges, I wish you would
make a point of looking up two old servants of ours who
returned there when we left France just before the invasion. I
should like to let them know that my husband and myself are
quite all right. You see, they may be anxious about us.'

After a while, it was decided for some reason or other that
the *salon*-runner was not really earning her keep. I have forgotten whether the reason was that things were going so well for
the Free French that she had become redundant, or were going
so badly that even a good *salon* was not going to make much
difference. It was decided to sack her. But de Gaulle's closest
advisers were worried—she was a woman still of potential
influence; the thing must be done with the utmost discretion.
'Discretion, General,' they said, and de Gaulle contrived to look
as though discretion were his middle name.

They cooked up the idea of a little tea-party at Carlton
Gardens where the General and one or two of the discreet
advisers were discreetly to break the news that, great as this
lady's services had been to the Cause, the Cause with the utmost
regret was compelled, temporarily it was to be hoped, to relin-
quish them. The discreet, sighing with relief at the fact that
things were going to go so smoothly, waited for her arrival. She
was announced. De Gaulle, uncoiling suddenly from his chair
like a long worm with a steel spring in it, strode beaming across
the room to greet her.

'A-ha! Madame,' he said, 'the first thing I want to tell you is
that you're sacked.'

Even months later he recalled with pleasure the expression
on the faces of the discreet advisers at that moment. It was
exactly the sort of thing that Zig would have done.

Our Gaullist campaign went so successfully that one day Mr
Brendan Bracken, then Minister of Information, openly attacked
and threatened me at one of those dreadful conferences of the
Houses of Commons Lobby correspondents which used to be
held several times a week. I liked Mr Bracken. He had a jaunty
kind of acceptance of the facts of war which was refreshing.
On the other hand I had been told (perhaps untruthfully, for I
cannot think he was the sort of man seriously to resent such a

remark) that he had been upset by my observation that a wartime Minister of Information was compelled, in the national
interest, to such continuous acts of duplicity that even his
natural hair must grow to resemble a wig.

And that same evening André Laguerre rang me up to tell me
that President Roosevelt, at some press conference or interview
in Washington, had, after sharp criticism of Gaullist policies,
remarked in passing that a great deal of the trouble and publicity was being caused by 'two small-time connivers in London.'

We founded on the spot the Small-Time Connivers' Club and
from time to time in the passing years, whenever conniving has
seemed slack, we have sought to increase the membership. But
as a result, no doubt, of laziness on the part of the foundation
members, the membership remains steady at a total of two.

Naturally it was not without a great deal of trouble, and noble
assistance from the National Union of Journalists, 90 per cent.
of whose members detested what I said but took a fine Voltairean
attitude about my right to say it, that when (after the fighting
men had driven the Germans and Italians out of North Africa),
it was agreed that a party of diplomatic correspondents should
be allowed to visit the scene, I was permitted to make one of
their number. I have it on what I consider good authority that
Mr Bracken—despite all—took a determined attitude about this,
and insisted that to exclude me would be a picayune sort of
politics. If it is true, I owe him a debt of gratitude. And, of
course, if not, not.

However, when we got to Algiers—we had been there I think
about twenty-four hours—two rather disconcerting things happened. The leadership of the pre-war Communist party of
France, a great parcel of ex-M Ps who had just been let out of
jail and seemed to have heard of nothing since August 1939,
made it clear to me that in their view Communist policy in
London towards de Gaulle had been grossly mistaken—the man
was a menace, an anti-democrat, and an embryo dictator. They
seemed, indeed, to be contemplating some kind of alliance—or
perhaps they already had such an alliance—with the Giraudists.
And I could not escape the discouraging impression that, because
the assassin of Admiral Darlan had been a Royalist extremist of
the Right, they disapproved even of that act.

The other upset to my schedule occurred when I was sum-

moned to the relevant British authority—the Information
people, I suppose, but I no longer recall who actually acted in
the matter—and informed that I was expelled from North Africa
and must take myself off within twenty-four hours. An aircraft
would have a seat for me at Maison Blanche on the morrow.

It seemed a sad thing to have come all this way and have to
return so soon. And I must confess that I was a good deal influenced by considerations other than those of political and journalistic achievement. The sun was wonderfully hot, and after the
war years in London Algiers danced in the sun like a dream come
true. I made up my mind that whatever happened I really could
not quit the scene so soon.

Moreover it was apparent to me that whereas the British had
allowed me in, and were quite prepared for me to stay, the
Americans were having an early attack of those security jitters
which later developed into neuroses really harmful to those
otherwise vigorous and healthy people, and had taken fright.
They were in fact raising Cain with the British for having
allowed me to become airborne Africa-wards in the first place.
One more example, they were saying, of the sloppy British way
of doing things. And the British were, at that moment, in no
position—certainly at least in no mood—to make an issue of it,
and find themselves quarrelling with their great and good friends
over the case of a Communist diplomatic correspondent.

It seemed best not to be, for the moment, an issue; in fact, to
disappear. I took refuge in the house of an elderly and heroic
Jewish doctor—a man who before the Allied landings had risked
his life over and over again in big and small (but continuous and
relentless) actions against the collaborationists and the Germans
and the Italians, and in whose house a part of the planning of
the landings had actually been carried out. He was not only old
but lame. When his big house was full of hidden conspirators
he had been used to spend hours and hours, from dawn onward,
limping wearily from market to market so as to buy food for a
dozen young fighting men without attracting undue attention by
the quantities he bought. I can think of no one I have ever
known who, in his courage, physical endurance, skill and cunning in the face of enemy attack, and ability calmly to cultivate
his cultural garden when he had a moment free from the threat
of torture, was superior to that man.

It was in his house that the assassination of Darlan had been planned, and the assassin had been hidden there for some time before the act took place. There had been, as there always is in such affairs, some sort of muddle and, although I naturally did not ask questions about it, I gathered that somebody had, as the saying goes, jumped the gun—the thing had not been supposed to happen in exactly that way or at exactly that time. However, as I say, this is simply an impression I gained indirectly in the doctor's house.

It was a fine house to lie low in—several exits available and a favourable concierge. My notion was that, by keeping out of the way and not making myself into any sort of test-case between the mutually embittered British and American authorities, I could probably avoid being physically thrown out of North Africa for at least a while, and at the same time—that house being the kind of house it was—could probably, in the ordinary course of conversation with the characters who stayed or visited there, find out more about what was really going on than I could have hoped to do in any other way.

I planned that after a time I would start making a test case in a slightly different way. The head of the Government was, after all, officially General de Gaulle. True, the British and American military were really in command, and true that in the event of any sort of serious physical showdown de Gaulle would be as powerless as a toothless dog. But nobody—not even the Americans—wanted that sort of showdown. And, at the same time, the General was very sensitive about his authority and rights. He would not, for instance, be much pleased at the intelligence that civilians were being expelled from his bailiwick by the British or Americans without so much as a by-your-leave to himself. It was my intention, at a suitable moment, to engage the General's interest on this point. But I had learned that André Laguerre, whom I had thought to find in Algiers, had been delayed, and I did not want to do anything decisive until he was there to advise and assist.

It would, evidently, have been foolish to allow the expelling forces to confine me solely to the house—rich mine of information though it was. It was necessary to go out and about a good deal, too. Once, by an accident—I just thought the place looked like a good bar—I found myself standing at the bar of the

Aletti Hotel which, as I knew, was the principal meeting place of the Anglo-American military. Regretting that I had come there, I yet thought it more prudent to drink my drink in a relaxed manner—especially as, by a happy chance, it was the time when the Anglo-Americans ate their lunch, and the bar was nearly empty. Then, in the glass behind the barman, I saw a brisk movement of khaki. I could not see the man's head but I could see his shoulders—a Colonel, no less. If he was a know-ledgeable kind of Colonel, I thought, he would have me picked up within a matter of minutes. There was nothing sensible to do other than just to go on quietly drinking. The Colonel was now so close to me that I could hear the sound his little bristles made as he rubbed his chin—Algiers was a bad town to get a good shave in. Unable to stand the tension any longer, I lowered my head to peek in the glass behind the barman and, having got this Colonel's head reflected in the mirror, saw that it was none other than my old and valued friend Mr Peter Rodd, a man of very likeably adventurous disposition who could be very serious, too. He had done, for instance, a lot of whatever little was done for the Spanish Republican refugees in France after the final hauling-down of the flag at Figueras.

I am not a very quick thinker, and must confess that for the moment it simply did not cross my mind that Mr Rodd had any right to the uniform he was wearing—that he was a genuine Colonel of the Guards. I assumed that he must be up to some-thing a little delicate, and therefore forbore to greet him. It might, it seemed to me, be embarrassing for him to have his life complicated by association with me. It was therefore he who had to make the first move, and it turned out that he was as pukka a Colonel as Colonels come.

I told him of my situation. As usual he was resourceful. Every-one, of course, knew that the landings in Sicily were due any day now. Colonel Rodd suggested that, if Algiers was getting too hot to hold me, a good idea might be to hire some British soldier's uniform, sneak aboard the vessel in which the Colonel was shortly to attack Sicily, get into a landing craft, and be the first British journalist to get ashore on this momentous occasion.

Although nobody would, I imagine, give Mr Rodd a prize in a run-of-the-mill discretion competition, in matters of moment he can be as discreet as a trainer a week before the Derby, so that I had to grasp what he had in mind from the merest hints.

It was, in many ways, an attractive idea, and I briefly entertained it. A shadow darkened my mind. I pointed out that whereas the whole of this hypothetical landing party, as it advanced to a point which one might call X, would be exposed to the fire of certain enemy forces, I would be unique in that, on arrival and discovery, I should be exposed also to the fire of a British squad which would shoot me as a spy. I said the thought perturbed me. Colonel Rodd was not at all perturbed.

'If anything like that looked like happening, after all,' said he, 'I could easily have a word with whoever was in charge. I'd explain the whole thing.'

I seemed to remember, from years of accidental association since Oxford days, that one of the things Mr Rodd is not is meticulously punctual. I was sure that he would come to 'have a word' with the man in charge. I was a great deal less sure that the fatal volley would not have rung out on some Sicilian beach about twenty minutes earlier. Regretfully I declined to pursue the project further.

André Laguerre arrived, and I arranged to be invited to lunch with General de Gaulle at the nominal seat of Government.

Just in case the Americans might pick me up on the way, I had asked André to take steps to ensure that they were aware that if they did anything like that they were going to be offering a deliberate affront to General de Gaulle. In consequence, I was rushed up the hill to the Residency in an enormous car with tricoleurs streaming from the bonnet and even from the top, a sub-machine-gunner beside the driver, and a couple of motor-cycle police roaring ahead and behind.

Conceiving that this was the occasion for a jolly good joke, de Gaulle had told his entourage that, for political reasons, he was entertaining that day a notorious Red hatchet-man. The possibility of an assassination attempt must not be excluded. Vigilance was essential. Remember what happened to Trotsky. The joke was a big success. When I entered the hall, and while I waited for my arrival to be announced, I noticed that at two points of the pseudo-Moorish style gallery which ran round it at a height some few feet above my head, dedicated men were kneeling, evidently in concealment, with pistols in their hands ready to blaze away in case this OGPU desperado should get up to any tricks. And at lunch, in addition to de Gaulle and myself, there were two Colonels who could scarcely attend to their food because they had been instructed to remain on the qui vive, watching my every movement. The general disregarded them—indeed they were so rigid with anxiety that I doubt whether they could have taken much intelligent part in the conversation any way—so that our talk was an interesting form of the tête-à-tête : tête-à-tête with bodyguards.

It was not to be supposed that the General would see fit to disclose the inner secrets of his plans and policies—and, even had he gone mad and done that very thing, the information would have been of little value. For he was not in any position to impose his plans and policies upon anyone, and, being a man of great political flexibility (the flexibility you sometimes find in men like de Gaulle who live, as it were, *sub specie aeternitatis* and can thus afford to treat the day-to-day wangle of politics with the contempt it deserves), whatever he might today think he was going to do tomorrow could, by tomorrow, be forgotten.

I detest 'interviewing' people, and it was therefore with relief that I reflected that anything in the nature of an interview was pointless. I did, on the other hand, want to make a final formal little bow to him; to say, just for the sake of having it said, what I felt about the exhilarating effect of his actions, his personality and his *mystique* upon the mind of the western world. He had, of course, heard the same thing over and over again, and I hesitated because I thought that a repetition from me might be tedious and spoil his lunch. However, one does not refrain from thanking one's host for the delightful party just because fifty other people have just said the same thing, so I said my piece. His courtesy —a virtue which always moves me and which I think is a part of that Charity that abides with Faith and Hope—was such that he pretended to be surprised and delighted by my tribute.

Once one is free of the confining and distorting requirements of the 'interview'—probably the most boring and useless dis- covery ever made by journalism, since the odds against any public man telling the truth for publication to a million readers can be calculated by anyone—one can get to the more serious business of finding out how the man's mind works, what is his basic attitude to this and that, what, in three words, makes him tick.

General de Gaulle, whom I had, of course, encountered in London, but always on strictly businesslike business, wanted, naturally, to have some talk about Communism. He asked me directly why I was—as I was at that time—a Communist. I told, him briefly, what I have already told in an earlier chapter of this book. Not much to my surprise—for I had a high regard for his intelligence, not to mention his inclination to prefer the disembodied theory to the sordid fact—he showed an immediate understanding of how I felt and why I felt it.

He added, thinking perhaps of all those out-dated Communist Deputies squabbling down the road, 'You don't think that your view is perhaps somewhat romantic?'

This seemed to be indeed the Devil rebuking sin. And I was in any case profoundly influenced by the fact that, so far as the resistance within France was concerned, the Communists were the toughest, supplest muscles of the movement.

There was no indication then of the post-war incapacity of the Communist Parties in Europe and outside Russia, to establish themselves prosperously even in territories where they had absolute power.

Yet to me it seems that the crime of the Communists in Hungary was not principally that they massacred people with tanks in the streets of Budapest. By the time it came to that, Russian control of Budapest could be considered as a matter dictated by the brutal necessities of world strategy.

The crime, monstrous in its fact and its implications, was that after nearly a decade of absolute Communist power, a majority of people was prepared to die rather than tolerate the regime. That rather than the military repression—there has been plenty of that on all sides at all times—is what gives to the Hungarian events their crucial, permanent, jolting significance.

7

The Long Train

GUIDED by hindsight, I should say that the attitude—mean, rigid and out-dated, as it seemed to me—of those quarrelsome and querulous Communist Deputies in Algiers may have effected in my subconscious mind a basic shift in my own attitude to Communism. It took a lot of the gilt off the gingerbread.

It is well enough to argue, as I have heard argued by people entirely opposed to the Communists, that from their own standpoint the Deputies in Algiers had a correct political appraisal of the situation. That is to say, they correctly anticipated that only de Gaulle could head off the victory of communism in postwar France, so that their first task must be to undermine de Gaulle.

It sounds like a good point until you recall that, as of now, the French Communists have not got to many of the places they thought they were going to after Liberation.

The question is a little more than academic, because the basic situation is one which recurs, and probably will keep on recurring, at various times and in various lands. In other words, if the Gaullist *mystique*—which was a *mystique* of France a lot bigger than the personal one of General de Gaulle—had fused, so to speak, with the Communist *mystique*, it is possible, barely possible, that something would have emerged which would have been neither Communism, in the orthodox sense of the word, nor Gaullism in the orthodox sense of that word, but something new and vital, as an attitude to life and politics, of the kind which those in the western world who reject defeatism and despair claim they are looking for.

At the time I had no very clear vision of this—simply a sense of disillusion and disappointment. I did report in

London that in my view the Deputies, who had after all been arrested and deported at the end of 1939, were living a long way behind the times. William Rust saw the point, and for a while there was sharp divergence between the policy of the British Party journal and the official line of the French Communist Party. Later, of course, everything got straightened out —in strict conformity with the French Party.

Revolutionary organisations which are deemed, as a matter of course, to be living in the future, are often more inclined than others to live in the past. It is paradoxical, but not unnatural. In fact, on reflection and first-hand examination of their problems, it becomes evident that in the nature of things they are required, for their own maintenance, to emphasize the past —their own past—more heavily than are conservative groups of long standing. Every political and, indeed, religious organization requires a 'myth'—I use the word in the most strictly neutral sense without any connotation of truth or falsity— and for the creation of a myth are needed both a goal, a more or less Messianic vision of the future, and a tradition, an iconic picture of the past. The newer the organization, the more sharply defined must be the tradition.

Heresy is a greater danger to a comparatively new and struggling organization, continuously threatened with disintegration from within or obliteration from without, than one long rooted in traditional soil. It is this fact which, within a revolutionary organization, inevitably weights the dice in favour of those who, like

> 'Hobbs, Nobbs, Nokes and Stokes combine
> To paint the future from the past,
> Put blue into their line.'

To propound a new idea must always be to incur the possibility of a charge of heresy, of 'deviation'. The onus of proof is on the propounder of such an idea. Exceptionally courageous and energetic men can do it, realizing that they are thereby not only challenging the Scribes and Pharisees, but also stirring the genuine terrors of those who obscurely feel that the slightest deviation from the route-map sketched by the founding fathers may run them all disastrously into the bog. And, one should remember, often enough it does. And among such, those who can do it most effectively are men who—like Lenin—have themselves become myths in their own lifetime, so that opinions which in others would be heretical, are stamped as orthodox almost before they are uttered.

There are also the professional heretics—most common in my experience among Scotsmen and Jews—who, often rightly, are deemed mere cranks by their colleagues. I am still a little awed by the recollection of a man I once met in Edinburgh after making some speech there. He told me that he was a member of—if I remember correctly—the New Scottish Labour and Nationalist Revolutionary Party. Its membership was five, it having only recently been formed after the breakaway from the Scottish Labour and Nationalist Revolutionary Party, which up to the moment of the schism had had a membership of sixteen.

I enquired the reason for the break. It was, said he, a matter of principle. Those sixteen used to hold bi-weekly meetings, and these continued for two or three months, with unanimity expressed on all occasions.

'Then,' said my informant, 'a few of us began to realize that we were living in a fool's paradise. We couldn't just put our finger on what was wrong, but it stood to reason, man, there must be something utterly tainted and rotten about an organization where everyone just agreed with everyone else all the time, so we up and quit.'

But, by and large, the innovators and the natural heretics are a lot less numerous than those prudent 'revolutionaries' who would prefer never to do anything that has not been done before; to whom, in fact, the mere notion of any possible new 'synthesis' such as might, conceivably, have been achieved at Algiers, suggests dangerous treachery. You often read of revolutionary statesmen who are supposed to be having immense difficulty in 'restraining hotheads'. In my experience, most of them have to spend a lot of their time prodding the mass of their followers into keeping less than a mile or so behind current realities. A man who kept a bookshop told me once that on the day of the Invergordon mutiny in 1931, he was beset with demands by eager comrades for a history of the Black Sea Fleet mutiny of 1917.

It was impossible, after Algiers, not to recall—and it seems to me always important to keep in mind—the observation of

Sainte-Beuve on the subject of people who do not adjust themselves to the times.

'What a number of watches stopped, during the revolution,
on this or that day of violent shock! Let us then try, even though
we may take no pleasure in the present time, to wind our watches
every evening and keep them right; it is an excellent mental
habit.'

A delicious example of what one may call the revolutionary-
traditionalist, was a Polish-Jewish tailor, an enthusiastic and
indefatigable attendant at meetings of the Communist Party
in north-west London. He rarely failed to intervene in debate.
His interventions and proposals rarely won general approval.

When shouts of 'No, no', and 'Nonsense' rose in volume, he
would pause and raise a commanding hand. Silence secured, he
would look round the room with a smile in which self-confidence
and pity were mingled.

'Comrades,' he would say, 'have you forgotten, do perhaps
some of you not even know, that once, in 1918, I carried a
message for Lenin from Minsk to Moscow?'

He sincerely believed that this achievement, which was a fact,
entitled him to a sort of plural vote in any gathering of the
faithful. I only once saw him put out of countenance, when
some irreverent new recruit asked whether the message had,
in fact, ever been successfully delivered.

In that latter part of the war, Communists were suddenly so
popular that it nearly hurt. Every district organizer seemed to
carry the Sword of Stalingrad in his brief-case. And I think it
can hardly be denied that the Communists, by their whole-
hearted—one could almost say reckless—devotion to 'the war
effort' during that period, really did constitute themselves a factor
of serious importance in the maintenance and increase of production, in the elimination of industrial conflict or friction, and
in the combat against 'war weariness' and apathy. They were,
after all, the most highly-organized and efficient body of 'mili-
tants' in the country. To put it no higher, the fact that they
were now prepared to pursue any course at all which would,
in their estimation, increase productivity for war, even though
it might involve the abandonment of all sorts of demands which
a couple of years earlier had been fostered and pressed by the
Communists themselves, meant that those in the factories and

mines who, war or no war, were intent on pushing forward this or that 'just claim' of the working people, were left without any leadership at all.

It was a curious experience to shift so suddenly from membership of a hated sect, to a position on a quite high-powered band wagon. It was fascinating to observe the varying types of people who calculated that this band-wagon was for them.

Apart however from the wave of cheerful opportunism, and although the development which now occurred was neither decisive nor permanent, it did have a peculiar significance as representing a novel, perhaps an unprecedented, fusion between nationalistic and communistic impulses in the British working class. On a tiny scale, it suggested the sort of situation that would have existed, if, by some no doubt impossible freak of history, Tsar Alexander I had seen England as a menace no less than France and chosen to fight both; if, as a result, Bonaparte and post-revolutionary France had been forced into alliance with the England not only of Pitt but of all those open or secret political societies and clubs which, only a few years before, had expressed the vastness of English sympathy for the Revolution.

Although, politically, I naturally welcomed the turn of events and the end of the nerve-wracking period between the signature of the Nazi-Soviet Pact and the outbreak of the Nazi-Soviet war, from a strictly personal viewpoint the new situation, as it developed during the following couple of years, left me feeling increasingly at a loose end. Things were suddenly so cosy that one had the sensation that nothing one might write was really necessary—everyone was rushing in the right direction anyway.

Furthermore, I have always had a good deal of difficulty in believing that the pen really is mightier than the sword, and although nobody in his senses—or only very few such—would actually welcome the idea of being physically involved in modern battle, (and I personally have an at least normal dislike of violence and danger), there were nevertheless many times when it seemed to me that to get somehow into battle would, in the widest sense, be preferable to writing interminably about the war effort.

Unfortunately, the *Daily Worker* was forbidden to employ a war correspondent. Nobody seemed to know just what was the reason for that. Some said it was the result of spite and alarm on the part of certain Labour Party leaders in the Government, who were gravely disconcerted by the increase in the prestige of the Communist Party as a consequence of the Russian war, and were anxious to do everything still possible to hamper the Party's organ. Others conveyed to us that the General Staff had put its foot down—on the ground that a Communist war correspondent would be either a Russian spy or an agitator, fomenting grievances among the troops.

I thought that if this were really the view of the High Command, one might circumvent the difficulty by applying for a brief turn of duty as a correspondent with the RAF bomber squadrons over Germany. If the General Staff suspected one of espionage, that could be overcome by allowing oneself to be held incommunicado on the airfield in the intervals between missions, and guaranteeing to write nothing of one's experiences over, say, Berlin, until an agreed time after the event. And the risk of one subverting the crew of a bomber must, I thought, be regarded as nugatory compared to the possible havoc one might wreak in the ranks of the infantry.

I wrote to the Ministry of Information to make this proposition, and spoke of it personally to Mr Bracken, who seemed to sympathize with my frustration, and I think supported my request, but was in the end unable to do anything further.

Later, with the assistance of friends in the Free French movement, I made considerable headway with a plan to get smuggled into France and attach myself to the most highly organized of the Resistance forces, those in Haute Savoie. Our idea was that I might remain with them for some months and, assuming survival, emerge at the end of that time with a story which, apart from its value to me and the paper, would be of value to them, too. This scheme also fell through—chiefly because my French, once very fluent, had rusted considerably during the war years, and in any case, however much I might improve it, I certainly could not hope to pass as a Frenchman and would thus render any group I might be with dangerously conspicuous.

In addition to all these frustrations, our charming little house in St John's Wood was blown inside out by a fly-bomb, so that life became physically very uncomfortable.

American researches have recently shown that several million dogs in the United States are suffering from schizophrenia, and that animals need tranquillizer pills and similar treatment, like anybody else. I made this discovery independently—indeed it was the only interesting aspect of the sordid business of one's house being bombed. Patricia and our son were fortunately living in Cumberland at the time, and when I got home—the bombing occurred in mid-morning—the only living things moving in the stinking mess were some bewildered rabbits which had been blown out of their hutches into the drawing-room, and the cat. She had been specifically my cat, attaching herself to me at all times and more or less disregarding others of the household. I was glad to see this friendly creature amid the lonesome wreckage, and greeted her warmly. She fled, shrieking, and as she ran into the sunshine I saw that she had turned from grey to bright yellow.

I had to wait until late at night, when she was exhaustedly asleep, to catch her—until then she eluded me with screams of fear and anger. I kept her prisoner in an undamaged cubbyhole under the stairs.

The house we had rented in Cumberland was on the estate of my friend Mr Wilfred Roberts who, it occurred to me, as an M P travelling back and forth between London and his constituency, was one of those who were still able to get a first-class sleeper on the Carlisle train. I had often enough spent from seven to nine hours jammed upright in the corridor of that ghastly train on fortnightly visits to Patricia, but I thought that to do so in charge of that stricken cat would propably break me down. Mr Roberts agreed to take her. A kind-hearted man, he presently let her loose in the compartment. She had an attack of madness and rushed round and round the little room, tearing and defiling railway property. He was covered with blood by the time he got her back in her box.

The cat settled down calmly enough in the Cumberland house, living mostly in the drawing-room, apparently relaxing. But whenever I came for the week-end, at the first sound of my voice she shot out of the window and hid in the vegetable garden, remaining invisible until I had gone. Food had to be put out for her under the gooseberry bushes. As soon as she heard me say good-bye, and the noise of the hired car taking me off to Carlisle, she jumped back into the house. Once, having forgotten something, I had to return after we had gone a mile or so. The cat was relaxing in the drawing-room. The windows were shut. At the sight of me, and without means of escape, she had a fit on the sofa.

The whole episode was moving. Some people said, 'it seems strange that, after being so specially attached to you, she should now tolerate others, but not you.'

It was, of course, not strange at all. I had been her God, her father-figure. I was also the provider of all food and comfort. Her attitude, indeed, was that which, according to Lévy-Bruhl, certain Malayan tribes ascribe to cats. Dogs, they say, are unlucky, because when they look at you in that attentive and, as you suppose, faithful way, they are really thinking 'If that man were to die quickly, there would be a funeral with burnt offerings, and I should get the bones.' Whereas the cat is praying for your prosperity, so that you will be able to afford more milk, and fatter and softer cushions to lie on.

But in this case, what had God, or Father, done? He had thrown a bomb. For, since he was responsible for everything, he must have been responsible for the bomb too. God, in fact, had gone mad. And that is a turn of events which might daunt any living being. Who can tell what further incomprehensible outrage he may commit? In such circumstances, to hide from God under the gooseberry bushes may be a melancholy proceeding, but is the only prudent course of action.

What with all this depression about the house and the cat and the difficulty of getting more actively into the war, I was almost exaggeratedly elated when, early in 1945, I found myself on a ship packed with diplomats; with hundreds of expectant mothers, brides of Canadian soldiery now being suddenly removed, by some War Office whim, to their new homes; with scores of journalists of numerous nationalities; with a sprinkle of expert intellectual mechanics from the garages where Anglo-American relations go for repairs; and with the customary number of professional spies—some masquerading as diplomats, others as journalists. The world being what it is, I dare say some of the expectant mothers were doing part-time espionage in order to defray the high cost of childbirth.

The journalists, the diplomats, the experts and the spies were all bound for the foundation meeting of the United Nations at San Francisco.

The vessel was quite large—around 20,000 tons, as I recall—but because most of the accommodation was required for the mothers-to-be, the rest of us were somewhat confined. The only 'public room' available to us was a small, perpetually crowded saloon. Otherwise, you could lie on your bunk listening to the repeated explosion of depth charges from the destroyers protecting our convoy (for it seemed that at this eleventh hour of the war the German submarines were seeking to put on a worthwhile *finale* to their show), and wondering what chance one would have if one of the submarines got through and the cry was raised 'women and embryos first'.

A voyage which might otherwise have been almost intolerably tedious was transformed into a pleasure chiefly by the accomplishments and charm of Sir John Balfour, who had been British Minister in the Embassy at Moscow, and was now being transferred to the same position in the Embassy at Washington. His impersonations of Stalin and Molotov were in themselves enough to take anyone's mind off torpedoes and a shortage of whisky.

I reminded him of how, years and years before, when I was a student in Budapest and he was Second Secretary at the Legation there, we used to play a game (his own invention, I believe) which might be described as a kind of literary Consequences. I have forgotten just how it was played, except that it involved inventing the title of a book, inventing a suitable name for the author of such a book, and writing a long review of this non-existent work.

This game we now revived, and for hours on end four or five of us sat at a table in the corner of the saloon, scribbling and passing our sheets from hand to hand in the manner of consequences. ('The Odious Paradox' was one of our titles. 'Now this, obviously,' remarked Balfour, 'must be a biography of Claud.')

The amusement of the game was enormously enhanced by its effect upon the spies who hung around the table with flapping ears and bulging eyes. The scene, they obviously felt, must *mean* something, must have some kind of international significance. How could it be otherwise than significant than to have there, huddled round the corner table of that rolling saloon, writing notes to one another, concentrating deeply or bursting into incomprehensible laughter, the new British Minister to Washington; the diplomatic correspondents of *The Times*, the *Daily Mail*; a notorious Communist; Mr Cecil King, the effective controller of the *Daily Mirror*; and Professor Catlin, who was believed by many to be on a secret mission from the Vatican to the State Department.

The spies' nerves were fraying fast. Day after day they crept nearer and nearer, breathing down our necks. At length Balfour, not a man to tolerate much intrusion, jerked round suddenly, his cigarette in its exceptionally long holder aiming like a lethal weapon at the peering eye of some Spanish or Swedish sleuth.

Startled and embarrassed, the sleuth stuttered out something about natural interest, just wondered what we were doing, whether it was a new game, or what?

'We are engaged,' said Balfour, 'in writing imaginary reviews of imaginary books.'

The sleuth tottered away, wounded. You could see that he felt his intelligence had been abominably insulted. Surely, he felt, they could have had the courtesy to invent a more credible lie than that?

We were in mid-ocean, celebrating, indeed, my forty-first birthday, when President Roosevelt died.

There were no Americans aboard, and the grave, perhaps momentous, event and its possible consequences were discussed and analysed gravely but calmly, like any other important and sudden occurrence. The experience of these last few days at sea, before we eluded the last submarine and ran safely into the harbour of Halifax, Nova Scotia, served, by contrast, to intensify its tremendous, explosive impact on the United States at that critical moment of its history. In England, as I have remarked before, it takes nothing much less than a major air-raid or a general strike to produce any immediately perceptible change in the social atmosphere. But the United States lives more externally, more expressively. In the electric streets of Chicago, in the gossip-laden muddle of a barber-shop, or the chillingly stream-lined and flamboyant luxury of a millionaires' club on a sky-scraper, no one could escape for a moment the awareness of this as an eve of great decisions. One was aware too—and a good many of the European visitors were more than a little scared by it—of the vast, dynamic confusion of American politics. Some of those who were confronted with it for the first time had the air of a person who has come to seek advice and support from an immensely rich and immensely respected uncle, and finds the old rip half drunk and boxing with the butler.

The journey of our special train across the Middle West, still (to anyone who feels strongly about people and history) one of the most exciting regions of the earth, was at times almost intolerably moving.

Our heavily-laden special had some sort of notice prominently displayed on its sides, indicating that it was taking people to the foundation meeting of the United Nations. In a natural way, the emotions aroused among Americans by the death of Roosevelt and the impending birth of the United Nations had fused in the public mind. From towns and lonely villages all across the plains and prairies, people would come out to line the tracks, standing there with the flags still flying half-mast for Roosevelt on the buildings behind them, and their eyes fixed on this train with extraordinary intensity, as though it were part of the technical apparatus for the performance of a miracle. Often, when we stopped at what seemed to be absolutely nowhere, small crowds of farmers with their families would suddenly materialize, and on several occasions I saw a man or woman solemnly touch the train, the way a person might touch a talisman.

Then I remembered how, many years before, when Dr Einstein first crossed the United States, the papers had carried stories of people who had come for miles just to touch the train in which the savant was travelling. In New York such people were derided. Since they knew nothing of higher mathematics, they must be the victims of hysteria. (In one place, it is true, a group of women were reported to have believed that if they could but touch Einstein's coat, their children's sicknesses would be cured. The same sort of thing, the late Michael Arlen once told me, happened to him when he visited the United States after the almost unprecedented success of *The Green Hat*. In his case it was buttons that people seemed to want, believing that a button from the clothing of such a man would be a charm and talisman—any button: jacket, waistcoat or fly.)

The attitude to Einstein still seemed to me a good omen. Naturally one might prefer that people should not be superstitious or hysterical at all. Just for the moment, at any rate, it cannot be denied that these tendencies exist. It was in my mind that if the people are going to be hysterical and superstitious about film-stars and dictators, it is at least somewhat encouraging —a movement of an inch or so in the right direction, than which no more can be realistically expected—that some of them some of the time should feel the same way about a man because they believe him to be the greatest thinker, the most learned sage, of the epoch.

Now people of this kind looked into the club car of our train, and one was disconcertingly aware that, in this normal collection of the competent and the half-crazy, the idealistic and the hard-boiled, the neurotic and the hum-drum and the drunk, those people outside were seeing a powerful instrument for the secur-ing of world peace.

The impact and implications of all this were both exciting and somewhat appalling. To an agitated mind, Salt Lake City came as a tranquillizer. It is one of those places which, despite having grown in the past hundred years from a conglomeration of covered wagons and tents to a major city, have not obliter-ated their origins—have left, perhaps, no physical trace of them, but have left very much alive the pervasive spirit of the *genius loci.*

In Philippopolis, Bulgaria, which, when I first saw it, in some odd way recalled Salt Lake, you are both soothed and stimulated by an atmosphere where the theories and controversies of ancient heretics—of the Paulicians, and of those ferociously pacifistic nihilists the Bogomils, who from their headquarters at Philip-popolis shot their inflammatory and subversive doctrines all the way to Albi and Toulouse—seem as lively and intelligible as the political doctrinal struggles of our own day.

Salt Lake stimulates a particular awareness of history's tightly woven pattern of fraud, courage, violence, idealism and trickery. And it thus serves to rescue the beholder from the temptation to suppose that the problems of human behaviours today are more intricate and startling than at any previous time.

A biographer of Brigham Young, the Mormon leader, has compared him to Moses, to Cromwell and to Bonaparte. And when you stand on the steps of the principal temple in that rich, eerie city of Salt Lake you do not find these comparisons absurd. There is that awful ring of mountains, that menacingly salty plain, and you think of the heroic scoundrel and murderous genius, stopping his followers in that abomination of desolation near the lake, and telling them that they were not going to gentle California or anywhere like that—this was the desert they were to make blossom like the rose.

It is interesting that many of those who wrote about Brigham Young, say, fifty years ago, apparently found much of his career and character shocking, contradictory, and in parts frankly incredible. These things would have been intelligible enough to political bosses in Chicago, but such men were not apt to write history. But they are intelligible enough, and indeed have a ring of familiarity, to people today with the merest 'headline' knowledge of the stresses and strains of revolutionary movements and revolutionary leaders.

His rise to leadership reads much like a bit of fairly recent history from west China or the Ukraine.

When, for example, Joseph and Hyrum Smith were bosses of the Mormons, Young already felt that the proper boss, the boss they all needed, was himself. By an accident, he and his only possible rival for the succession—a man named Rigdon—happened to be away from Carthage, Illinois, on a June night in 1844 when the Smiths were in jail there. Leaders of an anti-Mormon mob in Carthage negotiated with the prison guards. The guards opened the prison doors, and the prisoners were lynched.

Young, who had a rather rare quality of being just as good in a political lobby as he was when out fighting the desert or the Army of the United States, rushed to headquarters and, after a brief, obligatory expression of sadness at the fate of the Smiths, immediately set about begging and exhorting the Council of Twelve (governing body of the Mormon Church) to recognize that Rigdon (who seems to have been a bit of an 'old' Bolshevik, not adjusted to the current situation), was out of line, a gross deviationist from the true doctrine.

Rigdon was expelled with contumely.

Among remaining potential thorns in the side of Young was the son of the lynched Joseph Smith who, in a move to head off Young, gave his support to a man named Strang, whom he announced as being 'King of Zion'. Strang established a 'kingdom' on Beaver Island, Lake Michigan. He lasted six years, with Young tunnelling under him all the time—or so, at least, it was alleged. At the end of that time public opinion on Beaver Island seemed to be turning pro-Young. A group of those whom Strang had considered his most reliable adherents shot him.

I remarked to Professor George Catlin, who had accompanied me on our little tour of Salt Lake City, that it was sad to reflect that three people out of five, on being questioned about Brigham Young, would admit that the real image of this astounding man —a far more typical American than George Washington—was obscured for them by some hazy miasma arising from the fact that he favoured polygamy.

That he was the first to introduce large-scale irrigation to the North American continent—he had stopped his people in a desert and he had to prove to them that you could make a desert work, and he did—and that, while developing this astonishing piece of real estate he did not hesitate to declare war on the United States, are facts overshadowed by the squabble about polygamy.

It would appear that Young had as cool an attitude to birth as he did to death. Polygamy meant more Mormons and, with the United States troops threatening the whole undertaking, more Mormons were what were needed. The way in which Young's polygamous doctrines were used against him in the eastern States is a valuable example of how, for strictly political ends, the 'moral' attitudes of a population can be excited and exploited.

The US Government under President Buchanan was not, it may be fairly safely surmised, much interested in how many wives Brigham Young or his entourage happened to have. On the other hand, the thought of a Mormon birthrate enormously exceeding, year by year, that of the rest of the United States was a matter of practical, indeed of military, concern.

But polygamy, being a practice which women whole-heartedly opposed, and to which men, too, in the eastern States and in Victorian England were forced to offer at least lip-opposition, (many of them, naturally, were merely furious at the thought of this Young getting away with a thing like that, claiming, it seemed to them, that having another woman was almost like going to Church for the third time of a Sunday), offered a stout stick to beat the Mormons with. It is always important in conflict to prove to the satisfaction of all the people on your side that the enemy is not only out to steal your land, or your cattle, or your market for cheap cotton goods, but is at the same time vicious and, as the Irish say, 'an affront to God'.

While taking steps to increase the number of potential fighters for the faith, Young was not slow in purging the unfaithful. In this he was providentially assisted by Jedediah Grant, who evolved the doctrine that certain crimes—such as conspiring against the Church of Young or trying to get way from the State of Utah—were so heinous that only 'blood atonement' could be considered in such a connexion.

Young—in this as in so many other ways, a thoroughly 'modern' man—at once saw that a political crime is worse than any other sort of crime. Private robberies, murders, and rapes are to be deplored. But they do not rate the full blast of horror kept in reserve for the politically hostile.

He considered the theories of Jedediah Grant, and reached the conclusion that, since nothing less than the sinner's blood will ultimately redeem the sinner, 'the cutting of people off from the earth, is to save them, not to destroy them.'

It is a doctrine of which people have availed themselves conveniently from, as the saying goes, the earliest times to the present day.

I reminded Professor Catlin of an occasion on which we had both been present at Geneva, when some hooligan correspondent of the Hearst press, comically anti-semitic, had forced his company upon us at lunch with Robert Dell and had said pontifically (he had been on a tour of the Middle East) 'Say what you like, Bob, there's certainly a case against the Jews.'

'Naturally my dear fellow,' snarled Dell, 'there's a case against everybody.'

And so, of course, there is a case against Brigham Young.

Our consideration of all these matters was abruptly cut short by the sudden arrival on the steps of the Temple, where we were talking, of a really enormous French woman who—it gradually became apparent—had been detailed by some French Intelligence man on the special train to keep an eye on Catlin. (The Intelligence man was a passionate adherent of the theory that Catlin was the bearer of some vital communication from the Vatican to the American State Department.)

Catlin—whether for practical reasons, or on account of an agreeably romantic tendency towards 'mystification'—had fed fuel to the leaping flames of this report by getting himself listed, on the official rota of journalists bound for San Francisco, as the correspondent of one paper in Reykjavik, Iceland, and of another in Agra, India. Or perhaps it was Allahabad. In any case, it was the kind of credential which makes security men and spies lift their eyebrows and whistle.

And now this French Amazon, bounding out of a hired car up the Temple steps, found him engaged in conversation with a bolshie—ostensibly about the Mormon irrigation of cabbages.

Not realizing at once her official motives, I supposed that she had fallen passionately in love with George, and started to make excuses to continue my tour of Salt Lake alone, leaving them together. The professor's attitude, his sardonic smile as he snapped his blazing blue eyes at me in signals of distress, above all his apparent desire to continue discussion of Brigham Young to an extent which might have satisfied the vanity even of Young himself, alerted me to the fact that he was in need of succour.

We told the French lady that there was much of interest to see in the Temple, that we would briefly borrow her car for an errand we had to do, and would send it back for her within a quarter of an hour.

We regained the safety of the train, which was still an object of wonder and admiration to those enthusiasts who were confident that peace on wheels was moving through their city.

A good many hours later we were all rolling into Oakland, across the Bay from San Francisco, where members of the Oakland City Chamber of Commerce greeted us and made clear that in their, perhaps more realistic, view we might be instruments of peace but could certainly be instruments of publicity for the money-making facilities of the city of Oakland.

8

Adjoining Buncombe County

MUCH of what might truthfully be said about the gathering at which the United Nations was founded turns out to have been said, about ninety years before the delegates assembled at the Golden Gate, by Dean Stanley in his exhilarating description of the Council of Nicaea which met in the year 325. Indeed I used sometimes to enhance a reputation, in orthodox Communist circles, for frivolity by asserting —truthfully I think—that for anyone needing to know how assemblies, congresses, committees and the like really work, the only absolutely required reading should consist of these chapters by Dean Stanley, together with Cardinal de Retz's analysis of the papal consistory of 1655, concluding with the election of Cardinal Chigi as Pope Alexander VII.

William Sargant, in *Battle for the Mind*, emphasizes as a principal thesis that the methods and physiology of brain-washing and religious conversion may proceed in a similar or even identical manner, quite irrespective of whether the object in view is to bring people to Wesley or Mao-Tse tung. Just so, the behaviour-patterns of assemblies and committees show similarities and repetitions which are traceable alike in the Kremlin, in seventeenth-century Rome, and the hall where the Urban District Council meets.

Dean Stanley quotes the wholesome remarks of the former Vicar of Kensington, John Jortin, who, after a long, cool, mid-eighteenth-century look at the way such things really happen, listed some of the motives by which assemblies—he was writing of Church assemblies, but he might have said much the same of a Congress of the Communist Party or the Republican Presidential Convention—may be influenced.

'They may be influenced', said Jortin in 1750 or thereabouts, 'by reverence to the Emperor or to his councillors and favourites, or the fear of offending some great prelate . . . who had it in his power to insult, vex and plague all the bishops within and without his jurisdiction; by the dread of passing for heretics and of being calumniated, reviled, hated, anathematized, excommunicated, imprisoned, banished, fined, beggared, starved if they refused to submit; by the love of peace and quiet; by compliance with an active body and imperious spirit; by a deference to the majority; by a love of dictating and domineering, of applause and respect; by vanity and ambition; by a total ignorance of the question in debate, or a total indifference about it; by private friendships; by enmity and resentment; by old prejudices; by hopes of gain; by an indolent disposition; by good nature and the fatigue of attending; by the desire to be at home.'

It might be healthy if anyone who ever goes to a conference of some kind and votes for something or other were to picture himself about the 1750's in the vicarage at Kensington, explaining to the incumbent why he personally was not seriously influenced by any of these considerations.

When, at San Francisco, I drew this assessment of motives to the attention of my friend Richard Bransten, a man crackling with political fire and blazing with goodwill, who later burned out and killed himself, he observed that, although the Reverend Jortin probably regarded it as too obvious for mention, one ought to add to his list the fact that people who attend this type of gathering are, more often than not, in hopes that their participation in history will be accompanied by some unique sexual experience or adventure.

That, I should say from experience, is a very true saying. At functions of the kind one is often reminded of the pro-consular-looking type in Rebecca West's admirable novel *The Thinking Reed* who, even when he was peering down a woman's V-neck at her breasts, managed to look as though he were thinking about India.

To recall—as an eye-witness—what actually occurred at San Francisco, and in particular the atmosphere of that historic Gabfest, jamboree and piece of global intrigue, is of some special interest now because, after a little more than a dozen years, the San Francisco get-together has already become one of the myths of history, in the sense that it is freely used by the advocates of quite opposite policies to prove their respective points. When things go badly for them, the supporters of one line of policy will declare that the whole thing originated in the rosy sentimentality displayed at San Francisco. When things go equally badly for the supporters of an opposite line, they will declare that it is all the result of the failure of the great powers at San Francisco to surrender their mean, old power-politics to the influence of the idealist spirit then potent and susceptible of being canalized for the good of mankind.

To the eye of the eye-witness, which may of course suffer a worse astigmatism than that of the hind-sighter, it was apparent that this conference, which has considerably affected everyone's life ever since, was being conducted on several different levels. There was a sense, and an important one, in which the affair was really a victory jamboree, in some degree hallowed and given an almost religious veneer by the thought that it was after all a celebration of the victory of the Good over the Bad —Hitler was by this time only a step or two from the patch of earth outside the bunker where they finally poured the gasoline on his corpse and set it alight.

The good word was that a new era was about to be inaugurated, and certainly nobody was inclined to deny that a new era might be just about what the doctor ordered. Like the inauguration of Presidents and the Coronations of Kings and Queens, the inauguration of a new era for the human race always draws a crowd. It did so at San Francisco. Orson Welles and Rita Hayworth came, and a lot of other people from Hollywood, and Anabaptists and Seventh Day Adventists came, and, for earthier reasons, lobbyists of every major industrial interest in the world came, and some of them divided their time between the big historical affair and a murder trial which went on concurrently, the accused offering as his defence for shooting his wife, the assurance that he had been 'somewhat drunk at the time'.

A lot of sailors, on leave from the horrors of the Pacific war, came too. Some of them stood in the streets gazing at the world's statesmen with reverence and hope—hope that they would be out of the horror soon, and that their sons would never have to get into a similar one. Others, sensing the jamboree spirit, got fiercely drunk in the forthright, whole-hogging American fashion and threw bottles at the most untimely moments—through the window of a room where some P R O was explaining to a startled Press that General Peron was a democrat at heart and that any-way his vote was badly needed, or into another room where (since this was the year when hearing-aids became *de rigueur* among American intellectuals) some European conspirator, who did not understand about hearing-aids, was trying to find a suit-able mean between a yell and a whisper in which to convey a profound observation of some kind to an American, suitably equipped, and impatient because the European did not appreciate the advantages of the device.

I found myself several times in that situation—and learned later, to my indignation that the supposedly super-communist I had been muttering and yelling to had been an F B I agent all the time. I saw his name, years afterwards, in the account of some trial. He had told me that British Communists—and such I then was—were, on the whole, as effete as the rest of the British people. Would I, for example, give him the name of any British Communist who was prepared to go in for really realistic stuff, like blowing up railway bridges, or the King? When I failed to do so, he made no secret of the fact that he had by now weighed me in the balance and found me wanting.

It was then, and how glad I was of it, that one of the sailors lodging across the court of the Palace Hotel tossed an empty whisky bottle through my window and hit that deaf *agent provocateur* just behind the hearing-aid.

An unfortunate thing about history—I speak deliberately of textbook history because that, despite the best efforts of the savants, is the only kind of history that the majority of people are exposed to, and they are exposed to it long before the savants have time to catch up—is that it has to present events as though they took place in a kind of vacuum; a vacuum in the sense that the student is left with the impression that on a given day the representatives of all the interested parties were sitting there thinking hard about the future of Libya, without reference to what may be termed the 'Jortin factors'—such as excessive heat, bottles through the window and Mrs X, or in some cases Master X, whose X-ly influence was palpable enough at San Francisco.

(It is, incidentally, interesting though not, I suppose, surpris-ing, to find homosexuality in, as it were, the front line of both sides in the great McCarthy v the Reds battle in the United States. The late Senator created in the public mind an impression that if people in the State Department who opposed him were not on Moscow's pay-roll, they were at least homosexuals. His opposition, rather belatedly, grew wise to the opinion—or at any rate the assertion—that homosexuality was the trouble with McCarthy. Quite possibly everyone was lying, and there is never going to be any means of proving whether they were or were not. The only point of historical, or perhaps one should say anthropological, interest is that out of that pistol you could still hope to fire a killing bullet.)

On this level, if you wanted to be socially and politically acceptable at San Francisco, you had to mind your Old World P's and Q's. You were about, for instance, to say, 'My God, doesn't a lot of this remind you of the old League?' It necessarily did, often enough. Often enough, this seemed to be where we came in. But to say so was to raise pained, peevish and even frightened eyebrows all around the room. The League had become a word of ill-omen, and there were many who quite evidently felt that to mention it could by a process of sympathetic magic put a hoodoo or jinx on the United Nations. If comparisons had to be made at all, the thing was to note how, despite a superficial similarity here and there, the great thing was that the *spirit* of San Francisco was so different from that of Geneva.

Paul Valéry, after the first World War, had written of the European Hamlet, pacing a vast terrace of Elsinore that stretched from the sand dunes of Nieuport to the Swiss frontier, and contemplating the millions of skulls 'And this one was *Kant; Kant qui genuit Hegel, qui genuit Marx, qui genuit. . . .*' The terrace was larger now, the skulls more numerous, the crack-up more awful. 'We cannot afford to fail' became one of the most wearisomely repeated clichés of the conference.

There were plenty of sceptics, but they were cautious. Nobody could escape the realization that millions upon millions of people in two hemispheres at least believed that the United Nations was going to save the world, and it was a belief which only a very cold fish could treat without respect. I heard an embittered Republican say angrily to a near-worshipper of the late Roosevelt, 'Trouble with you people is you believe in the human race. It'll let you down.'

'God's let me down damn often,' said the other, 'but I go on believing in him.'

In the view of the sceptical, San Francisco was all very well as a pious demonstration of faith and hope, but they felt that no real decisions could be taken here, because all the important ones had already been taken at Yalta. Their theme song was a parody of Bing Crosby, written for the annual revue staged by the Washington Press Club.

> 'Yalta! Yalta! Yalta!
> Winston, Joe and I.
> Yalta! Yalta! Yalta!
> Congress don't you cry.
> Yalta! Yalta! Yalta!
> Shut the other eye.
> You are going my way—
> That's a Russian lullaby.'

It is always with a slight shock that one realizes in how short a time the novel can become the commonplace, the speculative surmise be transformed into a mental platitude.

A somewhat ruthless-minded friend of mine from the US State Department used to shock people at San Francisco by asserting that the central feature of world diplomacy then and for a long time to come must be the inevitable effort of British policy to cause dissension and division between Washington and Moscow.

'You British,' he used to say, 'talk as loud as anyone else about unity and continuance in peace time of the wartime co-operation of east and west, but you just can't afford to have it played that way—or at least you think you can't, which comes to the same thing.'

He took the view, so familiar now, but startling to many at that time, that the real problem of British policy during the decade following the end of the war would be to provoke 'all trouble short of war' between the United States and the Soviet Union. For, he admitted, war between 'the big Two' would be even more disastrous for British interests than a 'deal' between them made without regard for, and indeed at the expense of, those interests.

This view of Britain's inevitable role was, naturally enough, shocking and offensive to such delegates as Mr Attlee—or, since nobody can say for certain just what Mr Attlee was really thinking about at San Francisco, people in his position certainly had to look as though they would be shocked and offended by any such notion.

Yet it was impossible not to notice that, among the British, indications of any sweeping agreement on major points between the U S A and the U S S R were apt to be greeted privately with a mixture of moral indignation and hardly concealed alarm. Rifts and sharp words between the Big Two were, on the other hand, equally often subjects of self-congratulation, as though representing victories for British diplomacy. Not that such sentiments were uttered. The correct formula was to remark how fortunate it was that, with some assistance from British experience, the Americans (such naïve fellows) were 'beginning to take a rather more realistic view of the Russians than the late President.'

The attitudes—some sharply defined, some vague—encountered among British officials and politicians at San Francisco vividly reminded me of similar attitudes encountered in the British Embassies in Berlin and Washington in the late 1920's. It was the period of the Arcos raid and the breach of Anglo-Soviet diplomatic relations, a period, that is, when Britain was pursuing an anti-Soviet diplomatic offensive with a vigour not seen since the ending of the war of intervention.

Public opinion in Britain took it for granted that such a policy must win the applause and command at least the tacit support of the United States. After all, for years British newspaper readers had been absorbing accounts—often shocking to the liberal-minded—of the 'red scare' in the States and of that anti-red 'drive', master-minded by Attorney-General Palmer, which, in its day, seemed as powerful and enduring a feature of American policy as MacCarthyism did thirty years or so later.

Yet it was almost exactly at the moment of the British diplomatic offensive against Russia that the Standard Oil Company took, first secretly and then publicly, decisive steps to establish the most cordial economic relations with Moscow. Mr Ivy Lee ('poison Ivy' according to an angry British diplomat), first of the modern type of Public Relations Counsellor, was mobilized for action. He was the man who in years of subtle propaganda work, much of it never detected as propaganda work at all, had transformed the image of old John D. Rockefeller in the American mind from that of an ogre or juggernaut, thinking nothing of spraying strikers and their families with oil and burning them to death in the interests of sustained production, into that of a kindly, socially-minded philanthropist, his eye ever on the public good, and the dissemination of useful knowledge. (By a fascinating dialectical process, what had started as a kind of diversionary 'stunt' dreamed up by the genius of Ivy Lee, later materialized as a concrete reality in the shape of the Rockefeller Foundation.) Mr Lee was now desired to apply his almost necromantic talents to the task of refurbishing, touching up, and in parts toning down, the popular 'horror' picture of the U S S R.

And at about the same time, the *New York Times*, through the medium of its able and enthusiastic Moscow correspondent, began to present the Soviet Union to the American public in a light which, though critical, seemed almost golden compared to the nerve-jerking effects the correspondent of the London *Times* was achieving from his peripheral listening post at Riga.

In 1929 and 1930, shuttling regularly between New York and Washington, I was often jolted by the contrast between the attitude of Wall Street men, who looked upon the U S S R with a minimum alarm, as in effect just another fast-developing area with a big trade potential, and the opinion, accepted as more or less axiomatic in the British Embassy in Washington, where Russia was viewed politically, and viewed as a menace. (It was always comical to watch Russian reactions to those diverse estimates. Officially, of course, the American businesslike attitude was the one to be applauded. The word 'co-existence' had not been coined. But a deal with Standard Oil, and Soviet gold bonds selling like hot cakes on Wall Street, were co-existence enough for the moment. On the other hand, there was something undeniably irksome in the American evaluating of the situation—something obscurely insulting, as though the Revolution and the doctrines of Marxist-Leninism were puerile incidents, temporary deviations from the ultimate forward movement of the world along businesslike American lines. The British, it could at least be said, took these things more seriously, more—so to speak—in the spirit in which they were offered.)

What was dangerous about the British attitude was the assumption that 'basically' and 'by and large' the American view was bound to be the same as the British, or at any rate that the Americans were bound to 'come round' to the British view sooner or later. It was dangerous because it was untrue in the first place, and more so because when people began to see where they had made their notable error there were going to be recriminations and dark suspicion.

There was, certainly, a vague sense in which the popular British notion of Anglo-American relations was true. But you could not assume it to be true in a sense in which it would at all times effectively govern political and diplomatic action, which is, after all, what matters. That it might somehow turn out to have been true 'in the long run' could be imagined; but, as Maynard Keynes used to say, 'the long run? the long run? In the long run we're all dead.'

At San Francisco the reaction of British officials to such an analysis of the position was apt to be first that the whole picture was chimerically false, and that, if it were found to contain elements of reality, that showed gross bad taste, even bad faith, on the part of the Americans. And at that they would recall with bitterness the attitude towards 'colonialism' adopted by Roosevelt that night at Casablanca when the Sultan of Morocco came to dinner with him and Winston Churchill, and his ludicrously naïve evaluation of Joseph Stalin.

They were not pleased when Molotov was, figuratively speaking, publicly embraced by Henry Kaiser, the great ship-builder, one of the most spectacular of Amerca's wartime industrialists. The pair toured Kaiser's shipyards together, talking no politics, but talking in particular about a gigantic scheme for Kaiser, once the Far Eastern war was over, to manufacture hundreds of thousands of pre-fabricated houses for shipment to Vladivostok and erection in Siberia.

At the time, it was one of the things Molotov liked to talk about. On political or diplomatic subjects he would—even in comparatively private conversation—go little further than to paraphrase, in slightly more informal language, his set public speeches. I knew him only very slightly, and had found him one of the few Russians whose conversation was really tedious. Others could be brilliant, profound, amusing, maddeningly paradoxical, childlike, or plain maddening. Molotov, had he not happened to be the Foreign Minister of the second most power-ful State in the world, and the harmonica which played the tunes breathed into it by the world's most powerful man, would have been a bore. And one does right to treat bores as genuinely dangerous characters, not merely on account of the debilitating ennui with which they enervate one's faculties, but because there is certainly something dangerously wrong with their men-tality, character and general relationship to life.

Often at San Francisco, when Molotov was chatting in private with a half-dozen people, I would hear someone making an effort to get him to discuss the wider aspects of the situation—the general picture of what later was called 'co-existence.' He sniffed through his pince-nez, waggled a dismissive hand and went on paraphrasing his last speech. I will say for the late Stalin that, according to what Michael Koltzov used to tell me, he too found Molotov a crashing bore. But Stalin, perhaps because of his keen interest in the proper employment of heavy artillery, not merely suffered Molotov gladly, but saw his positive value. He took, I was told, a sadistic as well as a purely political pleasure in watching some foreign diplomat being pounded by Molotov's monotonous barrage.

Partly because so many important delegates and officials came from 'austerity' areas—the mountains of China, the starved underground of France, not to mention the dreary subsistence levels of England—the San Francisco Conference put into prac-tice on the largest scale the belief, the most cherished article of faith among diplomats, negotiators and promoters through the ages from the Homeric heroes to Krupp, that without free wine and women you either get nowhere, or get somewhere more slowly than otherwise.

Nobody seems to analyse this belief—though I dare say some advertising agency has at this minute a team working on it. The principle is thought too obviously axiomatic to require discus-sion. Yet it is in reality complex, raising innumerable and profound problems of human behaviour. 'Under the influence of an excellent dinner followed by a port which, etc., etc., Lord X relented . . . .' The motif recurs in innumerable novels; so often indeed that a person who had done nothing but read novels could be excused for supposing that if you could only lure an

Under-Secretary for something or other, or the owner of a uranium mine to your home and offer him something rather special, he would be as wax in your hands. (When I was about sixteen there was a very general belief among boys of my age that if you could but get a girl to come to dinner and at the end of it manage, unperceived, to drop cigar ash into her coffee, she would be not merely willing to jump, but insist on jumping into, bed with you. The only problem, it seemed, was to get the money for a good cigar—and of course good cigars were a lot cheaper then than they are now.)

Everyone knows the old American definition of a statesman as 'a politician who stays bought', and nobody has any difficulty in appreciating the effect upon history, ancient and modern, of the straight, time-saving cash bribe, whether it follow the pattern of Louis XIV's annual subsidy to Charles II; of gross over-payment for the avowable part of the services rendered; or of the crude, but pyschologically sure-fire, packet of crinkle slipped across the desk at moments of recalcitrance or indecision.

But if you ask the Moribundian Foreign Minister does he really think that another round of champagne and peacocks' tongues is going to have the Ruritanian Ambassador signing away his country's claim to the Mudd enclave with a smile, he admits it seems rather unlikely.

Agreed; the idea is preposterous. Agreed, too, certainly, that in our own day, as in the past, many vital decisions have been made by statesmen, generals and captains of industry which would have been made otherwise, even in a quite contrary sense, if those responsible had not been drunk at the time. Everyone can call to mind dozens of such instances. And the Elizabethans, as is known, were half-tipsy most of the time—they had to be unless they chose to go through life parched, or die of disease from infected water. But what, apropos of San Francisco, we have under discussion here is not the broad, general influence of alcohol-intake on history. In the cases just referred to, the people concerned would have been drunk anyway, using their home supplies to put them in fettle to face the Irish Question or the submarine menace or the challenge of Japanese cotton goods. That situation has very little to do with what may be termed the mellowing process, or technique of the lush-up, in which A is supposed to gain his ends by offering B rather more of what he fancies than will do him good.)

What then is the true incidence of the lush-up upon what, ultimately, goes on? Some man from the Treasury or the Guaranty Trust Company sternly replies, 'You over-estimate the importance of this aspect of affairs. Serious matters are not affected by that type of thing.' In which case the Foreign Offices and Plenipotentiaries and the tycoons with their costly Public Relations Counsellors are all barking up the wrong tree, are ignorant of what makes things tick, and wasting their time and money. It seems to be not very probable.

Certainly the United Nations was launched on an ocean of champagne, whisky and vodka, and there was scarcely a noon or eventide at which some diplomatic or financial organization was not giving a mammoth cocktail party designed to cause at least some proportion of the guests to act, think, speak or write otherwise than they would have done had such an entertainment not been offered. It was *de rigueur*, naturally, to express boredom, deplore the exhausting multiplicity of these routs. The only absolutely sincere complaint I heard was that of a friend of mine who was a solitary drinker. He complained that the stamping and babble and pop-pop from the banqueting rooms of his hotel disturbed the peace of his intimate sessions with the bottle.

The Americans, perhaps because being on their own ground made it easier, made more play with girls and young women than other delegations. Shortage of shipping space being what it was, it would have been difficult for others to compete in this department. Where they did so, they had to rely on the overtime work of typists and secretaries.

But the State Department and other organizations concerned with influencing official or public opinion abroad had worked hard at deploying women on the propaganda front, and they had a fine range of such troops, capable of appealing alike to the man crudely in a hurry, and to those who liked to feel that true romance was burgeoning for them between the huge oysters under the flat, drifting mists of evening, and the touch of an expert American hand on the percolator as sunrise hit the top of Tamalpais. Women who could awake this conviction in the breasts of diplomats and publicists, however far from home, were not two a penny. Some of the best qualified had to be officially detailed for secretarial or social work in San Francisco, while their husbands, without leave or travel priorities, toiled on at their end of the war effort in Washington or New York, in a situation which made the troubles of Uriah the Hittite look trivial.

Sometimes it was nearly eerie to watch Chinese and Saudi Arabians watching the San Francisco of 1945—for many of them their first contact with America or, indeed, any part of the western world. It was exhilarating, too, like being swung aloft by a crane and enabled to view the turmoil of the place and time from a fresh angle. Such a crane hooked itself into my belt one late afternoon in that roof bar, called the 'Top of the Mark', which, glowing like a jewel with fine carpets and woods and metals and a rainbow of liquor bottles, commands one of the most dramatic prospects in the world from the pinnacle of the Mark Hopkins Hotel.

I sat down to appreciate it, and found myself beside a Chinese of about my own age, appreciating too. He wore a beautifully-tailored suit of what seemed to be some fine silk. His hair and shoes shone smoothly in the Pacific sunset. He looked as smooth, as untouched by hardness or hardship, as if he had lived for years and years in places like the Mark Hopkins. Nevertheless, he was appreciating, and had a light in the eye. We fell into conversation. At the end of a quarter of an hour, it appeared that a topic which particularly interested him was the civil war in Spain.

'When I lived for some years,' he said, 'in a cave in Szechuan, as a guerrilla fighter you know, I read a book about it—it had been translated into Chinese from the Russian edition. But it was by an Englishman, a reporter who had also fought in the Spanish Republican Army for a while.'

'You recall the author's name?'

'I don't know how you'd pronounce it in English. It seemed like . . . .' He gave a fair rendering of the name Pitcairn.

'That,' I said, not even pretending to be calm at this coincidence and at the thought of my book, which I did not even know had been translated into Chinese, being thumbed by those legendary guerrillas of Szechuan, 'is my *nom-de-plume*, I wrote it.'

Nor did he try to live up to any myth of oriental impassivity. On the contrary, he shouted with an enthusiasm which made an explosive noise even amid the roar and buzz of the Top of the Mark at cocktail time.

We cut all other appointments and talked for hours, while the melancholy outlines of Alcatraz blurred into the ocean. As soon appeared, he, so far from having lived in the Mark Hopkins half his life, had spent many of his years, fighting in West China, living in the caves for months on end or, with ragged columns of poorly armed men, struggling over terrible tracks on barely credible route marches—forays and agonizing retreats and evasions.

No Communist, he was in the fullest sense of the word a fellow-traveller, on foot and in philosophy. He had been, ever since his late student days, fighting first in the seemingly hopeless battle against Chiang Kai-shek, later against the Japanese, after the temporary alliance between Chiang and the Communists to which Chiang himself was later to attribute his downfall.

To talk on this and many subsequent occasions with this man was to experience that delicious stirring of the brain which comes only from converse with someone whose experience has almost nothing in common with one's own, but yet has been looking intently at the same scene, so that the events you have both been observing from such distant points form the link between you. Few things are more refreshing than to discuss a given situation with someone whose basic assumptions are not yours. He startles you every minute, and you him. Each of you has to take another look at what had seemed so obvious, so shopworn. It is the kind of conversation in which there is no such phrase as 'of course.'

It is stimulating in the way Greek and Latin—and, I have no doubt, Arabic and Hindi—prod and stir you in a way no modern language (whose basic assumptions are the same as those of your own language) can do. The first time you, as a schoolboy, discover firstly that the Latin word 'honor' is not a translation of the English word 'honour', and secondly that the Romans did not have any single word meaning just what 'honour' (except in the Birthday or New Year sense) means in English, you are up there on that over-publicised but still exciting peak in Darien.

Adding oddity to our meeting was the discovery that we had been born within a mile or two and year or two of one another in Pekin—I, as he joyously pointed out, in the British Legation, headquarters of the rapacious, imperialist foreign devils. And here we were talking in San Francisco, because he, fighting along with the Reds in the West China mountains, had read a book of mine about fighting along with the Reds in the Spanish Sierra.

The last time I saw him was the night of farce and nervous ulcer when we had both been invited to make—with a couple of others—a radio broadcast of reminiscence, comment and view-exchange—a meeting of minds for the public benefit. Anyone is at liberty to state that in their opinion the notion of a Chinese fellow-traveller and the correspondent of a British Communist newspaper being invited to get on the American air and chat is too fantastic to be given credence. The person who finds it so is unaccustomed to the abrupt changes that can occur in American political weather.

However, the event did not come to pass, because by that time both of us had come to take the technical and mechanical efficiency of the United States for granted. That is an arrogant mistake. One should enjoy it, but not lean on it too heavily.

Leaving the Top of the Mark in plenty of time to drive to the studio, we found that the lift had gone out of action. Few things are more daunting than to prepare for a mile-a-minute vertical ride so silent that a Senator's polite hiccup is disturbing, and find that what you are going to have to do is to undertake a leg-killing trek down the stairs. On the faces of many whom we passed, or even, occasionally, met sweating up that Matterhorn of stairs, there was the look people have in films about the breakdown of civilization or the shape of things to come.

Late, we rushed to the hotel car-park where my friend's car was parked under ideal conditions of security and freedom. The hotel gave bona-fide guests some gadget which they fitted into the ignition (or thereabouts) and this raised, for a sufficient number of seconds, an invisible electric ray which barred the exit to car-thieves and anyone else without the proper gadget-accreditation.

The place was, in a word, burglar and car-thief proof. Nowadays it is called automation.

On this particular evening it chanced that the ray itself had somehow become stuck—you worked the correct gadget, but it still loyally, though mistakenly, turned off the ignition every time you got to the exit. We had to climb out and get the whole ray turned off—a serious business, because it meant the quick mobilization of humans to take on its functions as theft-preventers,

Then we shot out into the streets of San Francisco and almost immediately something went wrong with the traffic lights, half a mile ahead. Traffic jammed and halted. I swore that I had actually seen a couple of men get out of their car and set out for their destination on foot. My Chinese friend said that I must be dreaming, no such thing could happen in America. We sat there in the stench and uproar of idling motors, half-deaf and being slowly poisoned.

'Let me tell you,' said my Chinese friend, 'in a cave in Szechuan this couldn't happen.'

Since all hope of reaching the studio in time was now lost, I told him the story I had just heard from a friend of Thomas Mann, with which world figure he was flying from New York to New Orleans, where renowned thinker and novelist Mann was to give a lecture.

At that time, any American officer above the rank of—I think —Captain, who wanted to hop a plane to go somewhere had the right to claim the seat of any civilian. At Asheville, Buncombe County, North Carolina, the plane made an intermediate stop. An American General and his aide fussed across the tarmac and said they had to get to New Orleans in a hurry. There was an impression that the Japanese could be landing any minute at Miami Beach. Thomas Mann and friend quit their seats and were left behind in Buncombe County.

Only when the General reached New Orleans was it discovered that the purpose of this intellectual soldier's dash to the city was to hear Thomas Mann lecture.

'Delicious,' said my Chinese friend. It made him happy because he was visibly thinking that in a cave in Szechuan that kind of thing couldn't happen either.

9

Mr Bevin and the Devil

IN the newspaper business it often seems that they wait until
you have just got the hang of something and then ask you
to go off to get the hang of something else. Essentially, it is
the same complaint you hear from Foreign Service people who
learn Turkish and get posted to Uruguay.

Perhaps, so far as the newspapers are concerned, this practice
represents an attempt to carry out the advice proferred to journalists by the late Lord Northcliffe—'never lose your sense of
superficiality.' I certainly was beginning to feel somewhat profound about the true stresses and strains of the United Nations,
to be aware of where the bodies were really buried which, when
ultimately dug up, were going to cause trouble. And then came
the news that a General Election impended in Britain, and on
the heels of it a cable from William Rust bidding me hurry
home, prepared to transform myself immediately from diplomatic correspondent to political correspondent of the *Daily
Worker*.

I thought there must be some mistake. I had always felt more
at home in the United States than in England, whose political
climate I have never more than dimly appreciated. Someone—
almost anyone—else, it seemed to me, could cover that British
election for them. Perhaps by reason of being a Scotsman, perhaps because of other circumstances of my life, my ear has
never been properly attuned to the way things are played in
England; the drama of English life subtly eludes me—so completely indeed that I am often tempted to the error of supposing
it is not there at all. Thus, compared with the big bout at San
Francisco, whatever was going to happen over in England looked
to me like pretty small beer, tepid at that. I wrote a careful cable
to Rust explaining that it would in every sense be better were I

to remain where I was. I inferred that his original instruction must have been the result of an impetuous aberration.

He replied: 'Return at once repeat at once.' I cabled again at length, and profoundly, touching on the world situation. He replied: 'Kiss the girls good-bye and take first available plane.'

A notion nagged at my mind, and I spent twenty-four hours or so in a state of indecision both exciting and painful. I was wondering whether the best plan might not be to remain in San Francisco so long as my American permit allowed, make arrangements—not by any means impossible—for the trans-atlantic transport of Patricia and our son Alexander, and then remove to Mexico where, during my stay in San Francisco, I had formed some useful connexions. Clearly in my ear I could hear the voice of Cacambo, giving his advice to Candide: 'We have travelled enough on foot. By the river-side I see an empty canoe. Let us fill it with coconuts, embark, and follow the stream. A river always leads to some place. And if we find nothing pleasant, at least we shall find something new.'

I dare say there are people who can recall truthfully just exactly what were the operative factors in some vital decision made in the past. Indeed it is something of a misfortune not to be able to do so. Years later people ask why one did this rather than the other, and expect a serious, well-informed answer. Not getting it, they suspect one of concealing something, and the word they will be using next is 'disingenuous'. It is not only troublesome, but makes one look either foolish or sly, but I have to admit that once the decision is made, the reasons for it—even the exact nature of the decision—tend to slide from my mind out of sight.

In determining not to go to Mexico instead of London I was certainly much influenced by the fact that, whereas at an earlier period of life the innumerable unknown factors would affect only myself, now they must be fateful also for Patricia and for a boy only four years old. Patricia, I gathered later, would pro-bably have welcomed the idea. She would have been dismayed, if at all, not by the difficulties of getting to Mexico, but by the nuisance of having to learn Spanish when she got there.

As for Alexander—but there was the rub. On so important a matter for his future, he had, as of then, no vote.

So without enthusiasm I chose London. Flying over the Rocky

Mountains and the prairies, I sank deeply into gloom. It was a state of mind to which I was but little accustomed. I hoped at first that it might be a hangover, something strictly physical, and fixed my mind on the thought that when Boswell believed himself suffering from moral despair or general *Weltschmerz*, his complaint was often nothing worse than alcoholic poisoning. But on making a tally of the drinks taken the night before, I could not feel such a conclusion justified. Something else must be making me feel unhappy. And watching the United States go by down below, I got an unpleasantly clear idea of what it was. I had begun to wonder whether I was not mistaken about the political shape of the world.

Years before, when I had first lived with and fallen in love with the United States, I had been vividly aware of what has so often been called 'the American dream'—and 'a faith' (to quote the first volume of this autobiography) 'that there was still room on earth for the kingdom of Heaven.' And when I had returned to Europe and jumped into the Communist Party I had been considerably affected by the idea—this was in the days of the great slump—that ultimately it would be Communism which would lead America to the next attempted realization of that repeatedly frustrated dream. It was perhaps less paradoxical than it sounds that I should have been more influenced on this score by the United States than by the USSR.

But now, fresh from daily contacts with innumerable American Communists, I became oppressed with a sense of futility. I do not speak of, or suggest, individual futility, though naturally there are as many fools and stumblebums in the Communist Party as anywhere else. A lot of those people were able, a lot of them brave, and many were both. But that, it seemed to me, as we came in to land for the stopover at Cheyenne, Wyoming, made the problem more serious. For if the individuals concerned were no more faulty than is to be expected, why were they demonstrably getting nowhere?

It was, of course, the sixty-four-dollar question, and I had no desire whatever to face it. It shadowed my mind as far as New York, but there the stiff breezes of necessary action blew it, for the time being, away.

For a political traveller such as myself, one of the principal *Sehenswuerdigkeiten*—a 'must' in any guide book—of New

York at that precise moment was Mr Earl Browder, top-ranking American Communist, under whom a bomb of international dimensions had exploded a few days before. Without a word of warning, he had been served notice that his entire policy, a policy imposed with almost ferocious rigidity upon all members of the American Communist organisation, a policy which in hundreds of thousands of words had been proclaimed to constitute, at last, the map which was going to show the path to the heights, was not only ill-considered and gimcrack, but was, furthermore, a blatant and disgusting betrayal of the interests of the working people of the entire world, a piece of sabotage and a sell-out.

The bomb, it may be remembered, had been actually detonated in the form of a published letter from the French Communist leader, Jacques Duclos, who directed against *le Browderisme* a flame of invective designed to sear the souls of all those American Communists who had not had the good fortune (as now appeared) to have been reviled and driven into political darkness by Browder himself.

It would be neither interesting nor possible to summarize accurately here what 'Browderism' meant. Some of its aspects were stimulating—the idea, for instance, explicit or implied, that the conception of a political party in the European sense is quite alien to the American scene, and that to insist on the existence of a Communist Party, electioneering and politicking as though it were a Republican or Democratic Party, was to mistake the character of the two latter : to equate them with European political parties, whereas in reality each of them is a coalition. The business of the Communists, according to Browder, was to unite and influence and help to guide the 'best elements' wherever they were to be found. (I am not quoting any stated thesis of Browder, only sketching what seemed one of his central themes.) He and his associates held even more 'heretical' views on the potentially 'progressive' role of what, before and after, was termed 'American Imperialism'. I forget what the Browder people called it.

But one could not talk to Browder for even half an hour without realizing that, deep and complex as were the theoretical issues involved, a major role in the development of the whole affair had been played by the personal relationship between

Browder and Franklin D. Roosevelt—or, as some would say, the influence of Roosevelt upon Browder.

The atmosphere of Browder's headquarters in New York was not a congenial one. In fact, although I tried to suppress the thought, the whole outfit bore an unpleasant resemblance to the picture of it which might be presented to the public by a rabidly anti-Communist satirist. During the few days I spent in New York I could not help being repeatedly reminded of the words of an enthusiastic but melancholy radical friend of mine who had once told me that he would have joined the Communists there were it not that one half of those directing operations seemed to be brashly ignorant, though genuinely prepared to die on any barricade that might be indicated, whereas the great thinkers too often proved to have acquired their comprehensive knowledge of Marxist-Leninism at the training schools of the F B I, in preparation for their work as spies and *agents provocateurs* within the organization.

Given the atmosphere of alarm, uncertainty and mutual suspicion created by the explosion of the Duclos Letter, the news that I was on my way up to what was referred to with unseemly reverence as 'the Tenth Floor' where the top men, including Browder himself, functioned, was received with a lot more interest than it deserved. It was supposed that I must be engaged on some major mission—bearer, perhaps, of some kind of counter-Duclos Letter. Nobody would have believed me had I said that I was just taking the opportunity to see an interesting man at an interesting moment of his career, and would have thought (perhaps rightly) that, if true, that was a very feather-pated thing to be up to.

For a man who has just been blown sky-high, Browder was calm—not resignedly so, but almost, one might say, exuberantly. It occurred to me that perhaps he had a rather more than normal amount of vanity in his make-up, and hence, though this might be the end of his immediate position and authority, found a lift, like the stimulus of champagne, in becoming the centre of a vast international shindy, which had significance not only for the Communist Parties but for much wider circles too, since it was to some extent a test and measure of what were to be the immediate post-war relations between the Communists and the rest of the world.

When he talked of his relations with Roosevelt this impression of vanity was increased. There were moments when one felt that Roosevelt considered that a fortnight without a chat with Browder was not a full fortnight. On the other hand it was quite evident that he really did know Roosevelt intimately, and his descriptions of the President's conversation were both vivid and uproarious. It was probably true that, in the circumstances of that time, it was of genuine importance to Roosevelt to have the general enthusiastic support of Browder, because such support enabled him to outflank other potential critics on the left of the Labour movement—if a thing was all right with the Communist extremists, who was anyone else to nark about it?

Each of them supposed he was taking the other for a ride. It was Duclos who declared unequivocally that the young lady of Riga was Browder.

Watching him, I reflected upon how lucky some people are to have faces which completely fit in with, and lend physiognomical support to, their policies. Browder's line was the essentially down-to-earth, domestic, native American character of American Communism—heir in mid-twentieth century to all the political revolts of the American Common Man against Wall Street ogres, heir to Farmer-Labourism and Bryanism. And his face could have sat for a composite portrait of that sort of American—rugged, honest, of course, but shrewd, too, and with a light of pawky humour in the eye: in a word, the lot.

A handy face to go campaigning with on his sort of platform. Unless it be, as I have sometimes thought, that the process really works the other way round, and that people are seriously influenced in deciding what line of country they are going to take by what, at some fairly early stage of the game, they see in their mirrors?

Naturally experience and so forth 'mark', as they say, a face. But what about the raw material? Appearances are very rarely deceptive, and people who look bluff yet shrewd often are. It may well be that every man is in some sense his own casting-director. It is certainly true in my experience, and I have tested this on many occasions, that, when you are puzzled as to what a man was really thinking when you spoke with him, what degree of truth or lie there was in his remarks, if you are mimic enough to reproduce on your own face exactly the expression that was on his when he said this or that, you often enough get at the reality of whatever was passing through his mind at that moment.

I found Browder a stimulating character—a talkative and indeed eloquent man who, in addition, could hear what you were saying without the aid of a hearing-aid and was even prepared to talk, without a too exaggerated fear of the tape-recorder. Nowadays, people—and perhaps in particular, Americans—are so conscious of tape-recorders that their talking chords get strangled. It is a standpoint I have never comprehended. And yet disregard of it has brought many people into grave difficulty. But it is no worse a difficulty than people have always had when they were seeking to communicate, one to another, something which the authorities might later hold against them. 'Walls have Ears' is an old saying. In those days people used to lurk behind, as it were, the arras. Now they have a microphone built into your typewriter or cunningly concealed in the electric light or wherever it may be.

The problem is the same. The theory that the microphone is more menacing than the arras seems mistaken. The development of the microphone, the near-tape, and even the distant tape—with which you can record a private conversation at a thousand yards or more—is a sometime tiresome, always interesting example of human relationship. To aver that the police must not listen to one's telephone calls is like averring that the hired help must not listen at the keyhole. They will go on doing it.

And, after all, nobody but a fool has ever—since the sixteenth century—written anything in a letter, or said anything on a telephone wire, which he would not wish the police to hear. Only innocent people do that.

And as one who has been tapped as much as the next man I would offer the opinion that all that tapping does is to waste one's time. From the point of view of the opposition—a business opposition or a police opposition, whichever it may be—that is an advantage. You have to go out and take a bus and wait till the engine buzzes before you can say the thing you were going to say. But that is about as far as it gets the opposition, and so long as the buses keep running it does not, seriously speaking—leaving aside the cops and robbers—get anyone very far.

In all the circumstances, there seemed not much to say to Earl Browder, although I did tell him that should he ever be looking for a job as either an actor or a newspaperman I would be happy to recommend him. He said that he would bear that in mind. I left him with the conviction in my mind that probably he was wrong about everything, but somehow seemed a more likeable kind of a man than most of those who were sharpening their knives for him a few floors below.

I told all that in London, but it was not popular. Even to have chatted in friendliness with the man Browder was a suspect act.

In London I felt even more disorientated than, in San Francisco, I had expected to be. And, despite the excitement and activity of the General Election, I was almost continuously aware of that shadow of futility, drifting back and forth across my mind, which had pursued me in the transcontinental plane. And I was in constant danger of becoming infected by that disease which to the propagandist is the most fatal of all—the disease of which the principal symptom is an awareness of having said or written all this over and over again, without, so far as can be seen, having had the slightest effect upon anything.

I have sometimes wondered since whether I really believed more than about 25 per cent. of the tens of thousands of words I wrote at that time. In fact—partly because the good propagandist for the most part really does believe what he is writing at the moment—I did so. Among the many wise sayings of Lord Northcliffe was that 'you can never successsfully put on the table of Demos what you would not put upon your own.' In other words, if you try to talk down to Demos, or to write with your tongue in your cheek, Demos will find you out.

True, I have argued with people who say that in approving of this Northcliffe saying and in approving, too, of what is called 'black' propaganda—deliberate invention, employed as a carefully judged weapon as, for example, in the case of the 'Revolt in Tetuan'—I contradict myself. I think not. Well naturally I think not, since nobody goes quietly along with a charge of self-contradiction. But, to put it reasonably, what I feel about it is that what matters is not whether the weapon is good but whether the cause is.

At this point somebody mutters something about doing evil that good may come, or the end justifying the means.

This obscurantist formula has clouded thought for a long time.

Nobody should. I would suppose, willingly do evil that good may come; and if the end justifies the means, then the means are good.

I can conceive of a person saying that those people who organized the big lie about 'The Man Who Never Was'—that corpse on the coast of Spain which deceived Hitler's General Staff—were doing evil, because they were (as one used to be told in childhood) 'acting a lie'. To believe that is to take up the position that telling lies—in the simple sense of deceiving other people—is worse than anything else you can do. Worse, for instance, than deliberately permitting Hitler to gain some advantage because you cannot bring yourself to tell him a lie.

It is not only a possible viewpoint, but a perfectly respectable one. I regard it as abominable, but respectable. But it is only respectable if you really hold it and stick to it. Assume then that you reject it. How can it be both good and bad to lie to Hitler? How, in other words, is the lie bad and yet its effects are good? And how then is this doing evil that good may come?

To which, the reply is made: 'But if you declare that, your cause being good, your means of defending it are good too, then you are setting yourself up as the arbiter of good and evil. How do you know your cause is that good?'

And to that anyone seriously engaged in the mêlée can answer no more than that either you believe in your cause to that extent, or you should go away and lie down in the shade— which, evidently, is a decision too. And should it turn out that you had underestimated the excellence of the cause, you would be committing an evil act by deserting it.

Simple thoughts of this kind—'simple' some would say in the Irish sense of the word, meaning vacuous—occurred to me repeatedly during that 1945 election.

Specifically what bothered me was the necessity for a whole-hearted, full-blooded support of the Labour Party.

One of the elements which make a General Election both farcical and excruciating is precisely this necessity for being whole-hearted about everything and everyone. It is a pretty widely accepted fact that you cannot go into a campaign saying, 'In my view, Mr X, though at heart on the side of the angels, somewhat stinks at the edges, so that while advising you to vote for him because his opponent stinks worse, I also advise you not to believe more than a very small proportion of what the man says.' That is not the way to gain friends for your candidate and influence people on his behalf. For the purposes of election-eering, the man is not only on the side of the angels, he personally is one.

The situation was, therefore, that because the Communist Party was so small—and why was it so small? was the question often and inevitably in mind—and had no hope of achieving power itself, the whole potential of the apparatus (not a small potential, because the apparatus was constructed of trained and dedicated people, people who would stay out longer in the rain than anyone else), was to be jerked into action on behalf of the Labour Party. Which, in turn, meant that one had to pretend to believe about eighty per cent of what the Labour leaders said. And that, when you came down to cases, meant believing in eighty per cent of what Ernest Bevin said. I had known Ernest Bevin, in a strictly professional capacity, for a number of years, and in my reckoning eighty per cent was a whole lot too much to believe.

I had watched Bevin at numerous conferences and congresses, watched for the moment when the sly, alert eyes of this John Bull in plastic would judge the moment ripe to switch from the sternly practical to the sob. Reporting any such event you could write, far down the page, 'Bevin lifts arms in Christlike gesture and declares "I am being crucified." Weeps.' You would rarely be wrong. He was a real John Bull, a professional Englishman, with the capacity of the professional Englishman—perfected through long years of colonialism—to have the tears gush from his eyes because nobody understood that it was only for the other boy's good that he was kicking him, or else it was in self-defence, because the wizened 'little boy' was a lot more dangerous, in reality, than he might look to those who did not know the facts. I have seen J. H. Thomas cry repeatedly, and muster votes by it. But Bevin's crucifixion was a better act—and pulled more votes.

I knew—and certainly it was no secret needing special sources of information to ascertain—that Bevin looked upon Com-munists and Communism in just the way that an old-time Methodist looked upon the Devil. Some of the time you are genuinely frightened of the Devil, and believe he may do you a mischief. Indeed, that fear is at the back of the mind all the time, and the dread powers of the Evil One justify anything whatever you may chose to do in opposition to him. Other times, you believe in the Devil but consider him merely a smart operator who has overreached himself. He has failed to realize that God is just a little bit smarter. And at other times again you are not worrying about whether there really is a Devil or not, but you see how essential it is that people who might be wavering in their support of you should believe frenziedly in that sinister old Satan who, unless they rush to your aid, is going to jump on your back and sear you with his filthy fire, carry you off— unless everyone will please rally round—to his loathsome pit. This is where the Devil becomes an almost lovable object—at least, an indispensable accessory. For people who might other-wise criticize you sharply, or even desert you altogether, have— if they have any decent human feelings at all—second thoughts when they get the news that you are at this very moment en- gaged in a crucial life and death struggle with sin, and that a vote against you is a vote for Mephistopheles.

All politicians, from Moscow to London or Washington, have to have an active Devil on the string. Perhaps, indeed, if there had been no Sparta, we should never have heard of Pericles.

In this election of 1945, Mr Bevin had a new and ingenious idea about his relations with the Devil. He put about the alluring notion that, after all the bother and fuss there had been about the fellow, he and his associates would very soon fix things so that the Devil, previously irked by social coldness, would be mellowed by a series of understanding chats.

'Left understands Left', said Mr Bevin, conveying to the voters who remembered Stalingrad that whereas the Tories would doubtless involve us in some kind of war, hot or cold, with the Soviet Union, the Labour Party would soon eliminate all that type of rancorous nonsense and achieve what a huge majority of the voting customers wanted, namely an enduring prolonga- tion of the wartime friendship between Britain and the U S S R.

The bitterest pill to swallow, so far as I was concerned, was to lend support to this gross—as it seemed to me—deception of the public. And yet, what else could be done? The Communist Party by itself could do nothing. And, though its vote in the country was tiny, it remained true that its influence in 'the Labour Movement' was powerful to a degree out of all mathematical proportion to the vote. So that if, for example, the Communist Party and the *Daily Worker* started to slur the Labour Party there was a possibility—at least it looked that way at the time, since no one knew just how big the landslide was going to turn out to be—that this small, but highly organized interior opposition might tip the scales. By hindsight it can probably be reckoned that nothing the Communist Party could have done would have tipped the scales. The Labour vote probably was in the bag. But that was not the way it could be seen then. We thought it was nip and tuck. And so we had to throw whatever weight we had to such men as Bevin who, I was convinced, would, so soon as they had attained office, use their special position in 'the Labour Movement' of the world to upset the possibilities of sane relationship between Britain and Russia.

'Left understands Left' was a good slogan—and like most good slogans was something between a vague aspiration and a downright lie. The 'Left' does not understand the 'Left'—and the whole history of the relations between the various branches of the 'Labour Movements' in Britain and on the continent during the first decades of the twentieth century proves it. Or, put in another way, the one sort of 'Left' understands the other sort of 'Left' so well that it fires from the hip on seeing just what sort of manœuvre other comrades are up to.

That is to say that either the 'understanding' is the understanding which exists between one hardened tactician and another, or it is simply not there at all. And Mr Bevin, far more experienced than I in that kind of business, understood it; must have understood it, perfectly. He cannot at any moment have thought that to move Transport House into Downing Street would improve the relations of Downing Street with the Kremlin.

On the contrary, as Mr Bevin demonstrated within a few months of the Labour victory at the election, he realized fully that one of the main functions of Labour in the immediate post-war situation was to carry out—as only Labour could—the essential British policy of driving a wedge between the USA and the USSR.

There was a moment when the cold war could, just possibly, have been averted. That was at Church House, Westminster, in the very early spring of 1946. Senator Byrnes was Secretary of State, and as a man of the Roosevelt era he was for friendly relations with Russia. To the United Nations Council meeting in London was sent Senator Vandenberg—a Republican Senator who, when even partially sober, was among the most intelligent statesmen of the western world. He was there to demonstrate the bi-partisan nature of American policy.

Mr Bevin at once understood that here and now was the moment to use the leverage of simply being Labour. A Tory Foreign Secretary might have sought to inaugurate the cold war without making much impact on the Washington Democrats. But if a Labour Foreign Secretary started to attack the Russians, what on earth was an American Secretary of State to do? Could he appear redder than the British Labour Party, which the Americans—as Bevin so well knew—assumed to be at least pink? He could not. Senator Vandenberg and Mr Bevin played the game perfectly. Here were a Republican and a British Labour leader, both agreed. And both agreed to lambast the Russians—the Devil, in fact. Secretary of State Byrnes, newly established President Truman—none of them had a leg to stand on. The cold war had begun.

All this was only dimly apparent to me during that 1945 election campaign. Nevertheless, every time I found myself suggesting to the customers that they should trust Bevin and his associates to 'cement' the Anglo-Russian alliance, to move, in fact, a little closer to Russia and no closer than was quite necessary to the United States, I felt embarrassed, the way anyone feels when he is not quite sure that he has the wrong bottle of medicine, but is very far indeed from being sure that he has the right one.

Bevin's policy, as had been evident to anyone in San Francisco, was the inevitable one for Britain to follow. It was possible for him to follow it more successfully than a Conservative Foreign Minister could have done just because he was allegedly of 'the Left'. It is axiomatic, and the examples litter European and British politics over the past hundred years, that in a democracy only the Left can afford to pursue a strictly Rightish policy. If the Right did it, the Right would be hounded from office and in extreme cases hanged from lamp-posts. When the Left turns Right it is, for a considerable time at least, invulnerable.

During the election, the customary comedy, to which, after many years in the Communist Party, I had become totally ac-customed, was played. That is to say, the Communists supplied much organizational ability, brain, and ability to stand about in the rain all night if that was going to catch one more voter, and the Labour Party supplied statements to the effect that it had no need nor desire for the assistance of the Communists whose tenets it most seriously repudiated.

There was one Greater London constituency, with which I happened to be closely in touch, in which the Labour candidate (and later Member of Parliament) was a paid-up member of the Communist Party, his agent was a Communist, the five people who worked in his office were Communists, and the only people who distributed his 'election literature' were Communists too. He did, however, have some kind of side-kick who thought he was running the affair, whom I found lording it in the office one afternoon when I passed by, seeking for a word of informa-tion. 'Daily Worker?' said this side-kick, with the air of a man who is on top of the world and intends to be reasonably kind to people who are under it, 'I'm afraid we can't give any in-formation to you people. Transport House is being very strict about that.'

I thanked him kindly for his awfully decent attitude and went on my way wondering whether he was an ordinary dumb-bell, a piece of apparatus straight out of Herbert Morrison's gym-nasium, or a super-stooge of the Communist Party.

I recalled a London County Council election at the outset of which Mr Morrison had issued a directive to Labour Party agents throughout the area, warning of the dangers of Communist 'infiltration'. The danger, said the directive, was that the pesky Communists would come and offer almost any sort of help— they would offer to address envelopes, scrub the floors, all for the cause. Two young men went to an election office in Stepney or Bethnal Green and said to the Labour agent they wished to offer their services. What, the agent wanted to know, did they propose to do? Could they speak, for instance, at street-corner meetings? They were shy, modest young men and they said they could not do anything like that, but they could address envelopes or even, in their enthusiasm, scrub floors.

The agent was immediately suspicious. 'Who exactly,' he asked, 'are you?'

'We,' said the ingenuous young men, 'are just members of the British working class.'

'Get out of here,' yelled the agent. 'I thought you were Communists from the first, and now I know.'

So, in 1945, we watched that well-known figure 'The Middle Class Vote', being wooed, seduced, and as near raped as a respectable Labour politician thinks it politic to go in a matter of the kind.

What troubled me was that we had aided and abetted. At the best we were going to be accessories before the fact—and I had a sufficiently clear idea of what the fact was going to be to produce a vast sigh of relief when William Rust (who, I think, knew just as well as I did what was the matter) suggested a trip to the Balkans.

Blue, red or grey, I love the Danube valley, and the Balkans are among my dearest homes-from-home.

I told Patricia that we should have a wonderful time except that our boots would be stolen. She bought a fine pair of boots in Rome, and in Belgrade, on the very first evening, they were stolen. My position as an authority on life behind the Iron Curtain—if it had ever been shaken—was by this episode happily restored.

10

The survivors

THE thing a Yugoslav had to be at that time was a hero. Of course, there were genuine heroes, too; men and women who, on a diet of nothing much beyond bread and faith, had performed miracles of endurance, courage and high cunning during the years of that awful war in the mountains. You listened to their stories with humility and excitement —humility because you felt sure that whereas they had gone right through that terrible alphabet of partisan warfare, you would have given up at F or G, or, giving your heart and nerve the benefit of the doubt, might possibly have struggled on to K. But there was always a point where you had to say to yourself, 'No, I couldn't have done that. At that point I should have given up.' I have often felt the same way talking to people who were in the army in Burma, and sailors from the Arctic convoys. And it is exciting, too, because such achievements can be said to prove that man is capable of moving, under certain circumstances, into a kind of fourth dimension—of breaking through and making nonsense of the supposedly final limits of what man can do.

But when everyone else feels obligated to live up to the heroic standard, the result is debilitating to the livers-up and exhausting to the spectator. It was inevitable that in Belgrade, for every genuine hero, there were ten incompetent bureaucrats who probably had been incompetent bureaucrats right through the war, but—on the general ground that the Yugoslavs were a heroic people—felt that they were heroes too, a status which entirely excused their incompetence.

A man loses your important telegram, or puts the wrong date on your travel permit, or reads you a thesis based on the wrong set of statistics, and is in no way ashamed of himself, because

147

his country has emerged triumphant from a glorious struggle.
It is an annoying aspect of group psychology, and can even be
dangerous to the group concerned. History and tradition can be
all very well, but they become a hazard when some oaf
at the Home Office bungles his business with complacency because somebody else brought lustre on him by fighting the
Battle of Britain, and a man who ought to be working overtime
in the City has no hesitation in playing golf instead because the
Armada was defeated and he is a neo-Elizabethan.

Even at that date no one could be in Belgrade and talk to
people in the Government or (which at the moment was more
important) the Political Police, without being more or less
obscurely aware of the terrific tensions which later were to be
openly disclosed in the break between Tito and Stalin. It began to
seem to me that for the correspondent of a Communist newspaper—and a correspondent with a long, long past into which, as
one of them accidently disclosed to me, the Political Police were
diligently digging—life in Belgrade was becoming altogether too
complex and even, perhaps, dangerous. I wanted to go to Albania,
but the Albanians—who were horribly suspect to the Yugoslavs
—would not give an entry permit until the Yugoslavs had given
a permit for exit to Albania. The Yugoslavs, it goes almost without saying, would not give their permit until the Albanians
had given theirs. I told them they were all getting Americanized,
which seemed to puzzle them, though it was no more than the
truth. Some people have chaos, and some have organization. Only the Americans have both. We went instead to Montenegro. The oldest man in Montenegro was in the plane too and
nearly killed us.

I forget just how old he was—well over a hundred, of course.
He was, equally, of course, a peasant and had a farm on a mountain side in northern Montenegro. Some publicity man, busy on
the campaign to get the peasants to deliver more food to the
towns, had had the idea of inviting this aged man to Belgrade to
see Marshal Tito. They brought him up by car, everyone said the
usual things (the greybeard had a gnarled stick and was photo-
graphed lunging with it at the Marshal to emphasize a point),
and now he was to have his first plane ride, to Podgoriza, nearest
airfield to his mountain farm. The central gimmick of the affair
was that the plane was to be slightly diverted so as to fly right

over his farm and enable him to see it from the air. He was much
pleased and excited. His chatter, as translated to me by an inter-
preter, indicated that what he felt was that by having his place
flown over by an aeroplane, and viewed by himself and fellow-
passengers, the place would be expanded and glorified. He was
particularly anxious that everyone should see a barn he had—
something special, apparently, in the way of barns. When he
occasionally stopped talking he had an ecstatic look, and seemed
to be laughing internally. Just wait, he seemed to be thinking, till
these folks see my barn.

The accompanying publicity man had a map with the farm
clearly marked, and consulted repeatedly with the pilot. Not
that the farm was very difficult to identify because it was the
only human structure on that vast and, at the moment, snow-
covered mountain side.

Now we were there, right above it. 'Look, look,' shouted the
publicity man. 'That's your place down there.' The old, old man
gazed down. He saw what you would expect to see, from the
air, some farm buildings with snow on the roof. But it was
not what *he* had expected to see. He took one look, and another,
half-shutting his eyes so as to be sure. In a harsh voice he said,
'Again. Go over it again.' The publicity man and the pilot
obliged. We circled, and went over it again. This time the
ancient was absolutely sure. He turned on the publicity man
with the look of a peasant whom somebody is trying to swindle
out of a pig.

'That?' he shouted. 'You're trying to tell me *that's* my place?
I've lived there all my life and you think I don't know what it
looks like? It doesn't look anything like that.'

You could see that at that moment of insult to his place—
his fine place which they were trying to tell him was this small
smudge of unrecognizable patches on the mountain side—he felt
himself confronted and outraged by the embodiment of all the
city-slickeriness of the world, them and their aeroplanes. He
snatched the gnarled stick and struck out at the publicity man,
and then he fought his way to the cockpit, hell-bent to belabour
the pilot, too.

The pilot, possibly himself a peasant by upbringing, thought
quickly and well. He gave the plane such a twist and a jerk that
before the gnarled stick could land on the pilot, the oldest man

in Montenegro had lost balance, fallen, struck his head on a seat just inside the cabin, and was carried out of the plane at Podgoriza still unconscious.

From Podgoriza to Cetinje we had one of those mountainous jeep drives which are physically wonderful but emotionally distracting and destructive. We had a fake hero from Belgrade, a wizened Russian who had to pretend to have been a hero because the Yugoslav did—though the Russian was really only interested in wholesale prices of wine, which he was either importing or exporting on behalf of some Soviet Wine Trust— and a Swiss who angered everyone by being excessively well-equipped without seeming to think there was anything excessive about it.

When it came on to rain he asked me why I did not put on my screen-wiper spectacles. I looked at him—he had seemed a pleasant enough young man up till then—and saw he had spectacles with little wipers, working away, back and forth and back and forth, keeping his vision clear. They were attached to some little battery worn in the lapel. What with the Americans and their hearing-aids, and now this Swiss with his glass-wipers, I became moody and resentful, and asked that nice, plump, harmless Swiss, in an offensive manner, how long it would be before he could dispense with himself altogether and wire together some eyes, teeth and other organs to be powered by electricity, without need of human intervention.

Fortunately, since he took electric spectacle-wipers for granted as a necessary part of human equipment, he assumed I was joking. He thought my wipers had probably been stolen in Belgrade. He was sympathetic. For how could a spectacled man hope to get about at all without that device? I said I had managed for about thirty-five years, and hoped to be able to blink my way through to the distant end of the vale of tears. For a moment all their hostilities were forgotten in a consensus that what they had here was a reactionary, an obscurantist. I was happy to have them stop quarrelling for a moment, even though the stoppage was occasioned only by a unified hostility to myself.

All the way to Cetinje people were edging towards fighting words—they wanted, respectively, to say that Stalin, Tito, William Tell and Magna Carta were sons of bitches, and had such words been spoken presumably we should all have had to jump out on to the half-frozen roadside and fight duels. But Cetinje met us before we got that far.

For my money, Cetinje is one of the nicest little towns in Europe.

Before we started for Montenegro, the only thing I could remember about it was that, at an early age, I had read somewhere that the King (the last King as it turned out) of Montenegro smoked 250 cigarettes a day. Until far into my teens that man represented to me Debauch. I was excited to be visiting the scene of his exploits.

Before we started, I had carefully looked up Cetinje in an out-of-date edition of the *Encyclopaedia Britannica* in a Belgrade library. It mentioned 'a very successful girl's school founded and endowed by the Tsaritsa Marie' and a road described as 'a triumph of engineering'. Other good roads, said the *Encyclopaedia*, 'give access to the richest parts of the interior. There is, however, little trade, though mineral waters are manufactured'.

By the time we got there, the triumphs of engineering had succumbed to still later triumphs—the bridges on the roads had been blown up by the Germans, the Italians, and the Partisans. There were no longer any 'rich parts' of the interior, and there was not just 'little trade', there was none at all. Nor, so far as I could find, were mineral waters still manufactured.

And yet that strange little town was a European history book. The majority of the buildings were mean, although another thing that the *Encyclopaedia* had said was true. It referred to 'a fortified monastery which was founded in 1478 but so often burned and rebuilt as to seem quite modern'.

But at the heart of the place there was a square or plaza surrounded by buildings which, by early twentieth-century standards, were not only neat but gaudy. These were the Legations set up, in the days when Montenegro was supposed to be a 'key-point' in European diplomacy and strategy, by the jostling Empires—the Russians, the Germans, the British, the Austrians and, above all, the Italians. Hardly anyone now remembers the savagery of those intrigues—intrigues in which people would blow children to shreds with bombs for the purpose of persuading 'world opinion' that someone else had done it, and should be punished accordingly. What may be called 'the Sarajevo technique' was first worked out in Montenegro, and you can nearly smell the blood on the floors of those pretty little palaces.

When I was there, one of them had been turned into a school for small children, another into a technical school, and a third —the former British Legation, I think—into an hotel where the Montenegrin Cabinet (to the great convenience of the visiting journalist) took its meals *en pension* at noon and evening, incommoded only by the presence of a former high-ranking officer of the resistance who had been accused of betraying to the Italians the presence of a partisan arms-ship in the Gulf of Cattaro. This officer, who may have been innocent or guilty —how could it be told?—used to sit in the corner of the room while the rest of us were at dinner, endlessly twiddling the radio. Once, I asked him why? He said that he thought that if he kept on twiddling, sooner or later he would pick up a dispatch saying that the ship in question had never been blown up at all, and then he would be happy and in the clear.

Since the episode had occurred two years previously, one could not feel optimistic on his behalf. And in fact, before we left a week or two later, he hanged himself.

The event, however, cast no deep shadow on the table. It was thought—the hanging—to be the kind of thing that might happen to anyone.

I have never known a set of Cabinet Ministers I liked so well as those of Montenegro. The Minister for Agriculture was a bird-watcher, but claimed that the best birds to watch were just across the Albanian frontier. Armed to the teeth we used to drive off across that forbidden frontier, a marsh full of huge, highly-coloured birds, and watch them. Once, after some hours of bird-observation, we drank a considerable amount of liquor in an Albanian pub. A man—Albanian or otherwise—spoke disrespectfully. The Minister pulled out a revolver and fired it four times into the rafters. I imagined that later on some comment would be made on the episode. It was never mentioned. Life, one could see, was being taken in its stride.

The Chief of Police who—I believe—was recently shot for some reason or other, looked like everyone's idea of an Irishman. His hair stood up on all sides of his head, he wore a belted mackintosh, and carried, rain or shine, an umbrella which was neither quite open nor quite shut. When drunk, he would laugh at Stalin.

The Minister of Transport was a different cup of tea altogether—very young, very romantic. And if anyone suggested that life is not romantic he had an answer to that, which consisted in telling you the story of his marriage.

He, before the German invasion, had been on a visit to Belgrade, and had gone to hear the singing in the Cathedral. The soloist sang. She was beautiful. He, from quite a long distance off, fell madly in love with her. He made enquiries. Who was she? She was a girl from Dallas, Texas, who had, in some Texan competition, won a scholarship for music study in Europe, and had chosen to work it out in Yugoslavia.

He found out that much, and then the Germans came. The young man joined the partisans. So, unknown to him, did the young Texan girl. One day they were crawling up opposite sides of a hill in Croatia, each believing that there were still Germans lurking there, and that at the top they would have to fire, when one of them saw the Texan he had last seen singing in Belgrade Cathedral, and the other saw this fine-looking Montenegrin.

They would have married immediately, had it not been for an order of Tito which forbade marriage among male and female partisans. The practice, it seems, had led to laxity.

But, the war over, they married, and there they were, very happy and very busy. Among the things that kept him busy— and personally I would put this at about G in the alphabet of how much you can stand—was the fact that he was supposed to arrange for the repair of all the bridges in Montenegro, but did not have any nails. Nobody in Montenegro had any nails. He had to arrange for the manufacture of wooden nails, and hold his bridges together with those.

In the meantime his wife, a beautiful girl who looked as though, instead of clambering up and down mountain sides shooting Germans, she had left Dallas the day before on the trans-oceanic plane, had started a music school and a children's theatre. She sang, too, on the Cetinje radio.

We went to see a play produced by the children of her theatre. None was above the age of twelve, and since they had chosen the play themselves, it was of a gruesome character.

Blood and guts poured from the entrails of kings on to the small stage. The audience, composed largely of children who had failed to get into the act, shrieked and pointed and whistled continuously. 'There's Maria,' they cried as Medea, Lady Macbeth, or whoever it was in the big long wig, tried to make her speech. This was a special performance for me, the Swiss, the Russian and Patricia who, in order to get a visa, was acting as an occasional correspondent of the Australian Consolidated Press.

After Act II had been drowned out in the noise, the producer in person bounded on to the stage. For eleven years old, he was the fiercest little producer I have ever seen. He said, 'You hooligans! You wretches! You betrayers of your country and of world culture! Do you not realize that owing to the wonders of modern technique and the electric telegraph, within a few hours your anti-cultural behaviour will be known to the general public not only of Britain, of Switzerland and the ever-glorious U S S R, but also of Australia?'

After that you could hear a pin drop.

It rained most of the time, so I spent most of the time in the palace of the former King. The drawing-room looked like a miniature Euston station—there were models of all types of locomotive set out on tables. The King had liked to play with them. The library, which had been my objective, was also difficult to disentangle, because it had been left just the way it had been in the old King's day. Thus, books on America were books on America, and I found the *Last of the Mohicans* jostling four volumes of the *Congressional Record* for 1908.

What with the ex-King's puffer-trains and the children's theatre it was tempting to settle down in Montenegro for good. The Minister for Agriculture actually did offer me some kind of job. In view of the later political upheavals it was no doubt fortunate, as a matter of personal survival, that I turned it down and allowed duty to call us to Sofia, in a train with broken windows, full of sheep-skinned peasants and poultry and flurries of snow.

At two o'clock on an icy morning, the central station at Sofia seemed like an uncomfortable end of the world. Bugs bit like stinging hornets, lice surged from the floor, much of it covered by sleeping peasants. There was no sign of any transport to the centre of the town. Nobody present, it seemed, could speak anything but Bulgarian. I got very weary of bending over snoozing men in woolly caps and jabbering at them in German until they shook their heads and dropped off to sleep again.

Then Patricia said, 'There are three men in felt hats. They look like our last hope.' I approached the group who, by the mere fact of wearing hats, achieved an almost cosmopolitan appearance. I tried German: no dice. French: total incomprehension. English: shaking of hats. Despairing and feeling a little mad, I addressed them in Spanish. Their eyes lit up. They understood, and replied in what was certainly intelligible as a form of Spanish—though a very strange form.

Volubly, their olive-coloured hands flying and fluttering, their dark eyes dancing, they gave us all needed information, volunteered to telephone for a taxi-cab. While we waited for it, I remarked that it was rather odd to find Spaniards here. They explained. They were not Spaniards but, one of them said, 'Our family used to live in Spain before they moved to Turkey. Now we are moving to Bulgaria.'

Thinking that perhaps they had been 'displaced' from Spain by the upheaval of the civil war, I asked how long it had been since their family lived there. He said it was approximately five hundred years. I did some quick reckoning and realized that their move had been made under the pressure not of Generalissimo Franco, but of Ferdinand and Isabella. They were the descendants of the Marrano Jews—Jews who had, in the centuries before Ferdinand and Isabella, renounced Judaism for Christianity, hoping thus to live and prosper in Spain. It had done them no good. They were routed out by the Inquisition and expelled just like those who had never bothered to get converted. But their language remained a kind of Spanish Yiddish. He spoke of these events as though they had occurred a couple of years ago. How long, after all, *sub specie aeternitatis* is five hundred years? They planned to live now by selling sewing machines.

A man from Mars landing anywhere in the Balkans at that time could have been excused for reporting back to his planet that a fighting war between Russia and the western powers was probable next week, and certain within a month. There in Bulgaria could be seen clearly enough the pattern of problems which have plagued Europe ever since.

The western powers, and their anti-Communist political allies in the country, considered, naturally enough, that their principal propaganda objective must be to prevent anti-Communists or waverers from becoming resigned, from losing the hope of change. Put like that, the policy sounded like a platitude.

But what in practice it meant, and had to mean, was that the western powers and their internal allies had to devote themselves to maintaining, by all available means, a state of maximum political and emotional tension. There was only one way to do that—namely by creating in the public mind the impression that a new war was imminent, that any day now 'liberating' forces from the west would turn up and turn the situation on its head. That, like it or not, was the only means the western policy-strategists could see of gaining and holding the attention of masses of semi-literate people whose attention was going otherwise to be occupied entirely by the Red Army.

As a result, almost everywhere you went in Bulgaria you met people who absolutely believed that within a few days or weeks the British or the Americans were going to 'advance'—or drop tens of thousands of parachutists from the skies. (Quite often, in the country districts, whole villages would be convinced not simply that it was going to happen soon but that it had happened already—everyone had met a man who had met a man who had actually *seen* British tanks or American artillery or something of the kind on the road a few miles away.)

Given the western objectives, it may have been the only possible policy, but on two counts it did not work out very well for them. On the one hand, since the parachutists, tanks, or atomic missiles never did turn up, precisely that mood of cynicism and defeatism among the anti-Communists which the policy was designed to avert, in fact, was deepened. And on the other hand, these western manœuvres, rumour-mongerings and other machinations provided the Russians and the Bulgarian Communists with a ready-made Devil: it was a Devil you see, or at anyrate hear running about the country, and his presence excused everything from political oppression to economic hardship.

Also, as always happens, a lot of people became, as it were, the prisoners of their own propaganda. I met British and American diplomats and military men in Sofia who, in a strange, hallucinated way, really did seem to believe that war was due to break out any minute. Many of them seemed to suffer from a kind of hysteria of anti-Russianism which, whatever its origins, certainly impaired their political judgment.

I had often noticed before, and in the Balkans the fact was particularly striking, that the supposedly superior judgment of 'the man on the spot' is a myth, and often a dangerous one at that. Particularly in England the idea of 'leaving things to the man on the spot' is popular and appealing. There comes a certain type of crisis, and in next to no time the Man on the Spot materializes before the public mind as a model of knowledge, understanding, common sense and practical activity, in sharpest contrast to the ignorant and woolly-headed pundits of Westminster and Downing Street.

In reality, as often as not you find that the man on the spot has spent dinnertime and half the night absorbing the lies poured into his ear by some half-crazed local adventurer with the gift of the gab, and is also itching all over his mind because the night before he was held up somewhere by a Russian patrol and turned out of his car and made late for an appointment and the bastards haven't apologized yet.

The Russians, of course, could afford, just then, to be a lot less hysterical than the westerners—they were on top, and keeping relatively calm. Years later, their actions in Hungary seemed to prove, among other things, that when things are going badly for them they are no more immune to hysteria than anyone else.

Even then, in the relative security of Sofia, the atmosphere of Russian diplomatic and military quarters was sufficiently electric and suspicious—reproducing, as we know by hindsight, the suspicions and awful tensions of Moscow under Stalin.

About a quarter of my whole time in Sofia was spent trying to arrange an interview with Georgi Dimitrov who, while I was there, made his triumphal return from Moscow to his native Bulgaria. The difficulties could hardly have been greater if I had been trying to arrange to assassinate him—or rather, the difficulties were there because it was pretty well taken for granted that any outsider who wanted to see a man of such eminence in the apparatus of world Communism might quite likely be intending to assassinate him.

Nothing prods and stimulates one's time-sense more healthily than the realization that some figure, some name which was a household word and played a major role in your own thinking and living for years, means precisely nothing to almost anyone more than about fifteen years younger than oneself. It is that way, I suppose, with Dimitrov.

In the blackness of 1933, with Hitler triumphant in Germany, the heroic figure of Dimitrov at the Reichstag Fire trial was a signal rocket, seeming to tell the world that the blackness had not after all triumphed wholly and for ever. He was the first man to show the dictators that, however big they were, a man with an idea could still take the stuffing out of them. Dimitrov, in fact, symbolized not only the struggle against Fascism, but the struggle of the thoughtful and the civilized against the philistines. Millions of people who were not Communists, millions, even, of anti-Communists were inspired and rallied by him.

At last, just as I thought I should have to leave Sofia without seeing him, I got a message—it was late in the evening—that he would see me. When? 'Now, at once. The car is waiting.' This sudden rush, after weeks of delay, was of course part of 'security'. There was a lot more of it before we actually saw him. In one car we dashed, zig-zagging confusingly half across the city. Then we changed to another car, and dashed zig-zagging and twisting through the streets in another direction. Suddenly we were in what seemed to be a cul-de-sac, with waste land on one side and a high wall on the other. Apparently the guard seated beside our driver had been a little slow in giving whatever signal he was supposed to give as we drew up. Four wiry little gunmen with black overcoats and white, furious faces jumped at the car like terriers, their guns covering us. There was a minute or two of tense, angry palaver before we were led from the car and through a gate which opened just long enough for us to pass. We crossed a dim garden, a door opened as briefly as the gate, and were were blinking in the brilliant light of an entrance hall which, in its furnishings and decoration, looked like an elaborate stage set for an Edwardian period piece.

A room upstairs, a library, where we waited for Dimitrov, continued the same rather disconcerting Edwardian motif. Then Dimitrov himself appeared. I do not know just what I had expected. I must have seen thousands of photographs of him.

Yet, perhaps because none of them were coloured, none had prepared me for the sight of a figure which not merely did not in any way clash with the 'period' atmosphere but actually enhanced it. It was as though we were paying a social call on some baronial crony of Edward VII in, say, Nice or Hamburg in the year 1906. I was even under the impression, for a moment, that Dimitrov was wearing a frock coat. His face was astonishingly pink and white, and of a texture and patina which suggested a waxwork. His moustache, carefully waxed, and extending an inch or more on either side of his upper lip, looked as though he had affixed it in the dressing-room a moment before making his entrance. His gait and his bow were courtly, his smile a perfect blend of interest, welcome and restrained dignity. It would have seemed more natural to address him as 'Excellency' than as 'Comrade'.

When I had said that I wanted to 'see' Dimitrov, I had meant just that. Formal interviews, for publication, with very prominent figures are, to my mind, almost invariably futile. Indeed, so far as the content of such interviews is concerned, the technique of posting the man a list of questions and waiting for him to answer in writing is more rewarding. I did not flatter myself that we should sit chatting intimately with Dimitrov about the Kremlin or war and peace.

I should have thought it even less likely had I known at the time just how thin was the ice he was skating on. Nor, so far as can be judged, did he. For in the course of this first encounter, he spoke favourably, even enthusiastically, of the possibilities of a Balkan Federation, a Soviet Socialist Balkan Union extending from the Adriatic to the Black Sea, and composed of Yugoslavia, Bulgaria and Rumania. For Bulgaria's most famous Communist leader to adumbrate such a plan seemed natural enough. Yet in fact the scheme was packed with political dynamite—for in Stalin's eyes, as later transpired, the whole idea was seen as a Machiavellian manœuvre of Marshal Tito, directed towards his own aggrandizement, and anyone who favoured the conception was automatically suspect of conspiring with the Marshal —still, of course, ostensibly on excellent terms with the Russian Communists—against the Kremlin.

The interview proper lasted about an hour and a quarter, but that was only the beginning. When that part was over, and

Dimitrov had retired, I sat—as had been agreed in advance—in the library and wrote my sheaves of notes into a coherent 'fair copy'. The interview itself had been conducted in German. My story was in English. Then a secretary came and translated the whole story into German—the only language we had in common —and took it away for Dimitrov to examine and revise. We left, being informed that I should be notified when to return and receive the revised version.

During the ensuing week, I visited Dimitrov either three or four times, I forget which, and at each meeting the same process was repeated and the interview, under this cautious mangling, grew duller and duller. I noticed, without at the time in the least appreciating the significance of the fact, that the Balkan Federation, which at first had bulked large, had by the end almost evaporated in a small cloud of generalizations.

Just before the final version was completed, Dimitrov made a public speech which said, almost verbatim, everything that was by then contained in my 'exclusive' interview. I felt how right I had been not to expect anything more than just to 'see' Dimitrov.

Journalistically, I suppose, a not very rewarding experience. All the same, I would sacrifice a lot of 'successful' interviews in favour of the total of four or five hours spent with that polite, Edwardian figure, offering a glass of cherry brandy as he scanned, on each successive visit, the translated text of our latest version.

He had the air, at such times, of a rather grand Oxford tutor from the Beerbohm period. And behind him, as he sat smiling gently beneath the huge chandelier, his hand extended occasionally to a red velvet bell-pull to summon a secretary, you saw the figure of the man who, alone in the dock at Leipzig, had turned the all-powerful Goering from accuser to accused—'You are very much afraid of my questions, are you not, Herr Reichsminister?'—had sent up those signal rockets in the dark, had, in fact, put under Hitler's arrogant foot the first and ultimately catastrophic banana-skin.

However, that was of no comfort to the people in the office at home, and the trip in general was proving of little value to them. This was partly because it had begun to seem to me that almost anything one could write which was not the sort of stuff that could have been knocked together out of Communist bulletins available in London was off the line, unpublishable.

I determined to leave for Rumania before London had a chance to send one of its peremptory telegrams of recall.

We crossed the wide grey Danube at Rustchuk, and landed on Rumanian soil—blissfully far, it seemed, from London, on the threshold of a country which had always loomed fabulously strange in my imagination.

As we walked up the quay in the crowd of peasants, gypsies, and soldiers from Rumania and European Russia and Asia, a clipped, authoritative voice at my shoulder said, in a tone that seemed to be warning me against any attempt to deny the statement, 'You are Cockburn Three.'

For a moment I had all the sensations of being caught out walking through the streets of Berkhamsted without my school cap, or cutting cricket.

Beside me was a man in the uniform of a British Major. But to me, he was a prefect, the head, in fact, of my House, and one with an inexorable will to keep up the tone of the school. He was keen on everything and wanted others to be, too. He had left when I still had two distant cousins at the school, both senior to me, so that he knew me only as Cockburn Three. (The substitution of 'Three' for 'Minimus' had been a proclamation of our school's modernity.)

He was now Military Attaché at the British Legation in Bucharest.

Still quivering somewhat, wishing I had at least shaved more carefully, and hoping—a futile hope—that I did not reek of the spirits some convivial soldiers had shared with me on the ferry, I followed him to the official car which he indicated. There was immediately a nasty altercation, nearly, it appeared, a brawl. The Rumanian Ministry of Propaganda had also sent a car to meet us, anxious that we should not be 'got at' at the very first moment by the British, with whom relations were at the time particularly bad. The Legation had had a similar idea about the Rumanian Ministry.

Looking more like a prefect than ever, the Major cowed the opposition party and we drove to Bucharest in his car, talking about a House Rugby match in which I had once scored 'a very useful goal'. He also, very courteously, told Patricia that, though cricket had not been really my game, I twice got into the House long-run team. 'And,' he said, 'he three times won the Essay Prize.' It was good of him. He felt, obviously, that though her husband might not be much to write home about now, she ought to know of these achievements in his past and give him due credit for them, off-setting his disgraceful opinions.

It was quite a long drive to Bucharest, and I had hoped that we might be able to complete a general review of our old school's football status, then and now, and get me brought up to date on news of how the House had been doing in the present season, in time for me to get some news and views on the situation in Rumania.

There was not much time, and the Major's news and views seemed to throw light rather on himself than on Rumania. He had reached his present position by a curious route. About the beginning of the war he had been in the Sudan, and had there applied himself to the study of Russian, on the ground that Britain would soon be at war with Russia, and a man who knew Russian would be in line for interesting work with our invading forces as they advanced on Baku. Things, as will be recalled, turned out differently, but his studies had not been in vain because they sent him to Russia anyway, on liaison work with our allies. His experiences in Moscow, and later here in Bucharest, had convinced him that the Russian and Rumanian authorities were unmitigated scoundrels, that there ought, if at all possible, to be a war with Russia, and that the Rumanian régime was likely to collapse very soon under the pressure of public opinion. The whole situation was nasty, and the Jews were responsible for it.

I could, of course, hardly expect that members of the British Legation would talk freely to the correspondent of a Communist newspaper. Nevertheless, it did seem to me that what had been, in effect, a Russian *putsch* to establish a pro-Communist Government in power, and their own helplessness in the face of events which they regarded as both disappointing and disastrous, had produced in them a sort of blindness, together with an inability to say or even think anything new about the situation, as though shock had brought on a painful stutter.

I found irksome, too, their almost sadistic pleasure in every item of information showing what a mess things were in—oil wells going to pot under 'workers' control', the harvest ruined by drought and peasant opposition to the Government. A mess was what the Rumanian economy and political situations were certainly in. (It was, I believe, a fact that when Vyshinsky dashed to Bucharest to dictate his orders to the King and establish a régime based on Communism, there were only a few thousand Communists in the whole country, the whole of the Central Committee was in jail, and of these, when they were released, a third or more had to be clapped behind the bars again because a quick look at the police archives showed that they had been receiving police pay as informers.) Still, if the oil wells were ruined and the harvest, too, it was the Rumanian people at large who were going to suffer. And the wastage of the earth's natural resources is a melancholy sight at any time.

The state of chaos in industry and finance was such that one went about the streets in a continual statement of amazement at the fact that life was carried on at all, that people survived.

Anyone who has reached the age of forty-five or thereabouts without being maimed, financially ruined, blown up, tortured to madness, or hanged, must, I opine, feel a general (though often unavowable) sympathy with other members of what may be termed 'the Abbé Sieyès Group'—people who, when asked like Sieyès, what did you do in the great war and revolution, are able to reply with modest confidence that they 'survived it'.

For many years, allowing my attention to wander from the successful people who have an apartment on the twentieth floor, and the failures who jumped out of it, I have brooded on the survivors—people who, according to the laws of probability, should be dead or in jail, and are not. What, just for example, in Easter Week 1916 were the chances of survival for Eamonn de Valera? Would anyone have backed them with any serious money? Certainly not. That wild-eyed fanatic was a gone coon if ever there was one. Yet he is still Prime Minister of Ireland. It is a disturbing phenomenon for those who think it wrong to back anything but an odds-on favourite.

It is, of course, hard to nominate anyone for membership of the Sieyès Group because, before your nomination can get printed, it is more than possible that a news dispatch from here or there will carry the sad intelligence that your man has died suddenly of Leftism, Rightism, or occupational ulcer.

However, I will take this chance and nominate for the Sieyès Hall of Fame Dr Petru Groza who, when I knew him, was Prime Minister of Rumania and is—unless something has happened*— at this moment still a powerful figure in Rumanian politics. As I recall, when I started writing this, he was the Speaker—or words to that effect—of the Rumanian Parliament.

'Bravo!' was the first word I heard Dr Groza speak. It was uttered in praise of an Italian dress which my wife had bought, *en route* to Bucharest, and was wearing at what, up to that point, had been a solemn kind of diplomatic reception. Groza made no kind of secret of the fact that he was prepared to throw all the Ambassadors of the world out of the reception line in favour of a pretty woman in a new Italian dress. And 'Bravo!' was the last word I heard from him—uttered in praise of my statement that after a week-end at his country home in what Philip Jordan used to call 'the heart of the Dracula country', I had no trace of hangover.

Far away in the nineteen-thirties, Groza was the youngest Cabinet Minister in Rumania. He was also among the four or five largest landowners in that country, and a director of between forty and fifty industrial companies. To be in that position in Rumania does not, one would think, foster idealism. It can even produce a certain earthiness. And it is a fact that Groza bought his clothes in London, and hired a boxing professional and a tennis professional from Berlin to keep him in form.

One day, during a Cabinet meeting, Groza slammed his portfolio together and said, 'Gentlemen, I resign. I am leaving this Sodom and Gomorrah of Bucharest for my estate in Transylvania. I shall not recross the Carpathians until things are very different.'

Everyone in Bucharest naturally thought it was a stunt. In fact Groza did go to his estate in Transylvania and did not recross the Carpathians for seventeen years. After seventeen years he recrossed them twice—the first time to be jailed as an anti-Hitlerite, the second to be installed as Prime Minister with the blessing of the late Vyshinsky.

When I met him he was somewhere in the late sixties, and had spent the morning of the day I first visited him running round the park for a mile or so, playing tennis, and then knocking down a man who was trying to assassinate him in the foyer of the Athenée Hotel. He seemed preoccupied. After the usual chat about world peace and the future of this and that, I found ourselves on sufficiently good terms to enquire what was on his mind. I explained that I much enjoyed talking with him, but did not want to disturb him if he were engaged in matters of State. He disclosed that he was trying to work out a means of playing a rather malign practical joke on an American Senator—a special envoy of President Truman, and publisher of, I think, the St Louis *Courier-Journal*, who was coming to check up on the state of westishness and eastishness in the Balkans.

It was a project—the joke, I mean—in which I felt able to offer some small assistance.

After several further conversations, he invited us to spend the week-end with him in Transylvania. We were all to go up together in his special train. In case anyone should be again lurking to assassinate him the special train left from a suburban station, outside Bucharest. The security arrangements were so complete that all the food for the journey was sent to another suburban station. We faced a journey through the night and the mountains with no provender other than a huge supply of hock which, fortunately, had been put aboard before the security people got busy.

Groza spoke perfect German and good French of a rather Teutonic kind. But his mind was restless, and somewhere towards three in the morning, as the little train—loaded only with ourselves and a horde of armed guards who kept tramping through the restaurant car fingering their pistols—snaked through the high mountains, he declared that the only language in which to conduct a serious discussion of life was Latin.

I had not spoken Latin for years, and always badly. To attempt to do so in the middle of the night after a five-hour diet of good hock was an exhausting experience. Groza, to my dismay, spoke it fluently.

His house in the mountains was a handsome place in the old Austrian style. The first thing my wife and I saw in our bedroom as we sought to relax after that extenuating night trip was a big printed notice in Rumanian, German, French and English. It said that guests were forbidden to smoke except in 'the Moorish lounge', that drinking except at meals was forbidden, that at the sound of the first gong before lunch or dinner everyone must assemble in the central hall, and at the sound of the second gong proceed to the dining-room. Anyone, said the notice, who failed to get into the central hall before the sound of the second gong would be excluded from the dining-room and get nothing to eat.

I lay on my back, smoking a cigar up the chimney like a mid-Victorian visiting his aunt.

The first gong went and we went down to lunch—all the guests were assembled under the eye of Madame Groza. The second gong went, and nothing happened for half an hour. At the end of that time Groza appeared, smoking a cigar, sipping a glass of vodka and enquiring why nobody else was smoking or drinking.

'Why,' I asked him when, after a day or two in that comfortable house, I knew him a little better, 'why put up these terrifying rules which nobody keeps or seems even supposed to keep?'

'Because,' said he, 'in Rumania unless we at least look as though we had some sort of rules people behave absolutely nohow. One must preserve at least the appearance of an ordered life.'

On the shelves of his study were as many as forty or perhaps fifty small diaries, bound identically in limp red leather. He had filled in a page or half-page every day of his life since he was ten years old. The first entry concerned his first visit, at that age, to London, with a note to the effect that the bus fare from Waterloo to somewhere in the City was two-pence. Much later there was a half-page devoted to his first meeting with Adolf Hitler.

'But all those seventeen years,' I said, 'after you left the Cabinet and sat down on this side of the Carpathians? What did you do all the time?'

'I cultivated my estates,' Groza said, 'I made a comparative study of the various religious and political beliefs of the world.

'And,' he paused to fill me another glass of vodka, 'above all, I learned to think dialectically.'

* As this book goes to press comes the news that Dr Groza —a Sieyès man to the last—has died a peaceful and natural death.

11

Emergency exit

OUR house began to seem lonely—with the end of the war people were passing through and passing on to somewhere else.

On Christmas Day that year they were still there, but not there like solid people who are going to be there next Christmas, but people on their way. Which, certainly, is the way people should be.

Otto Katz—of whom I have spoken before—came. He was on his way back from Mexico and going to Prague, where, after a spell as a foreign adviser to the Government, he was hanged. Egon Erwin Kisch came, also from Mexico, and also on his way to Prague where he was going to be Mayor, and soon die.

Alice Astor came, but she was already almost on her way to the United States. She suffered from the reputation of being the fourth or fifth richest woman in the world, and had been married by Prince Obolensky, and Hugo von Hoffmansthal and others, and strenuously wooed by the Communist Party.

She was a woman of a sad kind of charm, and a child of misfortune. She had a big house in Regents Park, and somewhere during the war period she had guilt—or someone told her she ought to have guilt—for living in that great big house when the fight for freedom was on.

So she found a little garage at the bottom of the driveway, and converted that into a tiny house—a living-room and bedroom and not much else except bathroom and lavatory. No kitchen.

So that when you went to dine there that winter, with the snow pouring down, the white (in the sense of anti-red) Russian butler and three maids had to run through the snow down the drive from the big house, bearing dishes full of the splendid foods cooked by the internationally-famous white (in the same sense) Russian chef. They, with the snow melting on their hair, would look at Alice with deepest sympathy—she was a victim of British austerity. And she would look at them in the same way—they too were its victims. She had the deepest sympathy for everyone—so deep that I sometimes thought it overwhelmed her. It paralysed the possibility of action.

Once she rang me up and told me that everything was getting a little bit too much, and she would like to come and discuss the whole situation. I asked her to dinner. 'But quietly,' she said. 'Very quietly,' I said.

What with one thing and another, it did not turn out so quiet, because at a cocktail party on the way to the little Soho restaurant I had chosen for our quiet talk we had accumulated half a dozen friends, one of whom was—during the course of the meal—struck over the head with an only partially empty bottle of wine by a diner at another table, and now lay on the floor, his blood mingling with the vile Algerian wine.

I apologized to Alice. 'Not,' I said, 'I'm afraid, quite the quiet talk we had in mind. All my fault.'

'Oh, but it's all right,' said Alice. 'It's quite all right. It makes me feel at home. It's *so* like New York.'

It was a true remark, but one of those which suggest that the remarker's sense of place and time is a little out of this world. Such sense does not bring them happiness and success. Such people, like the philosopher in the poem, are apt to be found to have 'pursued truth like a beagle, but they ran so much faster, they sprinted right past her.'

I was not in the least surprised to read in the newspaper some time back that Alice's lawyer, after his last visit to her—visit, that is, by a high-powered man very much from within this world —had left her will, worth so-and-so many million, on a seat in the New York underground train. It was the kind of thing that was almost bound to happen to Alice—almost as though her endearing spirit and qualities had reached out from some instant between earth and heaven and told that lawyer that to lose a multi-million will was all right; *so* like dear New York.

Hans Kahle was there. He had been, when I first knew him, a refugee journalist in Paris. But before that he had been an officer in the Hanoverian Guard, or some Regiment of equal prominence, so that when the Spanish war broke out he had been able to quit Paris and come down to Spain to be a military man again, and a divisional commander of the International Brigade.

He was a man with that mixture of sourness, panache, hardly conceivable courage and sentimental despair which is associated with the best sort of Prussian. I had met him for the first time at about midnight of the night in the suburbs of Madrid when the International Brigade first went into action from somewhere in University City. He had under his command about twenty Hungarians, some of whom had come across Europe hanging on to the rods and buffers of the international expresses, a company or so of German refugees from Paris, and a mixed bag of heroic odds and sods from nobody knew quite where—nor were they very anxious to explain.

After the Republican defeat, and his escape to England, he was, as I recall, shipped off to Canada as a German, which he certainly was. When I last saw him, he was on his way back to Germany, where he became Police Chief of Mecklenburg, in East Germany, a post he retained until he died of occupational ulcer.

Alan Hutt and his wife were there. He was a man to whom you had to talk fast and funny to be as fast and funny. He is, I have been told by everyone I have spoken to who knows anything about such matters, the greatest English expert on typography and layout after Morison of *The Times*.

The William Rusts came, of course. Rust was, I should reckon, among one of the half dozen liveliest, supplest and toughest Englishmen I have ever known. He came from the area of the Elephant and Castle and was as English as that implies. And like the real cockney and the real Lancashire man, he seemed— though he spent a part of his life in Moscow and another part in Spain—nearer to the type of Englishman who puzzled and often frightened Europeans in the eighteenth century than many of those who feel that they have been born too late and that the eighteenth century would have suited their talents better than our own does. He was a character who could have walked through the world of Brecht's *Threepenny Opera* with success; with the probability that he would have imposed his ideas, policies and human wishes upon a lot of people before they decided that he was too dangerous to have around and put him away.

Even his clothes warned you to be careful—he wore well-cut,

conservative suits. His unrevealing, square, plumpish face was almost equally misleading. So, too, was a certain pleasure he took in poking his short nose into corners of society which to him—as a proletarian Marxist from near the Elephant—had a gamey reek, and might, in their decay, yield something useful to the political buccaneer. You could put it in another way and say that he had a streak of snobbery. Probably that would be true. But snobbery—the real, basic snobbery of Voltaire and Marcel Proust—is only an accentuated awareness of the gradations of society, a form, in other words, of class consciousness. To the class-conscious millionaire, an ex-miner like Khrushchev has a special interest, not simply as a big man in the Kremlin but because he is a proletarian. To the class-conscious proletarian, a millionaire is interesting just because he is a millionaire. Only the insensitive, the unaware, are not alive to these interests. The rest are out with their butterfly nets scooping in the specimens. Rust's butterfly net was never inactive, though he felt the need to justify his hobby by explaining that it was all for the good of the cause. Which, oddly enough, it very often was. I have seen him take a hostile Tory Peer for a political ride which made the giant dipper look tame.

He had the humility of the truly assured. When he first came to the *Daily Worker* he had, and he knew it, a reputation—so far as writing was concerned—as one of the dreariest and most arid of the Cominternists. On his first day in the office, as Editor, he called me into his cubbyhole and said, 'Look. This is what I want to say.' He showed me a couple of sheets of his writing. 'It's stiff and it stinks. Could you see if you can do anything with it? I mean,' he said, with a cock of the eye and eyebrow which conveyed both an appeal, if you chose to answer it, and an announcement that if you didn't so choose you could stuff it up and he would get by without your help, damn your eyes, 'if you could put it the way people will read it.'

He used to look at his notes and my treatment day after day as carefully as a good girl in a cookery school. And one day, when I watched him through a door he did not know was half-open, I saw him writing away with the touching expression of the child who at last has learned just how the manufacturers make the toffee so that it does not stick to the dish.

He died of high blood pressure at a meeting of the top-level committee of the Communist party. And, short of dying in battle, which he might have preferred, I dare say that—had one ever suggested to him that excessive blood pressure engendered by a difference of policy was what would lay him low—he would have said, with sincerity, that that wouldn't been a bad way, either.

Numbers of the new Labour M.P.s used to come to our house at that time, and they increased my sense of isolation, of being, somehow, in the wrong place and needing to move on to somewhere else. These, being for the most part members of the left wing of the Labour Party, were people whom the *Daily Worker* and the Communist Party had, in degrees varying from the very small to the decisive, helped to elect. Talking, and sometimes working, with them, I was aware of a lack of sympathy on my own part which positively startled me.

It was easy enough, of course, to find reasons superficially satisfying to oneself; as, for instance, that some were grossly on the make, others insufferably conceited, and others more pusillanimous than anyone has a right to be.

I recall a remarkable occasion, and one which was sufficiently typical, when one of the innumerable 'revolts' in the Parliamentary Labour Party was in progress. These 'revolts', usually against some phase or other of Bevin's foreign policy, occurred about once every couple of months, and followed a scarcely varying pattern from the moment when the optimists declared that this time it was serious, and Bevin would have to mend his ways, to the later moment when the whole thing faded away, leaving Bevin and his policy unshaken and unchanged.

On the occasion I speak of, no less than fifty—I think it was more like eighty—Labour M.P.s had put their names to a resolution, highly critical of Bevin, which was to be debated at the regular 'secret' weekly meeting of the Party.

Since, this time, they had not merely gone about the lobbies talking of mutiny, but actually signed something in black and white, even my hard-learned scepticism softened. This time something really was going to happen. I hung about, waiting for the meeting to be over and the story of it to 'leak'—which it normally did about fifteen minutes after the secret session was over.

To my naïve astonishment, it transpired that not eighty, not fifty, not twenty or ten of the bold 'rebels' had voted against Bevin in favour of their own resolution. The number of such voters had been three.

I tackled a number of the un-rebellious rebels in the lobby and asked them how come? Their answers were singularly revealing of the way such matters are really conducted. One of them said that in the course of the long discussion his feet had got hot and swelled. He had been in pain, and had left the room to remove his shoes for a few minutes and let his feet simmer down. 'And would you believe it,' he said, 'when I got back in there, the vote had just been taken?'

Two of them said that, after all, the voting on a resolution was unimportant—the debate itself, they said was the important thing, and they assured me that Bevin had been 'visibly impressed'.

Another had a more ingenious explanation of his failure to vote. 'It was obvious,' said he, 'that even if a large number of us voted for the resolution we should still be in a minority. And that would be an encouragement to Bevin. But if nobody voted for the resolution, or even abstained, in fact if we all voted for it, Bevin would have no clue to the true size of the rebellion, and that would frighten him.'

Rendered somewhat dizzy by this line of reasoning, I tried to envisage the consequences of its application to political struggles in general.

It was the kind of episode which constantly occurred, and to watch such events and write about them was naturally frustrating. But gradually I began to have to admit to myself that my lack of sympathy with the Labour men was not so straightforwardly political as I had pretended to myself. In any case, evidently, it was foolish to object to Labour legislators on the ground that they did not act like Communists. But I began to realize that what I found increasingly unsympathetic was not merely Labour but the atmosphere of English life in general—and that, as I came more slowly to understand, included the 'climate' of the British Communist Party and the *Daily Worker*.

People have asked me repeatedly—and the questions are natural in a period when the fact of Communism and everyone's relation to it are the central features of the world's political, social and intellectual life—how precisely I came to move into the Communist Party and how precisely I came to move out of it. Numbers of friendly reviewers dealing with the first volume of this autobiography mildly complained that it did not answer the first part of the question. That surprised me, because I had supposed that the whole book, all the way from nursery to the Spanish war, was, in fact, an answer.

A difficulty is that, with many examples before them, people are accustomed to expect something abrupt, sensational and Pauline in the way of a conversion—some explosion on the road to Damascus capable of explaining so drastic a decision. Things do, certainly, quite often happen that way. I can only say that in my case nothing of that sort occurred, and it would be misleading even to suggest that it did. And I am forced to give the same sort of answer, highly unsatisfactory to many people, and to some both offensive and suspect, to the second half of the question too. I daresay if I had been at the *Daily Worker* at the time of the Russian attack on Hungary that kind of 'explosion' would have occurred, and I should have quit in a blaze of disgust. It would be agreeable, but also dishonest, to state categorically that such would have been the case. It would be a respectable thing to assert. But no one can with honesty assert just what they would have done in circumstances which never arose. I can imagine, as a theoretical possibility, that— just as, at the time of the Communist change of line at the beginning of the war, a principal factor influencing my decision to stay with the paper was a perhaps overdeveloped sense of loyalty, and distaste for leaving the outfit when it is under fire— so, even under the pressure of events in Hungary, I might have taken the same kind of decision. I think not, but there is no way of knowing.

As things were in reality, there was no more of an explosion on the way out than on the way in. It was a gradual process, involving countless factors which were by no means all 'political' in the strict sense of the word.

It would, again, be respectable to pretend now that I was already alert to and horrified by the proceedings of the Stalin régime in Russia. There would be an element of truth in that, but not the whole truth. The fact was that like innumerable non-Russian Communists—and it is an important fact to keep in mind—I was sheathed, so to speak, against indignation and dis-

gust regarding many atrocious events in Russia, by two suits of
protective clothing. The first was the fact that during a great
part of my life I had listened to anti-Communists telling the
wildest lies about Communism and Communists, and on occasion had even seen the lies being manufactured. The result was
that even when they told the truth one almost instinctively
rejected it—certainly one treated it with a scepticism tougher
than one would bring into play on other issues.

Almost exactly the same thing happened, during the early
years of the Nazi régime in Germany, to people who had been
pacifists during or soon after the first world war. From books
and pamphlets by leading Socialist publicists like Arthur Pon-
sonby, they had learned a lot about the seamy side of wartime
propaganda. They had discovered that a good many of the most
hair-raising 'atrocities' supposed to have been committed by the
German troops in their advance through Belgium had never
happened. They discovered that the story of the Germans boiling
down the corpses of soldiers to make soap or other fats—a story
beautifully calculated to horrify British people, always easily
disgusted by the picture of the ruthless scientist outraging decent
humanity—had, in point of fact, been invented for the purpose
of horrifying the Chinese and arousing their anti-German
sentiments.

The people most affected by such revelations were, naturally,
those who during the war itself had taken such propaganda at
its face value and now felt that they had for years been the
victims of a confidence trick. The result was that, having once
believed too much, they now believed too little. They thought
the stories of Nazi atrocities were inventions, too.

The other protective suit was of a different material and texture. It was woven principally of two beliefs. One was the belief
that after all, on balance, the Soviet régime was, so to speak, on
the side of the angels—that is to say that despite many deviations and shortcomings its mere existence was an asset to the
oppressed of the earth, a challenge and a threat to the oppressors.
In my view, and in the view, obviously, of millions of people
from India to South Africa to the Southern States of the U S A,
there was a most obvious truth in that. But out of that belief
grew a second article of faith which was more dangerous—the
conviction that, in such circumstances, actions which would be

violently condemned if performed by any other régime must be quite differently assessed when performed by the Government of the U S S R.

Anyone can see and say that that is a dangerous attitude. But to recognize it as such does not solve the dilemma of—in particular—the western intellectual looking for peace, progress and the fall of the Bastille. For, the moment he accuses the Russian Communists of some hideous malpractice, he finds himself to his horror in the approving company of half the leading ruffians of the western world, people of whom he feels certain that, given half a chance, they would behave in the same way themselves. It is like advocating the abolition of capital punishment and being patted enthusiastically on the back by the bloody hand of a man who has just murdered a child.

The dilemma is real. It is part of the more general one described by Jean-Paul Sartre: 'If the Communists are right, I am the loneliest madman alive. If they are wrong, there is no hope for the world.' Certainly that is not a comprehensive account of the true situation—nor, I suppose, did Sartre mean it to be. But it is a true account of a common and not discreditable state of mind.

So far as my strictly political 'doubts' about the Communists were concerned, they were concentrated less upon whatever evil the Communists might be performing than upon the good which they seemed, at so many points, unable to perform.

At that time, certainly, one could attribute this lack of performance to the aftermath of war. Nevertheless, after viewing the chaos of Rumania, the comparative stagnation of Bulgaria, and, above all, the arid desert of East Germany, the doubts nagged at me. Very well, so it was true that these conditions were the direct result of war and revolution. But I, after innumerable conversations with a wide diversity of people in all those territories, found myself afflicted with a painful uncertainty as to whether the classic Communist formulae for ultimately solving the difficulties were really calculated to bring home, as they say, the bacon.

Viewing the British scene, I found my doubts more obtrusive. It is always disconcerting, after long immersion in a particular kind of activity, to come up for air one morning and wonder whether you and your fellow-workers are getting anywhere at all. We ran faster and faster, and seemed to remain almost exactly in the same place. If Marx was right in noting that the crucial thing is not simply to understand the world but to change it, we seemed to be changing very little.

For example, to descend from the general to the particular, the circulation of the *Daily Worker* at about this period was not merely not rising, but falling. Well, of course, that was very easily explained—it was due to the war ending and the consequent change of political atmosphere. It was an explanation, all right, like another. But was it an excuse?

The size of Communist representation in Parliament, fluctuating at that time, so far as I recollect, between one and two, could also be fully explained: the voters almost everywhere were certain the Communist candidate could not win the seat, so to avoid wasting their suffrages they gave them to the Labour candidate instead. A very truthful account of the position. But just what *made* the voters so certain that the most sensational victory the Communist was likely to achieve was the saving of his deposit? Worse still, what made the voters' prognostications 98 per cent. right?

Newspaper propaganda designed to reach 'the masses' is a strident affair, and in political propaganda of that kind you have to keep telling people that you are winning. They may not, after a look at the form book, believe it, but at least they are supposed to believe that you believe it. But it becomes irksome to be endlessly proclaiming the imminence of victories which do not, in fact, occur. You find yourself annoyingly reminded of the old Sam Goldwynism—the one about the time, during the depression, when some banker in New York rang him up in Hollywood and asked, 'How's business?' 'It's wonderful,' shouted Sam, 'it's tremendous, it's impressive, it's colossal—but it's picking up.'

It would have taken a powerful microscope to detect just where our business was picking up, and powerful microscopes of that kind were in demand among many of the leadership and rank and file alike. Others preferred the telescope through which you could see Chiang Kai-shek being routed, and the Chinese Communists sweeping that mighty country. To some this brought immediate solace. But when you took your eye from the telescope and looked, say, at the results of a County

Council election in Britain, the change in the view could give you a painful headache.

A more personal feature of this depressing scene was my growing conviction that, although some British Communists were doubtless proving immensely effective somewhere, my own effectiveness was sinking towards zero. Often I experienced that nightmare of the publicist in which he finds himself condemned to shout exhortations, warnings, funny jokes, and alarming disclosures down a telephone line with nobody at the other end of it. They have put down their receivers and gone to the pictures or a meeting of the Labour Party.

It was clear to me that if the circulation of the paper was falling, or at least was failing to rise, the fault must be to a quite large extent mine. I was the most experienced writer there, I often wrote more of the paper than anyone else, and both before and during the war my writing had admittedly been effective, had had an impact—occasionally a major impact. I had a fairly clear idea of the nature of the fault. Just the same qualities, it seemed to me, which had made me an enthusiastic and effective commentator during, say, the period of hunger marches and anti-Fascist brawls and riots in London, Paris and Marseilles; the period of the Spanish war; the electrically sultry period of Hitler's advance from Munich to the war; the period of the war itself—these qualities and dispositions appeared in some way to unfit me for what were called 'the tasks of reconstruction'. For the first time in my life I realized what people mean when they use the term 'maladjustment'. Hitherto I had supposed it was something that only happened to other people.

It is all very well to recognize a fault, but it is not really much use when you recognize at the same time that it is a fault which it is now far too late to correct. I used to reflect that had I, for example, in years gone by, taken more trouble to study and steep myself in the history and essential character of the British Labour movement, had I exerted myself more vigorously to comprehend the British character, I should be better adjusted to the situation. But there was no time to start doing all that now.

I was thus in the unpleasing position of a man who has volunteered to help drive a car over rough roads and now finds that he has forgotten how to change gear and rather suspects that the car has taken a wrong turning anyway.

More personal reasons, too, played a rôle in bringing me—some time about the late summer of 1946—to the point of, for the first time, seriously considering a move.

Patricia—it was a few months before our second son was born—was even more aware of, and oppressed by, a sense of futility and boredom than I was. She had always been more clear-headed than I about many aspects of the situation. She did not, to the full extent, share my propensity—often useful—for treating action as an end in itself; for acting, in fact, without asking ultimate questions; for taking hasty decisions and then behaving as though the decision to follow this course or that had been the product of the most careful weighing of pros and cons. She was therefore more irked than I by the unanswered questions with which my political path was littered. And she resented more than I did all kinds of evasion and double-talk—every occasion upon which, after some impending possibility had been denounced as disastrous for weeks before it happened, it was suddenly 'proved' to be a boon-laden victory after it had occurred.

I had been in Paris attending some conference or other of Foreign Ministers, and she had gone for a short holiday at her parents' house in Ireland. On the evening of our mutual return to London I told her suddenly—I had never even hinted at it before—that I was thinking about the possibility of dropping everything and starting an entirely new life. I had expected her to be startled. Instead she coolly remarked that she had noticed for months that for me the savour had gone out of things, and that as for her she had reached the same conclusion, but had not liked to mention it.

'The only thing is,' she remarked, 'what exactly would we use for money?'

It was undoubtedly a ticklish problem. The pay at the *Daily Worker* was still small, though, in contrast to the sort of thing that had happened in my early days there, it came regularly week by week. But it was possible to supplement it considerably by writing for Communist newspapers abroad—notably in Poland and the Balkans. Also I could, very occasionally and under a plethora of pseudonyms, sell an article or short story to a non-political magazine, though my American outlets, which had been very profitable in the pre-war years when a known Communist could still sell to non-Communist publications in the

U S A, had clogged up at the beginning of the war and never re-opened. Patricia had a small allowance from her father. I have forgotten what precisely our average income, including my earnings and Patricia's allowance, amounted to at the time—I suppose about £600 or £700 a year, which would be reduced to somewhere between £200 and £300 if I quitted the paper and left London.

Furthermore, after years of more or less strenuous and some-what specialized political journalism, I knew that it would take some time to develop, as it were, new muscles.

We had, naturally, almost nobody with whom we could dis-cuss the position. Of course the people at the paper would have felt, quite sincerely, that the only proper course was for me immediately to go to them with my doubts and problems, so that a 'full and frank discussion' might be held. It would have been the correct Communist way of doing things. Equally sin-cerely, I felt that it would achieve nothing useful whatever, and must inevitably produce exasperation and suspicion on all sides. I could not see myself successfully explaining the nuances of my attitude in acceptable terms. The nuances, so important to myself, would, like certain wines, 'travel badly' into strict Marxist territory. The fact that I did feel that way was incid-entally a proof that, despite all those years at the paper, I had not, after all, become a very good Communist. I thought that the more I kept my ideas and purposes to myself, the more I should be likely to save both myself and them a terribly lot of trouble. It was therefore impossible to take counsel with more than one or two intimate and truly reliable friends.

Among them, it was Patrick Hamilton, the novelist and play-wright, who, so far as I was concerned, did most to ease the strain. (I should much dislike to saddle Mr Hamilton with any responsibility whatever for my own decisions and actions. He had none—unless it is a responsibility to offer another man's mind a convenient chair, so to speak, to sit down in while it thinks.)

He had never been a Communist. As a passionate anti-Fascist, with a world reputation solidly based on the plays *Rope* and *Gaslight*, and such eerily wonderful novels as *Hangover Square* and *The Slaves of Solitude*, he was constantly approached by what the Americans call 'Front' organizations. However, the thought of joining anything made him shudder. The notion of just having his name listed as one of fifty vice-presidents of something, even though assured that he would never have to attend a committee or other meeting, brought on a terrible attack of agoraphobia. I have heard many people described as 'shy'—usually as an excuse for some sort of boorishness. Nobody, I used to think, knew what shyness could really be until he had met Patrick Hamilton. But in his case the word, so far from describing any kind of boorishness, indicated a sensitivity towards other human beings which for him frequently produced actual pain.

I believe when he was very young this sensitivity had been an almost continuously painful liability. With great deliberation he turned it into an asset. An American Army officer who had just read *The Slaves of Solitude*, in which a principal character is an American Lieutenant stationed in England, once asked me how long Patrick had been attached to the American forces—he thought he must have been on some 'cultural liaison' work or other, and in the course of it acquired his knowledge of how such a man as his Lieutenant thought and acted. I knew Patrick had never had any such job, but I did ask him about the Lieutenant. He said he had 'listened occasionally to American officers talking in bars in Henley', and I should think that was the literal truth. Just as some people can listen to a voice once and an hour later mimic it perfectly, so Hamilton could listen, without even seeming to listen, to a half-hour's conversation going on at the other end of a bar and afterwards not only reproduce its content and cadences, but intuitively deduce from it the whole nature of the talkers.

At one time, indeed, this extraordinary capacity got him into a ludicrous piece of trouble. Somebody who had read *Hangover Square*, and remarked on the perfect drawing of the Fascist-type villain of the piece, said that obviously at some time or another Hamilton must have been connected with a Fascist organization, or at least have gone about a lot with Fascists. The story spread. Its truth was taken for granted. And finally William Rust, who knew that I was a close friend of Hamilton, cross-questioned me sharply about this alleged background, supposing that Hamilton might be a crypto-Fascist even now, skilfully milking me of Communist secrets.

Even Rust, a man of suspicious mind in such matters, had to admit when he finally met Hamilton that the notion was singularly laughable. It was like attributing crypto-Fascism to Charles Dickens, with whom—in his general attitude to life, society and 'the masses'—Hamilton had close affinities. Even his faults, including an occasional facetiousness of style and an inclination to the 'pathetic fallacy'—both of which I personally rather enjoy, but are faults none the less—were, I believe, derived from Dickens.

Our first meeting, some time about the beginning of the war, had been agreeably farcical. Hamilton, who was moderately well-read in Marxism, and was always hoping to reconcile Marx —and the goings-on of Communist organizations—with his own native, warm-hearted and sometimes sentimental or romantic radicalism, had a brother-in-law who was a Liberal Member of Parliament, and he pestered this legislator with profound and awkward questions on matters not included in the ordinary M.P.'s curriculum. The brother-in-law shook him off by introducing him to the Communist M.P., William Gallacher.

Saying that the thing to do was for him to meet Communist writing chaps like myself and Walter Holmes, Gallacher brought him down one day to the *Daily Worker* office in City Road. Always panic-stricken at the eleventh hour by the prospect of any new human contact, and on this occasion additionally terrified by horrid visions of a couple of grim-minded pamphleteers, ever alert to chloroform and pierce with deadly pin anything looking like an intellectual butterfly, Hamilton—as he told me afterwards—actually considered deliberately falling off the tram before it got to our office. Had his companion been anyone else, he could at least have insisted on dashing into the Eagle and knocking back three or four double whiskies in readiness for the ordeal. But his guide was Gallacher, most prominent and ardent 'dry' at Westminster. He did not dare make the suggestion.

At that time the whole staff of the paper, except the Editor, sat together in a large barn-like room which, to Hamilton's fear-inflamed eye, seemed the embodiment of rigorous austerity. We too were embarrassed as Hamilton, his knees trembling, tottered across the room towards us. Gallacher's idea of an introduction was to say, 'Well, there you are. All intellectuals together,' and then stand back, smiling benevolently, and waiting for us to get on with it.

Luckily we were obviously busy at the time, and I cut the embarrassing encounter short by suggesting a meeting a few days hence. Shepherded by Gallacher, Hamilton tottered thankfully out again, resolved, at that moment, to cancel our appointment as soon as possible. He felt he had already had one narrow escape, and that his nerves would hardly stand a longer session, consisting probably of a discussion of the Novelist's Duty to Dialectics or something of the kind, washed along its course by draughts of tea.

On the tram back to Westminster, Gallacher said meditatively in his powerful Scots accent, 'You know, it's a very funny thing about those two men, Cockburn and Holmes. They're fine lads, fine writers. They've both of them given up a lot, a whole lot, for the sake of our paper, And yet, would you believe it now, they *drink*.'

Patrick Hamilton let out a yelp of surprise, pleasure and relief, which Gallacher took for a very natural cry of disappointment and dismay.

'They do?' said Hamilton, determined to get the thing stated without risk of misunderstanding.

'Like fishes,' said Gallacher.

In consequence, Hamilton gave up the idea of cancelling his appointment, and a few days later we sat for two hours in a public house near the office, being twice admonished by the woman behind the bar for laughing too loudly and disturbing the regular customers.

Right through the war years we used to meet a couple of times a week, and now I found nothing more soothing and stimulating to do than to discuss with Hamilton the intellectual and political situation in which I found myself. Looking back, I think I must have bored him a good deal—it is nearly impossible for people engaged in making decisions vastly important and exciting to themselves not to assume that, vividly and dramatically presented, they must appear equally important and exciting to someone else.

A supreme advantage of these conversations was the bearing they had on a major factor in the situation which was neither strictly political nor strictly personal—the, so to speak, literary question. The problems of writing 'as such'—if one may be permitted the expression—had always, in the various phases of my life, played a role at least as important as the problems of politics, although hitherto they had been inextricably twined together, almost indistinguishable one from the other. But now it seemed to me that I had come to the end of a literary as well as a political tether—though it was hard to tell whether political dissatisfaction had promoted dissatisfaction with my writing, and a sharp longing for new fields of writing, or whether it was the other way round.

Nearly a year had passed, and my second son, Andrew, was four or five months old, before Patricia and I made up our minds that, if we postponed the move until we had carpentered together some assurance of future financial security, we should perish of economic paralysis in London. We decided to sell the balance of the lease of our flat, which brought in a few hundred pounds, and take off for Ireland at the earliest practicable moment.

There remained a vital tactical problem to be solved. I was naturally anxious not to do harm to my old friends and associates at the *Daily Worker* by making any kind of spectacular exit. It would, I thought, be unbearable to become the centrepiece of a press furore in which I should inevitably be treated as a kind of Kravchenko, dashing out from the Iron Curtain to write *I Chose Freedom*. Maybe I really was 'choosing freedom', but, in my case, that seemed no good reason for biting the old comrades.

(I remarked once, a long time later, to Mr Osbert Lancaster, that it would be nice if he could help to persuade some of the Fleet Street chiefs that I was tired of having people expect that at any moment an *I Chose Freedom* was coming from me. Twirling his moustache and rolling his eyes in his fascinating manner, he said, 'But you might, you know, write an interesting little book called *I Chose the Galway Blazers*.')

I have nothing much to hold against the people who spend twenty years or so in the Communist Party, and presently dash out, tearing hair and beating breasts, to tell the waiting world what a murderous brothel they have been living and working in all that time. They are entitled to do that. But as a man in Youghal, County Cork, said to me one day, when Douglas Hyde or some other refugee from the salt-mines came to address the populace, 'Jesus, Mr Cockburn, he was warning us all against Communism which none of us ever thought of. And him, to hear him tell it, a member of that same organization for fifteen or twenty years or whatever the devil it was. Wouldn't you think now, Mr Cockburn, he'd do better tell the story down in Prague or some place like that?'

I see no sense, from anyone's viewpoint, in these—however sincerely felt—confessions. The brain-washed westerner who talks to the Chinese and Russians cuts very little ice among people intelligent enough to pull any political weight. And the same is presumably true of people turning the other way round. If a man was fool enough to be fooled by a lot of fools whom he now declares to be fools, and furthermore was fooled for years on end, should any intelligent person pay much attention to his testimony?

In considering that kind of people, one is constantly reminded of the girl in Norfolk, Virginia, who was suing a man for alleged rape. The Judge said to her, 'When did this rape occur?'

'When did it occur, Judge?' said she. 'Why, hell, it was rape, rape, rape all summer long.'

The easiest way of avoiding that undesirably spectacular exit seemed to be to fall gravely ill of a diplomatic illness. When you are in reasonably good health, there is a certain charm in the process of selecting which illness you are going, diplomatically speaking, to have. In earlier days the whole business was, I imagine, easy. If the worst came to the worst you could say you had brain fever—that undefined disease which so often hurried mysteriously to save the plots of so many Victorian novels. With the advance of modern medical science the thing becomes more difficult. In my experience, modern medical specialists do not worry unduly if you die, but they feel uneasy if they cannot record in some detail what you died of.

The more I studied possible diseases, the more difficult it became to find one which would really fill the bill. For, the moment I made public the news of my ailment, a posse of high-powered Communist Party doctors would be rushed to my assistance. I might even be offered a trip to a rest-home in the Crimea. And even if they failed to discover that there was nothing seriously wrong, in the end I should have to be cured, and perhaps offered some months of unexacting employment—in charge, perhaps, of the *Daily Worker* library, with permission to write one article a week about Fascist Tito, or Beria, watchdog of the Russian people.

At this point a miracle occurred. I had (a strange thing for me) been sleeping badly, and used to take sleeping pills occasionally. One day I asked a friend of mine who, although not a doctor, was a distinguished chemist, whether he could recommend a pill which would induce sleep but would not, at the same time, give me an agonizing stomach-ache at the moment of wakening.

He enquired about the pills I had been using, enquired about the stomach-aches and said, 'I will get you some pills, but what you have to do is to get in front of an X-ray. What you have is a pretty severe stomach ulcer. The symptoms are unmistakable.'

He explained about some ingredient in my pills which, if you happened to have stomach ulcer, touched it up and made you writhe.

It seemed too good to be true, but my friend fixed up an emergency X-ray for me in some laboratory, and when we got the pictures there it was—a genuine, entirely undiplomatic ulcer.

Just in case anyone thought this was a put-up job—which was of course exactly what everyone was going to think—I went to one of the big London hospitals and had another X-ray done there. The result was the same, and, this time, as it were, official. The doctor who told me the news was quite surprised. Possibly he had never before had the experience of telling a man he had a bad ulcer and seeing the man beam with pleasure and thank him warmly for the information.

In face of that neutral evidence, everyone agreed that a long rest was essential. I pointed out that as luck would have it I knew of a place which was ideal for the purpose.

In point of fact, Patricia, Alexander, and Andrew in his basket, had already flown to Ireland. The removals men had made preliminary arrangements for shifting as much of our furniture as had not been blown to bits in the house we had had before. And a few days later I was on the Fishguard-Cork boat, *en route* for the ancient town of Youghal, a town standing—like the poet Cavafy in E. M. Forster's description—'at a slight angle to the universe'.

12

In a far country

JUST once in a longish while you find you can write yourself an order for a pair of seven-league boots, and you travel
inhumanly far in next to no time. It is only eight hours or
thereabouts from Fishguard to Cork, but on the quay there
in Cork I knew at once what kind of boots I had on. For whatever a person feels about Ireland—likes it, loathes it, or it merely
blurs on him—it is a long way from England in all directions.
Here and there it is a little nearer to America, but is a long way
from there, too.

In the car to Youghal that day I re-lived the sensations of
being seventeen and travelling for the first time across Central
Europe. Not, evidently, that there is the slightest resemblance,
physically or otherwise, between Ireland and Central Europe. It
is simply the 'other-ness', the difference between this or that new
sort of life and whatever rut you have somehow jerked yourself
out of, which brightens the eye of the beholder. And you can be
in a dull rut at seventeen as easily as at forty-five.

There are people who deny that there is any essential difference between being in one place and being in another. They are
sincere. They use their seven-league boots without reference to
geography. They, perhaps, need only to take their 'first look into
Chapman's Homer' to travel far and fast. Myself, I have always
found that geography helps.

Long years before, I had been, so to speak, suspicious of
Ireland. There had been times when I had been inclined to
believe that the whole place, except just as a physical entity,
had been invented for the aid and comfort of philosophical
reactionaries, of the Roman Catholic Church, of the enemies of
dialectical materialism, of the mystical, of people equipped for
the modern world with a wide range of all-purpose whimsies.

I had been in the island only once before, about 1933 or 1934, and the experience though stimulating had been confusing. It had not done much to assure me that Ireland was in the known world at all.

I had gone to Belfast to report for the *Daily Worker* on some situation which had arisen there, and after a couple of days it was Saturday and I had nothing to do before catching the early afternoon train to Dublin. I volunteered to go out with other members of the organization selling the *Daily Worker* in the street. (In those days a great part of the distribution of the paper was done by volunteers.) They gave me a bundle of papers and I wandered off, finding myself after a while in the dock area. There were numerous rugged-looking proletarians in sight, and the prospect of sales seemed good. Shouting my wares, I approached a group of these workers, who, when they heard from afar what I was selling, turned to look at me with an interest which roused my keenest hopes.

About ten seconds later, I was made fully aware that they were certainly interested in a man selling the *Daily Worker* and what they wanted to do with him was throw him into the nearest expanse of deep, dirty water. I had to run fast and, in avoiding the deep water into which those hairy Orangemen wanted to throw me, I was forced to jump into an expanse of shallow dirty water and splash my way across it while they stood on the slip, cursing and deriding.

When I got back to the organization's headquarters I spoke with bitterness. The man in charge said, 'I suppose we should have warned you. That's a tricky area for us, just at the present time. You see those fellows think Communists and people connected with the *Worker* are somehow agents of the Pope.'

I took the train to Dublin, and got there that evening in time to attend a mass meeting of transport workers who were on strike, and their sympathizers. The meeting had been organized by the Communists, who were supposed to be 'behind' the strike, too. The time of the strike happened to coincide with that of the Roman Catholic 'Missions', and the Roman Catholic population had heard many exhortations against and denunciations of the Communists. About half-way through the meeting it was attacked by a compact mob, some of whose members had their faces masked with white scarves, and some carried open razors. They were singing 'God Bless our Pope'.

To my surprise, the stalwart transport workers dispersed almost without a struggle, just melted away. I found myself sheltering in a doorway with the secretary of the Communist Party. I complained. 'In London or Glasgow,' I said, 'people would have fought back. Why have they run away?'

'They've not run away at all,' he said. 'This is Dublin, and that's the military men going home to fetch their maps.'

He looked me over and saw that I was carrying a copy of the *Daily Worker*. 'I wouldn't display that carelessly just at the present time,' he said. 'Most people around this area think anyone with a *Daily Worker* must be an agent of anti-Christ.'

His warning came too late. A passing member of the attacking forces had spotted the paper and run down the street to get reinforcements. He thought probably that we were two look-out men for a big gang of Reds in the building behind. We saw the main body coming just in time, separated, and ran for it. I ran a long way until I was sure there was no razor close behind me, and then decided to go to the Communist headquarters—it was, as I recall, over a bookshop—and get the full story of whatever had happened or was thought to be going to happen.

I had been there talking and listening for but a few minutes when a man rushed in with the news that a huge mob bearing torches had formed in procession and was marching on the building. The same thing had happened once before, and the then Communist headquarters had been burned down.

There were a dozen of us in the place now, and my companions started grimly to barricade doors and windows with heavy tables, cupboards and chairs. The building itself, it could be seen, was mainly constructed of wood, and my instinct was to say that in my view the thing to do was to drop all that and get out of there as fast as we could go. On the other hand, I was the only non-Irishman present, and I could understand clearly enough, from the dedicated air of those around me, that to make such a suggestion would seem to them a low, materialistic, weaselly kind of thing to do—the sort of thing that might be expected from a non-Irish source. It would be a loss of face for Britain. So, feeling that perhaps after all the pattern of the universe contained a little bit somewhere where I was fried to a

crisp by Christian enthusiasts in a wooden house in Dublin, I
joined energetically in the task of barricading one set of pieces
of wood with another set. Wood, wood, I kept thinking. Everything in sight so combustible.

We had a dry-rotted sofa wedged pretty firmly against a dry-
rotted door, and there was plenty of light for our work from
the approaching torches, when a man came climbing through a
side window from the roof of some shed or outhouse.

He was a big man on the strike committee. More important
still, from my viewpoint, was that he was a Scotsman with an
Irish-sounding name, and I knew him well.

'And what,' said he, 'are you doing?'

My companions said that we were preparing to 'sell our lives
dearly'.

'Is the place,' said this newcomer, 'not insured?'

'It is,' said they.

'Then get the hell out,' said he. 'What in hell are we waiting
for?'

And as we crept across the roofs at the back of the house in
the fitful light of those torches I had occasion, not for the first
time, to thank heaven for that state of mind which carto-
graphers seek to define as Scotland.

Patricia, when I told it to her years later, much disliked that
story, feeling that, since the Scots seemed to come out of it
better than the Irish, I must have misunderstood what was happening, got the facts wrong. In course of time she had, certainly,
abated my suspicions of her country. She, after all, was a long
way from being a whimsical philosophical reactionary. And in
any case it was now, paradoxically, just that 'other-ness' of
Ireland, that fact of it standing at 'a slight angle to the universe',
which jolted and stimulated the mind. The question whether one
was 'in favour of' or 'approved' this or that aspect of Irish life
and activity did not arise at all. The point was that, right or
wrong, wise or silly, these things were not running along in the
ruts of British or American or European life. I felt what I had
felt talking with my Chinese friend in San Francisco—here was
a place where nothing was 'of course'.

We came into Youghal, running along beside the ocean
where the thrust of the Blackwater's current fights the Atlantic
tide. Here on the left, we had two neat new textile factories,

claimed to be the most up-to-date boxes of machinery in the
entire island, supervised technically by imported experts from
Lancashire. A few hundred yards up the road behind them are a
wishing-well and a magic tree where, surreptitiously, some
people still hang rags torn from their clothes as they did before
the Christians superseded the Druids. Some few hundred yards
farther up the same road is the site where, in Ireland's last war
with England, three men of the Irish Republican Army let off a
land mine under the first truck of a British column. They had
information that the truck was full of ammunition, but at the
last moment there had been a switch and some boys belonging
to the band were blown up instead.

At this end of town were the hotels, some with spacious
names like 'Pacific' and 'Marine', and one called, with scrupulous
honesty, 'Railway View'. It recalled a time when you could any
day see an ocean, and a big river full of salmon and bass, and
distant mountains, but to look straight out of the bedroom or
dining-room and see a railway station was a worthwhile
experience.

After that, the road narrowed to where the real Youghal lay,
longitudinally squeezed, between the river and the hill; a beautiful, gnarled town where history smells as strong as blood.

It took us six weeks to find a house for ourselves, and more
than two months to have it made habitable. For, as is natural in
a country which has lived in a state of colonialism for centuries,
there is a shortage of small country houses; everything seems
either too big, with hundreds of acres of land, or too small. And
for equally historical reasons many, many houses are derelict
People got poorer and poorer, or emigrated, leaving the house
to very poor relations, who could not afford to do otherwise
than let the roof cave in above them.

The house we found, on a hillside a mile and a half from the
town, had once been the summer residence of the Mayors of
Youghal. Why, with so small a town around them, they needed
a summer residence at all is not exactly known. It is supposed
that in hot summers the open sewers and gutters stank and were
deemed unhealthy. At other seasons, the house and its courtyard
were used for the collection of tribute from the country. The
tributary cattle were brought in and penned in the yard behind
a gate with powerful stone pillars. A little above the house there

was a square watch-tower. When I say 'was,' it is still there, like
the house, but in those days—the early sixteenth or late fifteenth
century—when the house and tower were built, the tower was
a look-out place for the soldiery who from there could give early
notice of any move by the natives to attack the place and
possibly recover their cattle by force of arms.

At right angles to this ancient house, which had thick, rough
stone walls and small windows and a general air of sturdy pre-
paredness for the worst, they built, in about 1740, another house,
on the spacious and elegant Georgian pattern, with wide windows twelve feet high in all the ground floor rooms. Through
doors on the ground floor or landing you step through a couple
of centuries from the old part of the house to the new.

For more than 130 years, the house was owned by some rich
Anglo-Irish named Drew. Then, one time in the latter half of
the nineteenth century, they began to smell something burning,
politically. Peasant revolt, or at least an outbreak here or there,
seemed imminent, and if it occurred here rather than there,
what was going to be the position about those huge windows?
Were they at all defensible against a determined attack by the
neighbours? It was judged that they were not, Thereupon the
Drews doggedly set to work to build something more adapted
to modern conditions of living. About half a mile away they
constructed a replica of a small mediaeval castle, with turrets
for observation of the enemy, very small windows, and slits to
shoot through or even, if it came to that, pour boiling oil
through. It took them over a year to build, and at the end of
that time they moved into it, abandoning their large rooms full
of light and air, and settling down in a posture of defence. They
had decided, in fact, that it was safer to live permanently in, as
it were, the air-raid shelter.

I said to Patricia that it seemed odd to take all that trouble.
Why, for instance, instead of building this other house, and
living—at least in their own estimation—in serious danger while
the building was going on, did they not go somewhere else; to
England, for example? Patricia was surprised. 'Well,' she said,
'for one thing, if they'd gone to England they wouldn't have
known any of the neighbours.'

When we found it, the house, or rather a corner of it, was
occupied by an aged man in a rusty black cutaway coat and a

stetson-type hat who gave the impression that he had worked in some capacity on the Mississippi river in the nineties. And he had, as a matter of fact, been a travelling salesman in Cincinatti. He was an energetic old man of great goodwill, but he was in no position to prop up the house. He lived, for the most part, in one room, where the ceiling was still intact, seated under an enormous crucifix, studying sacred books in Latin. The lower part of the house was invaded, not by neighbours now, but by fowl of many kinds, and sometimes by cows.

Very soon after we had taken the house, he died, and for a while it was hard to get anyone to work late around the place on account of his ghost. I never saw it myself, although I do not, in principle, disbelieve in ghosts. But I have never been able to understand why it is still so very generally supposed that ghosts are malign and therefore alarming. If the person who has now become a ghost was benign in life, why should he be sinister on his *post mortem* appearance? I used to argue thus with one or two of the workmen who seemed distressed at the thought of the old man possibly wandering about the passages. I convinced no one, and I think they probably supposed I was making up all this stuff about benign ghosts for the purpose of getting them to work overtime. There are, of course, explanations for this alarmed attitude towards the dead, to be found in many mythologies. What is odd is only that this fear should almost universally triumph over any other feeling about ghosts. Some ghosts are naturally terrifying. At Lep Castle in Ireland there is a ghost of a headless sheep which stinks horribly. A dog, confined for the night in the room haunted by the sheep, went out of its mind and jumped through the window to its death.

We were just settling into the house when an unpleasant thing happened. The U S Senate Committee on Un-American activities, or some cognate body, issued its list of the two or three hundred most dangerous Reds in the world, and included my name. It seemed an uncomfortable thing to have happen to one in the heart of Catholic, passionately anti-Communist, Ireland.

There was, obviously, a way to appease everyone—namely by taking this American attack as a peg from which to hang a violent renunciation and denunciation of the Communists and all their works. But this, as I have said earlier, was a thing which

I felt it would be both dishonest and undignified to do. I did not think that anything would justify anyone saying things that would be quoted with approval by, say, Senator McCarthy, and I am happy to say that nobody I knew even suggested that I should, though an action of that sort on my part would have made life rather easier for my Irish friends and acquaintances as well as for myself.

To make any worthwhile statement or generalization about just how 'tolerant' or 'intolerant' is the 'climate of opinion' in the Irish Republic, you would need to spend years and years getting the evidence—and at that you would probably find at the end of it all that you had done grave injustice to some man who felt himself spiritually or economically hounded and persecuted, or else to some nobly fair-minded Roman Catholic priest.

It is, however, factual, I should suppose, to state that if I had been living in a village in Bohemia at the time when, a year or more later, the Czechoslovak Government denounced me as a sinister organizer of the western Intelligence Services and arrested several score people in Prague for the crime of having once met and talked with me, I should have been subjected to a lot more inconvenience than I was in Youghal after that Senatorial denunciation.

Indeed in Youghal I was subjected to no more inconvenience than a dubious look here and there, and eager looks from those who felt that a certain amount of drama had been injected into the situation. The way I like garlic, the Irish like drama. It is no use people telling me that too much garlic spoils some food; I daresay they are right, but I have never been able to get too much garlic, and mostly not enough. The Irish seem to feel that it is hard to get enough drama. Presence of a dangerous Red provides drama, regardless of what you feel about this subversive fellow personally. I am sure there are many people who would rather have a murderer in town, to observe and talk about, than a person who provided no food for thought and conversation.

One or two little informers had an unusually good time. They would sit in the secret 'snug' which almost all Irish bars have, taking note of my conversation with these and those in the public bar. It gave them a justification, one might say, for their existence.

C.T.L.—N

With no harm done to me, the plot and conspiracy of which I might be the centre kept going for months—even for a couple of years. It was the Freemasons who formed the hitherto missing link. Personally, I have never been sure whether there are any Freemasons in Youghal at all. But, as I have remarked before, every politician and every political or religious organization needs a Devil. In a country where there is only the tiniest minority of Protestant opposition to the Roman Catholic Church, a Devil is more necessary than usual. It must be that, though the Protestants are few in numbers, and outwardly weak, yet they have a power of secret organization, through the Freemasons, which renders them nevertheless a menace. There were said to be four of these menacing Freemasons in Youghal. At one period of my life in that town, it was noted by alert people in search of drama that sometimes a certain well-known Protestant would meet me in the street, draw me discreetly aside, and press into my hand a document or documents. It was fairly evident what was happening. This Protestant, clearly, must be an agent of the Freemasons. The Freemasons, of course, were using the whole Protestant Church as a front organization. But who was using the Freemasons as a front organization? Unquestionably the Kremlin. And here was Mr Cockburn, attested Kremlin agent, getting from this go-between reports from the Freemasons on how the evil work was progressing.

I could almost have wished it had been so. For, as I pointed out when I heard the story, the 'go-between'—though he certainly was the sexton of the Protestant Church—was also the local process-server. He handed out the writs to people who were being sued and were supposed to appear in court. Those were the documents which, as a result of high expenses and low earnings during our first year or two in Ireland, he all too often had to press, as discreetly as possible, into my hand.

Being true, and susceptible of demonstration, this explanation of mine was annoying to many. It knocked a piece of drama right out of the middle of the situation.

For a long time, the only people who seemed at all seriously interested in my real or imagined activities were the people at the Special Branch of the Criminal Investigation Department at Scotland Yard—or perhaps their interest was prodded by M I 5. That was all natural enough—it is the business of people in such organizations not to believe in the existence of the needle unless someone has obviously tried to hide it in a haystack. It would have been very little use seeking to persuade them that even in this day and age it is not impossible that a man may decide that there is something unsatisfactory about his way of life, decide, therefore, to quit the *Daily Worker* and the Communist Party, and take up some other form of activity. I used to hear a good deal about their interest in me from some members of the Garda in Cork whom I knew. Once, one of these men asked me if I would be good enough to step round to the Garda barracks in Cork and give them a little help. I need not, of course, he said, answer any questions, but it would be kind of me to do so.

It then appeared that a query, I gathered of a pressing nature, had come from Scotland Yard. The Yard, was aware, said the message, that I had recently travelled to London, and that I had travelled by boat and rail from Cork via Fishguard to Paddington. So far so good. But by what means, the Yard wanted to know, had I travelled the thirty miles from Youghal to Cork?

The Cork men said, rather apologetically, that naturally they liked to do their opposite numbers at Scotland Yard a good turn when they could. Furthermore, they supposed that by instituting wide enquiry in Youghal, they might be able to find out whether, on that day a month or so ago, I had taken the train, or the bus, or had hired a car—or perhaps been driven to Cork by a friend.

I said I would try hard to remember, and would they in the meantime be thinking what particular form of mania could have induced the people in London to make such an enquiry at all.

I thought and thought, but could not for the life of me recall what vehicle I had used for that journey. And they thought and thought, and could not for the life of them conceive why Scotland Yard should give a damn what sort of vehicle it was. Could they suppose I had a secret aeroplane?

As one of the Gardai said, 'Isn't it just awe-inspiring to think of all those fellows over there worrying about did you take the bus or the train? They've always told me your police are wonderful.'

In view of all this, it occurred to me some time later to ask Mr Erskine Childers, then Irish Minister of Posts and Telegraphs, whether my telephone was tapped in Ireland as it always had been in England. The moment I had asked the quesiton I thought perhaps it had not been in the best possible taste to introduce shop talk of this kind at that time and place. The time was about four in the morning, and the place a champagne bar in a huge tent in a deep glen of the Wicklow mountains where a very fine party was in progress to celebrate the twenty-first birthday of our hostess's eldest son.

However, Mr Childers seemed to think my question natural enough. He said he thought no, my telephone was not tapped. He said he had a list of tapped numbers somewhere, and anxiously slapped the back pockets of his tail-coat in a gesture of exquisite courtesy, as though to indicate that he had indeed been remiss in not carrying the list about in his dress-clothes in case of meeting someone who wanted to know was he on it or not. 'I don't remember ever seeing your name,' he said earnestly. 'There *is* a small group of homosexuals in Tipperary that the Guards are keeping a very careful eye on. But I don't think they're worrying about you.'

He had his back to the tent's entrance and, as he said these words, did not see, as I did, a two-seater sports car being driven furiously from the lawn outside into the tent, the driver shouting threats of death and destruction to all. Although fortunately checked by the edge of the dancing-floor, raised a few inches above the lawn, the car, at reduced speed, came on, and seemed likely to mow down everyone standing by the champagne bar. I leapt at Mr Childers and dragged him aside with such violence that we both almost toppled to the ground, and I felt sure that in that instant he was reflecting that it might have been more prudent to have kept a closer eye on me, too.

As things turned out, few were hurt by the angry man in the car, though many were dismayed by the occurrence, and in particular the members of the Garda who had turned out in considerable force to police the affair, and done so efficiently, but had, understandably it seemed to me, not taken any special precautions against one of the guests using his car as a projectile against the others. Looking over the situation in the first light of dawn, the head of the local Guards said to me, 'D'you know what it takes to deal with modern life, Mr Cockburn?'

I said I did not.

'It takes,' said he, 'the brains of Gladstone and the balls of a Munster Fusilier.'

It was a sage statement, and you felt that these symbols of supreme intellectual and physical powers could hardly be bettered.

Despite the interest of Scotland Yard, it was happily nearly a year before I heard the voice of London demanding a public statement of what I was up to. It interrupted a conversation I was having with my father-in-law about Sir Roger Casement.

Across a couple of pages of a recent biography of Sir Roger Casement fleets the figure of 'a certain Major Arbuthnot', offering as he does so a glimpse of what emerges as one of the few humane characters on stage during the savage last act of that terrifying melodrama.

He was my wife's father and it was in his house in Youghal, where Raleigh used to live and Spenser wrote part of the *Faerie Queen*, that we had previously stayed for some months while we looked for a house of our own. And as I came to know the Major well, I had come to feel that luck, which had played so many dirty tricks on Casement, had, at the very last moment, at least tried to proffer Casement a consolation prize by arranging for this civilised man to appear.

The biography tells how, when the friends and relatives of Casement are being driven from pillar to post, unable to force from the wooden-faced bureaucrats, some stupid, some sadistic, some ignorant, even where the prisoner is being kept, this 'certain Major' suddenly comes on to the scene, tells them where Casement is—namely in the Tower—and tells them, as a matter of urgency, that before they think of politics or the legal position or anything else, they must get him new clothes. Casement in the Tower was wearing the same clothes in which he had set out in the submarine from Germany, and the Major had that kind of simple human intuition which reminds you that there are times when a change of clothes can be more important to a man than patriotic fervour or the prospect of death.

As a Major of the Scots Guards, doing a turn of duty at the Tower, Major Arbuthnot was in personal charge of Casement. He was the genuine kind of High Tory who believes that orders and regulations and forms in triplicate are probably all very well for keeping the machine running, and preventing other people from getting out of hand, but should be ignored by people like himself if they happen to interfere in any way with what seems to him good to do at the time.

There were strict orders from on high that no one, not even of his closest relatives, was to be allowed to interview Casement without the presence of the officer on duty. Political plotting was feared. But Major Arbuthnot was, so to speak, socially conditioned against paying much attention to those 'on high'— particularly if they happened to be, in his far from humble opinion, a lot of incompetent and probably corrupt politicians on the make. His chief interest in them was to wonder how on earth they had got there, and since his view of politics was that of an eighteenth-century landowner, the answer came to him in one word—jobbery.

Thus, when the relatives of Casement begged for a little time alone with him, the Major broke all regulations and granted the request.

Some of Casement's last hours after his condemnation and before his execution were occupied in conversation with this same Major who, partly because to do so was, for him, artistically irresistible, and partly to ease the loathsome relationship of prisoner and warder, spent the time making a portrait of the doomed Casement, and discussing it with him in a manner to suggest that after all there are more interesting things in life for civilized men to think about than the circumstance of one of them getting hanged for alleged treason.

It seemed to me when Major Arbuthnot told me about it—I had noticed the Casement portrait on the wall of the library at Myrtle Grove where we were sitting—one of the few alleviating episodes in an otherwise wholly horrible series of events. But despite the interest of the story, I have to admit that my attention was a little distracted by the fact that all the time on a table beside us was lying a telephone receiver through which a distant voice at intervals clacked, screeched and seemed to implore.

I suppressed my curiosity about the disregarded telephone receiver until the end of the Casement story, but at length asked the Major whether he noticed that the receiver was off the cradle and that someone seemed wishful to talk with him?

'Oh that,' he said comfortably, 'that's the *Daily Express* office in London. They rang up an hour or so ago wanting me to tell them whether you had joined the Roman Catholic Church. They thought, too, I might supply them with some comments on my son-in-law, the formerly notorious ex-Red. Awfully intrusive.'

Although he could affect, at a moment's notice, the attitude of the aloof aristocrat who hardly knows what a newspaper is, and in any case deplores the existence of 'the popular press,' Major Arbuthnot had, in point of fact, once worked on a part-time basis for the *Daily Express*. At that time, shortly before the death of a relative who later left him a quarter of a million, but was taking some time about it, he found himself rather pressed for money. He was a friend of Mr Blumenfeld, the Managing Editor of the *Express*, and, from discussion between them and (I suppose) many others, emerged the notion of the original *Beachcomber* column. The Major was, I think, the first *Beachcomber* —at any rate he edited and to a large extent wrote the column at an early period, when it had the character of a humorous column of satire and gossip.

Unlike most people today, he believed in the reality of unearned income as something to be relied upon, but felt uneasy about earnings. He thought that once you were in the position of earning money—except of course in the Army or Navy— 'they' would somehow contrive to do you out of your pay. He therefore made an arrangement with Mr Blumenfeld that his money was to be paid in cash as soon as each *Beachcomber* column was completed. He would finish the column, collect the money from the cashier, and get a taxi to Paddington where, on the days when he was working in Fleet Street, he had a special train awaiting him so that he could be sure to reach Windsor in time to go on guard duty at the Castle.

He had also, since 1912, been a regular contributor to the *Morning Post*, so that his pretended astonishment at the 'intrusiveness' of journalists was not very convincing.

He was, however, genuinely anxious to save me from annoyance. And as one who knew something of the newspaper business it pleased him to think of the face of the man at the other end of the telephone. When they had first rung him up he had expressed enthusiasm—asked them just to hang on while he went and fetched his 'notes', speaking of these non-existent notes in a manner which suggested that for months past, ever since my arrival, he had been assembling some very juicy comments on me. Then he had simply laid down the receiver, pottered about the garden, and finally returned to talk with me about Casement.

The Dublin correspondent of the *Express* had, as a matter of fact, already rung me up—also wishing to know whether I had been received into the Roman Catholic faith or was aiming to be so received. News editors have an occupational tendency to believe that anything that has recently happened is due to happen again, and since two prominent Communist journalists, one in New York and the other in London, had walked out of Communism into Roman Catholicism, they thought I must be going to do the same thing. Also, no doubt, they were victims of the widespread popular fallacy that there is some mysterious affinity between the Roman Catholic Church and the Communist Party. Just what this affinity is supposed to be I have never been able to ascertain, unless it be the existence, in both organizations, of a certain discipline—a fact apparently so alarming and sensational to some that it overshadows everything else.

I had been on the, so to speak, intrusive end of the telephone often enough to know that if you give a good newspaperman an inch he is capable of giving you half a column of hell, so I told the Dublin correspondent 'No comment, no story.' Nevertheless, he insisted that he should drive the 150 miles or so from Dublin to see me. I urged him, as one newspaperman to another, to consider whether he would be able to justify the expense account, and he said the London office was crazy about the story and he thought he had better come on down.

The Major finally put the receiver on its cradle and we went and sat in the pond garden, confident that if they rang again and the eloquent Irish butler answered it the resulting confusion would be enough to baffle even the skilled men of the *Daily Express*.

But in the town that afternoon I was suddenly cornered by the Dublin correspondent with two cars—the second of them a Dublin taxicab filled with a photographer and his apparatus. The correspondent proved to be a very nice man indeed and when, after some drinks off the record, he said it was a pity that I still kept saying 'No comment, no story', I began to feel badly about his expense sheet.

I cautiously amplified my remarks, and in exchange for my mild co-operation he agreed to let me off the photographer. Unfortunately this photographer was tremendously keen and energetic, and possibly had had a slight overdose of American newspaper films and seemed to think that he was being done out of his big moment. He pretended to agree to the 'no pictures' arrangement, but lurked. And when the correspondent went off to Dublin the photographer pursued me up hill and down dale.

I ducked him, and reached my house by a secret route, but a half-hour later heard imprecations and general uproar. Rushing to an upper window I saw that a girl who at that time worked with us had suddenly espied the keen young man squatting in semi-concealment just inside the back gate, his camera trained on the house. With a vague idea that he must be up to no good —invasion of landed privacy by vulgar Anglo-Saxon press, perhaps—she had snatched up a pitchfork which chanced to be resting against the stable wall, and charged.

I was alarmed, partly because I thought it might be disadvantageous for me if the *Express* got a picture of my landed privacy being defended with a pitchfork, and partly for the more altruistic reason that I knew, as the photographer did not, that she was a powerful athlete and if she got anywhere near him with that pitchfork he was done for.

I yelled so loud that he retreated just in time. He continued however to lurk in the roadway until moved on by a local Garda who knew nothing of newspapers and cared less, and supposed him to be loitering with intent.

I was happy to see later that the Dublin correspondent had got enough material to sweeten his expense account. It filled the William Hickey column, and made me sound fairly mysterious, without being embarrassing.

It made my house sound rather bigger than it really was, my whole establishment more imposing. And I much admired whoever wrote the column for being, I should say, the first man who ever made a bicycle sound a shade sinister. 'For transport to Youghal,' he wrote, 'Mr Cockburn rides a bicycle.' In the context, the reader might well wonder what sort of a blind this was. Perhaps behind those mysterious walls lurked an armoured Mercedes, not to be used 'for transport to Youghal' but for some less avowable purpose.

C.T.L.—O

13

Something new

IN a fable of R. L. Stevenson, the old man says to the young man, 'Why are you weeping?' 'I am weeping for my sins,' says the young man. Months later, they meet again, and the young man is still weeping. 'Why are you weeping now?' asks the old man. 'I am weeping because I have nothing to eat.' 'I thought it would come to that,' says the old man.

The first task, not easy, was to prevent it coming to that. We had reached the island and 'the natives,' as explorers say, 'were friendly.' But from where we sat, it looked as though it would be a hard climb to reach the essential coconuts. During my long years as a 'red' political journalist, all other connections with the journalistic and literary world had slowly but inevitably broken down. And it was not difficult to surmise that if I now appeared waving some kind of new leaf and asking to be paid to write on it, there would be considerable askance-looking by many. Every agent, publisher and Editor will truthfully tell you how import-ant it is to build up a name. But the two names I had built up reeked of politics and subversion. It was necessary to act as though one were twenty-one years old, just down from Oxford, and trying to break into, as the saying goes, the writing game.

(The only alternative was to write the familiar 50,000 words entitled 'My fifteen years in a Snakepit' which would certainly shake the coconut trees but would be otherwise undesirable. '*Nec propter vitam vivendi perdere causas,*' my father used to quote from Juvenal when the possibility from time to time arose of doing something lucrative but distasteful. It had been, as I recall, a somewhat alarming principle for his dependants—we thought that once in a while we would not mind seeing him taking a chance on losing the 'reasons for living' and just live.)

Salvation came in the shape of Mr Richard Bennett, at that

time editor of the monthly magazine *Lilliput*. He liked my writing, and had no political inhibitions. At the same time, he and I
believed—we may, of course, have been wrong—that some
backward individual on the business side of *Lilliput*, might
not like to have a person of my background writing for their
paper. I became Kenneth Drew. The necessity for writing pseu-
donymously became still more apparent after I had made some
financial calculations and reckoned that, at the rate *Lilliput* paid
in those days, I would need to get at least two pieces into the
magazine every month, and sometimes more. Without cast-iron
pseudonyms that was going to raise a lot of eyebrows.

So I was not only Kenneth Drew but James Helvick and a man
called Patrick Cork and, I seem to remember, Hector Hamish or
somebody of similar name, and a couple of others as well. Coconuts thudded down, sparsely but just adequately. Later, Hulton
Press launched a new weekly called *Leader*, which was understood to be going to revolutionize British weekly journalism, and
Drew—I think it was he—wrote a long series of articles for it.
It was a good paper, and I dare say it would have revolutionized
British journalism if given the chance.

But one of the curses of contemporary British journalism is
the increasing power and influence of a lot of people who know
nothing about journalism, but have persuaded numerous proprietors and shareholders that they are in possession of statistical
gadgets and Geiger counters which, properly read, reel off the
news of what the public wants. They conduct polls. They make
surveys of 'representative groups'. They dip their thermometers
into the water as assiduously as attendants at a thermal bath.
Then they go to the proprietors or the advertising managers and
report that three per cent. of men earning more than £1,800
annually are allergic to science fiction, or crazy to read more
about yachting or love. Naturally they get the right answer some
of the time, though no more often than people using common
sense and intuition instead of statistics and polls. But since everyone has an eerie awareness that he does not really know what
the public wants, anyone who appears with a definitive and
didactic statement on the subject is reassuring.

The result, all too often, is a kind of paralysis of the editorial
will. An editor has no business to be worrying himself sick about
what the public wants. He should be thinking about perfecting

and producing what he wants and then making the public want it, too. The contrary principle can produce a situation like that existing at the kind of 'progressive' school where nobody tells the boys and girls what they ought to be at, and these pupils live in a confusing and, ultimately, mind-destroying vacuum—no orders, no order, no standards, no compulsive framework, no guidance, but instead a lot of pestering questions from teachers, designed to ascertain whether the pupils would like more cinematography in the curriculum, or would prefer that more time be given to Physics, Old English or Advanced Salesmanship.

Somebody proved that *Leader* was appealing to the wrong income groups, so that despite the energy and ability of its Editor, Sydney Jacobson, who fought hard to save the paper from needless extinction, and to give it at least a fighting chance, I learned in Ireland that there were not going to be any next six months— they were folding it up immediately.

In Fleet Street today this kind of thing is going on all the time —not necessarily in the extreme form of closing an entire paper on the strength of the statistical men's thermometer readings— but in terms of intrusion by these figure-stuffed bath attendants upon editorial responsibility. They tend to unnerve the editor as he tries to get on with the real job of giving the public the courage of his convictions.

A guest at my house wrote, at this time, in the visitors' book, a description of what he called the Literary Colony at Youghal. He claimed to have met Frank Pitcairn, ex-correspondent of the *Daily Worker*—a grouchy, disillusioned type secretly itching to dash out and describe a barricade. There was Claud Cockburn, founder and editor of *The Week*, talkative, boastful of past achievements, and apt, at the drop of a hat, to tell, at length, the inside story of some forgotten diplomatic crisis of the 1930's. Patrick Cork would look in—a brash little number, and something of a professional Irishman, seeking, no doubt to live up to his name. James Helvick lived in and on the establishment, claiming that he needed quiet together with plenty of good food and drink to enable him to finish a play and a novel which soon would bring enough money to repay all costs. In the background, despised by the others as a mere commercial hack, Kenneth Drew hammered away at the articles which supplied the necessities of the colony's life.

Theoretically, the slow building of contacts and mending of fences required at least four or five visits to London each year, but it was evident that such visits often resulted in an expense of £100 to earn £150. Besides, I did not want to go to London more than was absolutely necessary, and when I did so always returned to Ireland with a sense of elation and relief as the boat docked or the plane landed. At that time I found it difficult to communicate with English people, more difficult than usual. Ireland, for all its 'other-ness' and its moments of fantasy, had begun to seem more real, or at least more intelligible, than England.

While Drew was keeping things afloat with his articles, I—as James Helvick—did in fact write a play and send it to Patrick Hamilton who telegraphed warm praise and took it to a leading manager. I was all for dashing to London and talking to the man about it, but Mr Hamilton's advice was not to 'rush things'. This not rushing took a couple of months, during which it was understood that, although nothing seemed to be actually happening, things were going well. At the beginning of the summer I had to be in London and twice had a drink with this manager, and it was deemed that at our next meeting I might venture to mention the play. Mr Hamilton told me a discouraging story about a playwright who had been forced to live, night and day for nearly two years in the bar at Claridge's because this manager had talked with him there and said, 'For heaven's sake don't move until you hear from me.'

All winter there was a crisis in the theatre, and to rush things just then would have been more fatal than ever. But there came a day when Mr Hamilton was going to stay with the manager for a golfing week-end in Surrey. He was going to take the script of my play in his golf bag. I was in London for a couple of days, and at about five on the Saturday afternoon Mr Hamilton was on the telephone from some outlying part of the managerial home to report that the game had been fine, the manager was in a good mood, receptive. Half an hour later the news was that the manager was lying on a sofa in the living-room with a drink beside him and the script actually *on his lap*. On a rug. 'On,' I said, 'or under?' Mr Hamilton dashed back to the living-room to make sure.

Presently the telephone communicated the terrific piece of

intelligence that the man was actually reading the script and had twice audibly exclaimed, 'This is bloody good stuff.'

As a result, the manager sent the script to his chief reader, whose report I saw. It said that the play was fine, very funny dialogue, an original situation, bound to appeal to the stalls and make money. I was back in Ireland when I heard this, and in our house there were rejoicings. Indeed, we bought a rather expensive hunter on the strength of it, and I went off to London again to see the manager.

He was geniality itself—the play was very funny, and his reader thought so too.

I was just starting a little speech saying how glad I was that he was taking it because there was no theatrical management in London I admired more, when he mentioned that of course it was not by any means the kind of play he was looking for at the moment—good, but not what he wanted. As I was leaving the room he came all the way round his desk to clasp my hand. It was very moving. With his disengaged hand he picked up a brown-paper backed copy of some play by somebody else, and said, 'I want you to have that.' I supposed I looked confused, stunned by the grandeur of the gesture. 'I mean,' he said 'I am giving it to you to keep.'

I thought of the new hunter now faced, like the other horses, with imminent starvation, and took my play to another manager. He congratulated me on a fine play with very amusing dialogue. I was just saying I was so glad he, of all people, was going to put it on because there was no management in London I admired more, when he remarked that, fine as it was, it was not at all the kind of thing he was looking for just at the moment. As I was leaving, he gave me two stalls for a play he had on.

A part of the next few months was spent in getting to know a Mr X in whose judgment Mr Y, the great theatrical manager, had implicit faith. 'If X likes it,' they said, 'you're home and dry.' Mr X said it was wonderful, very amusing dialogue, and then went to hospital for some weeks. When X came out, Mr Y, overstrained by having had to carry on without Mr X's judgment, had a nervous breakdown and went to hospital for some weeks. When he came out, Mr X said he would give him the play to read, but without mentioning his own opinion; he wanted Y's unbiased judgment, in which he had implicit faith. Mr Y read it and said it was fine, but he did not care to do anything about it unless he could have X's opinion. But X unfortunately had gone to the United States on an extended trip. Y went on to talk appreciatively of the nerve hospital where he had been, and I dare say if I had stayed with him a little longer he would have told me not to hesitate to use his name if ever I felt the need of accommodation there.

I thought that while awaiting further developments on the theatrical front, and keeping Kenneth Drew's nose to the grindstone, I might get somewhere by taking one theme from the play and turning it into a novel, *Beat The Devil*, by, of course, James Helvick. By the time the novel was written and published in Britain and the United States, it could certainly be said that things were definitely not going so well.

Our house in Ireland began to look more and more as though it had been invented by Somerville and Ross. Since we had not yet finished paying for the earlier structural repairs we could scarcely get the contractor to embark on a new series. Odd job men did their best, but the task was too great to be handled on a 'do-it-yourself' basis, and rain poured through the roof and ceilings.

The sexton-process-server, supposed link between Cominform and Freemasonry, was out to see me repeatedly. And the men wandering about the grounds were not guests or employees, but sheriff's officers, mentally pricing the horses and threatening to drive them off and sell them.

By great good luck, we decided that since there appeared to be nothing we could immediately do about this situation, the sensible thing to do was to let the process-server and the Sheriff's men carry on as best they could, and accept an invitation to stay, for the Dublin Horse Show week, with Lady Oranmore at her house in the Wicklow mountains. It was a big house party, and my pleasure was particularly great when I heard that my old friend Mr John Huston, film director, was coming.

He arrived in Dublin very late one night, and joined our party at a Hunt Ball there. At about four o'clock or five o'clock in the morning, around the time people start stripping to the waist and jumping off the balconies blowing hunting horns, I started to talk to Mr Huston about my novel. At such a time, I was well aware, Mr Huston would prefer to talk, for instance, about horses in their many aspects : things to hunt foxes on, things to put your money on.

However, he is a volatile man and I was afraid he might suddenly get a telephone call from Beverly Hills and fly off to Hollywood before anyone was awake after the ball.

Something of the kind nearly did happen a day or two later, because after he had promised to read it I found I had forgotten to bring a copy with me. At the last moment I found, and rudely snatched back, a copy which I had recently inscribed, in terms of the sincerest admiration and affection, to our hostess. She said it seemed rather sad to have been in possession of a tribute like that for such an unexpectedly short time, but surrendered the book for the good of the cause. Then I seemed to remember that Mr Huston—when travelling without benefit of secretary— might very likely lose just one copy. Just as he was leaving for the airport, I found that there was another copy in the house— warmly inscribed to Mr Terence Kilmartin. He, too, acted for the good of the cause, and I threw the two copies into Mr Huston's car as it started up the driveway.

Mr Huston is a good friend and proved it when he started to read the book the moment he got to London. Two days later I had a guarded message from his secretary to say that he was so absorbed in it that he had had a bad fall as a result of reading it while walking down stairs.

A week later he was back in Dublin. Mr Huston is one of those blessed men who, if they like your work, say so clearly and repeatedly. Such men know that, like Wilde, an author can stand any amount of flattery provided it is gross enough. Nor was his praise inhibited by any niggling fear that he was putting the price up. His own affairs were, as I understood it, in a considerable financial tangle at the time—it was, I think, just before the enormous gamble he had taken on *African Queen* paid off. He and Humphrey Bogart had a company called Santana which could buy the film rights of the book and arrange major financing for it afterwards. He said there was an ideal part for Bogart in *Beat The Devil*.

Thinking of my experiences with the theatrical managers, I imagined that about now there would be a long pause during which, for weeks on end, nothing would happen of a character satisfactory to creditors and Sheriffs. Our enthusiastic conversation took place at breakfast in Dublin. While I was talking to his wife, he was scribbling something. It was, I found a little later, a long cable to Mr Bogart in Hollywood, speaking in glowing terms of the book, advising him to buy the American edition instantly, and assuring him that in Huston's opinion they should buy the rights immediately too.

Partly for the purpose of talking about the possibilities of the screen play, partly because he wanted to ride in new country, we arranged that the Hustons should come down to Youghal at once and stay with us for a couple of weeks. From Mr Huston's hotel room, I rang up our home. The number was unobtainable. I became flustered. Mr Huston sat on the bed, watching me with sardonic sympathy.

'It's happened to all of us before,' he said softly.

He was the kind of man who knew from experience how easy it can be to run into a situation where the authorities cut off your telephone on account of the payments being long overdue.

At Youghal we had to keep our hats on part of the time as we talked about the screenplay, because of the leaks in the roof. Meantime, the local post office was handling some of the longest telegrams seen in those parts since the Easter Rising—cables between there and Beverly Hills. Finally a firm offer came—for a larger sum of money than I had seen for a very long time indeed, if ever.

'Look,' Huston said, 'this is a firm offer, but in Hollywood terms it isn't so damn big. Not so damn big at all. If you hang on, and especially if the book goes well in America, you can get three or four times that figure.'

I said, thinking of many phases of his career and of my own, 'Listen, we've both of us known times when ten dollars, cash on the barrelhead, now, is worth a whale of a lot more than a hundred the week after next.'

'If it's like that,' said Mr Huston—and considering the drip, drip from the roof it was not very difficult to note that it was just like that—'what are we waiting for?'

If the hunters and ponies had known what was happening they would have danced in their stalls.

Mr Huston's purchase provided a breathing-space, a space for contemplation of the world at hand, and for experimental writing and, so to speak, writing drill, or practice, having the same purpose as that of a person learning the piano and playing scales on it. For me, after that long spell of polemical propaganda and high-pitched reporting, this type of practice was particularly necessary for the purpose of loosening the joints, strengthening muscles grown flabby from disuse, and improving the ear.

I went on, of course, writing articles and wrote, too, another novel—*Overdraft on Glory*. It was on a theme which had teased and entertained me for years and years, ever since, just after Lindbergh's Atlantic flight, I had attended preparations for the first, and even more dangerous East-West flight. Only one journalist was permitted after all had drawn lots—to go on the flight. The chosen one, whom I knew well, was, at that time, living in a swirl and welter of romantic and sexual complications. Until the moment when his name was drawn out of the hat, it had appeared that some disastrous explosion must be going to take place any minute. A wife or a girl or another girl would shoot herself, or some other terrible scandal would occur and the man's career would be ruined. But now the position dramatically changed. Within a few hours, this journalist was either going to be illuminated by a blaze of glory, world-famous as the first journalist to fly the Atlantic, or else—as seemed to most observers more probable—he was going to be dead in the Atlantic ocean. In face of that awe-inspiring situation, how could anyone be so petty as to permit the final hours before the event to be marred by merely personal passions? In an exhilarating mood of exaltation and apprehension, all three of the young women concerned in the matter forgave one another, forgave the intrepid man. They not only forgave one another everything, they each confessed to things the others had never heard about. Then they forgave one another for these things too.

It was uplifting, and it reached a noble climax in the bar at the airport during the last hour or so before the plane was due to take off. Glory, in life or posthumously, was assured, and it shone benevolently on all, transfiguring them. At length the plane was ready. Final farewells. A couple of hair-raising last-minute confessions from our death-or-glory man. The plane left. The rest of us went back to the bar for a little more champagne, and all raised their voices in assurance of their love and esteem for one another and the hero. We had been there not more than an hour or so when a strange rumour swept the airport. It became a certainty. The plane making the transatlantic attempt had been forced to turn back. Serious engine trouble. It landed. I could hardly bear to watch my friend as he stepped out on to the tarmac and back into this appalling situation. But perhaps it was only a brief delay? Death or glory might still be swiftly achieved? Not so. The technicians reported a radical defect—it would take weeks to find out just what it was, and weeks more to correct it, if it ever could be corrected.

In the years since witnessing that episode, which had all the terrifying character of true farce, I had seen the pattern repeated over and over again: sometimes farcically, sometimes comically, sometimes even tragically. Wars, of course, reproduce it continuously. People think they are on embarkation leave and then the battalion stays in England after all. Not always a matter for relief. Or, on a nobler plane, a man renounces all to enter a monastery and then finds the monastery will not admit him. The pattern repeats itself on a great number of levels.

I enjoyed writing that book, which got a few 'rave' reviews in Britain and the United States and then flopped like a shot duck. I agreed with those critics who had acclaimed it, but I had to admit that my five-finger exercises had evidently not been carried out strenuously enough. I had failed to convey to most people, including most of the critics, just what air I was trying to play.

An Irish neighbour, to whom I had mentioned that, so far as sales were concerned, the book had been pretty much of a failure, made a heartening remark. 'The way to look at it,' said he, 'is to think what a wonderful thing it is for anyone living in the soporific air of the Blackwater Valley to complete a book at all—any book, good, bad or indifferent. It is amazing to have kept awake long enough to do it.'

He spoke with earnest sincerity and admiration for my achievement.

'Look,' he added, 'at Edmund Spenser. Walter Raleigh had him to stay with him in Youghal here to write the *Faerie Queen*. How much of it did he get done? A few score lines only, so far as anyone knows. Then he took to sleeping longer and longer, and in the end had to get out of the place before he could even begin on the other umpteen thousand verses.'

Apart from the lulling climate of that lovely valley, there are other factors which sometimes seem to make writing in the country more arduous, more of a strain on the brain and emotions than in the city. What it amounts to is that part of the time the writer in the country is subjected to a series of interruptions—like alarms of foot-and-mouth disease, fences falling down, or a catastrophic drop in the market price of turkeys—which in the city do not impinge. From these, it is true, I was to a very large extent protected by Patricia who, in addition to being an expert with horses and turning a wilderness of scutch grass into a garden a whole family could live on, took other farm problems, of which she had no previous knowledge, in her stride.

But when you have shaken off those problems of life in the country, or rather have handed them to someone else, you are sitting there thinking, and your skin creeps slightly with the sensation that there is absolutely nothing between you and eternity—not some eternity in the future, but all round and behind you. You have the feeling you had as a child when nobody would tell you what there was beyond the place where outer space ended. A simple sensation, but eerie, too.

In our part of Ireland the sensation was heightened for me by the awareness one continuously had there of what may be called the presence of the past. There are, of course, innumerable places where what are called 'antiquities' are as numerous as here. But even in, say, Rome the past seems to me to be keeping its distance, and allowing itself to be judged and studied with a certain detachment. Here in the country it is not so. In the story circle of the Druid wood at Blarney—a place which perhaps was sacred even before the Druids adopted it—you are tumbled, almost as though you had been physically pushed, head over heels into pre-history. The trees there, forming the grove in which is situated the ring of sacred stones, have been demonstrated by arboreal experts to be older than any other trees in the world, with the exception of the Californian redwoods. The grove, and the stones—the fact that this was a sacred place thousands of years ago—are, one can hardly doubt, the true explanation of the legend of the Blarney stone. Every century has had a different account of the origin of the belief in the stone's magical powers—explanations which are mystical, religious or matter-of-factually political according to the prevailing climate of thought. But there would have been no legend about the stone's powers if it were not associated with a holy place, though nobody knows what first made it holy nor how distant, primitive and furry were the first worshippers.

Across one of our fields runs the outline of a rath—a line of underground dwellings built, probably, as a fortification and defence against early Scandinavian invaders. They, too, had to abandon airier ways of living and take to the underground shelters, and they seem very close.

This lurking and sometimes intrusive presence of the past might perhaps be supposed to weaken or dull the impact of the present. The contrary is the case. This crowding in of history serves instead to intensify a consciousness of the pressures and contradictions of life and society in the present.

Perhaps that is why people are so repeatedly moved to discuss over and over again the 'Irish character', or the 'pattern of Irish life', as if there were a uniform character or pattern. It is hard to say whether such speculations are more tedious when undertaken by Irishmen or by eager foreigners. But they do have the value of being an acknowledgment of the fact of a peculiar obtrusiveness in Ireland of basic problems of life and thought which elsewhere can be muffled, or forgotten, in a brisk jog-trot down well-rutted roads.

The only pattern of Irish life that I can discern is the pattern made by a series of diversities and the sharpest contradictions. There is no statement that can be made without it soon becoming apparent that its opposite is true too. Not that one statement is a lie and the other true—both are true. It could be said that this is the case everywhere, and to pretend otherwise is absurdly to exaggerate the peculiar quality and position in the world of that island—not its peculiar place in past history, its peculiar place now.

Certainly such contradictions are part of the dialectic of life everywhere. The point is not that they exist uniquely in Ireland, but that—perhaps because of the physical smallness of the area and population—they are muffled by nothing. In other words, you are forced daily on to your mental toes. You are forced to take note that nothing about human life, thought or activity can be taken safely for granted.

In such a situation, all sensibilities are heightened. For example, when I remarked to someone that—viewing the development of Communism and the Communist parties, and in particular the agonizing development of events in Hungary—from Ireland, I reacted to them more violently than I probably would have from any other watch-tower, he immediately assumed that I was alluding to some obscure influence upon me of the circumambient Roman Catholic air.

I meant nothing of the kind—and, indeed, that particular atmosphere might possibly have had an opposite effect. I meant simply that the 'other-ness' and the vivid contradictions of life seen in the Irish microcosm must increase one's awareness, and prod one almost brutally from any kind of mental slumber in which one might ignore the shifting realities of the world.

You can doze off in that way in England—sometimes in a kind of resignation to a situation which at so many vital points appears to be out of control by any influence you might help to exert. In the United States and the USSR, the habit of the mental doze is more dangerously widespread, though the fact that millions of people are taking a siesta from original social or political thinking is greatly obscured by brilliant technical achievements. But, as Professor Blackett, President of the British Association for the Advancement of Science, said recently at its meeting in Dublin, technology and science cannot take over the functions of politics in the widest sense of the word. There comes a point where social and political thinking, social and political action, have to deal with the human situation, however advanced or backward its technological position may be.

Ireland, good and bad and dubious, can be a cure for the siesta-habit, a stimulant stronger than any tranquillizer a person might be tempted to take. One looks at the world and thinks again of Cacambo's remark to Candide, urging him to take a chance on getting into the canoe and going somewhere. 'For if we find nothing pleasant, at least we shall find something new.' A man said to me in some agitation, 'But suppose the world exerts itself to find something new, and then it is horribly, abominably unpleasant?'

I said that in my view nothing could possibly be more unpleasant than what the world would get if it failed to find something new.